POLITICAL ECONOMY *and* STATESMANSHIP

POLITICAL ECONOMY *and* STATESMANSHIP

Smith, Hamilton, and the Foundation of the Commercial Republic

PETER M^cNAMARA

NORTHERN ILLINOIS
UNIVERSITY PRESS

DeKalb 1998

© 1998 by Northern Illinois University Press

Published by the Northern Illinois University
Press, DeKalb, Illinois 60115

Manufactured in the United States

using acid-free paper ♻ ∞

All Rights Reserved

Design by Julia Fauci

Library of Congress
Cataloging-in-Publication Data
McNamara, Peter.
Political economy and statesmanship : Smith,
Hamilton, and the foundation of the
commercial republic / Peter McNamara.

     p.   cm.
Includes bibliographical references and index.
ISBN 0-87580-228-1 (alk. paper)
1. Economic policy. 2. Smith, Adam,
1723–1790. 3. Hamilton, Alexander,
1757–1804. I. Title.
HD87.M38 1997
338.9—dc21
97-12499
CIP

To Carol, Isabella, *and* Adelaide.

CONTENTS

ACKNOWLEDGMENTS

WHAT GOOD THERE IS IN THIS BOOK owes much to those who have helped me along the way. Robert Faulkner and Robert Scigliano supervised the dissertation that is the basis of the present study. The comments and criticisms of friends and colleagues have been helpful. John Danford and Peter Minowitz deserve special mention. The John M. Olin Foundation and the Harry and Lynde Bradley Foundation provided generous financial support. Rob Anthony, Susan Bean, Dan Coran, and the rest of the staff at N.I.U. Press have shown great professionalism and even greater patience in helping to bring the project to a conclusion. Rachel Hurst, Sally Okleberry, and Stephanie White gave me much needed help in preparing the manuscript. As did Ryan Jensen who also helped prepare the index. There are two other debts that I must acknowledge. Richard W. Staveley first kindled my interest in political philosophy. For that I will be forever grateful. My final debt is to my wife, Carol, who was involved in every aspect of the project and who provided me with the encouragement necessary to complete it.

EDITIONS *and*

ABBREVIATIONS

for the Works of Adam Smith

Citations to Adam Smith are to the Glasgow edition of the works and correspondence of Adam Smith, published by Oxford University Press and reprinted by Liberty Classics. I use the following abbreviations in both the text and the notes; complete citations are in the Bibliography:

EPS	*Essays on Philosophical Subjects*
LJA	*Lectures on Jurisprudence,* Report of 1762–1763
LJB	*Lectures on Jurisprudence,* Report of 1766
LRBL	*Lectures on Rhetoric and Belles Lettres*
TMS	*The Theory of Moral Sentiments*
WN	*An Inquiry into the Nature and Causes of the Wealth of Nations*

I use the following short titles to specify works included in EPS:

Account	"Account of the Life and Writings of Adam Smith," by Dugald Stewart
Astronomy	"The Principles which lead and direct Philosophical Enquiries; illustrated by the History of Astronomy"
Physics	"The Principles which lead and direct Philosophical Enquiries; illustrated by the History of the Ancient Physics"

POLITICAL ECONOMY *and* STATESMANSHIP

RECONSTRUCTING POLITICAL ECONOMY

SCHOLARS IN A VARIETY OF FIELDS frequently have had occasion to compare Alexander Hamilton and Adam Smith. In the field of international political economy in particular, the two men are often introduced as early exemplars of the two sides of a long-standing and ongoing debate about trade policy.[1] Smith is presented as the advocate of free trade, whereas Hamilton is the advocate of state interventionism, particularly to protect infant industries. Hamilton is presented either as a forward-looking policymaker reacting to the needs of a new industrial era or, less flatteringly, as simply a representative of eighteenth-century mercantilism. With few exceptions the comparisons are perfunctory and give way quickly to discussions of supposedly more sophisticated recent theories.

I want to use the Smith–Hamilton comparison for a much broader purpose—as a contribution to the construction of a truly *political* economy that would supplement or, perhaps, replace mainstream neoclassical economics. The need for a political economy is widely recognized among scholars and policymakers across the political spectrum. Among those at the left-liberal end of the spectrum, a political economy is sought as a corrective for both the lack of realism of neoclassical economics and the inability of neoclassical economics to address moral concerns. These criticisms of neoclassical economics usually issue in a political economy that takes the form of government planning with the goal of regulating and humanizing capitalism.[2] Many conservatives and libertarians also detect a lack of realism in neoclassical economics, but they single out for criticism the tacit assumption made by neoclassical economists (and left-liberal planners) that politicians and bureaucrats, in sharp contrast to ordinary citizens, are selflessly devoted to the public good. Public-choice theory is the most ambitious effort so far to remedy this defect of neoclassical economics. It recommends the introduction of strictly limited government and greater reliance on voluntary exchange to achieve social goals.[3]

The approaches of both the planners and the public-choice theorists have serious defects. The left-liberal planners are correct in seeing much of neoclassical economics, including its basic assumptions about the operation of the market, as hopelessly unrealistic. They are also correct in pointing to the limitations of the notion that facts are the stuff of science, whereas values are beyond the reach of science. Indeed, so-called radical or Marxist political economists are correct in seeing the fact–value distinction as cloaking a large number of value assumptions that favor capitalism. Planners, however, neglect not only the question of the practicality of their own plans but also the incompatibility of their plans with the notion of limited government so critical to the liberal tradition. Partly in response to the schemes of left-liberal planners, public-choice theorists have delivered a sobering message about the problems of planning. Yet most, perhaps all, of their insights were known to the likes of a Smith, or a Hamilton, or a Madison; and, more importantly, much is lost in their effort to create a unified political science and economics. The assumption that "rational self-interest" is the only relevant human motivation, the assumption that underlies public-choice theory, is particularly problematic because it rejects a priori the possibility that citizens and statesmen have other important motives. This problem is most evident when one considers the difficulty of explaining the motives of a Smith, or a Hamilton, or a Madison simply in terms of rational self-interest.[4]

The task of constructing a new political economy is beyond the scope of this book, but the comparison of Smith and Hamilton points to a number of paths for future inquiry. What is required for a new political economy? Colin Wright has ably described political economy as the area of inquiry that encompasses both the interdependence of political and economic things and the normative questions that arise from that interdependence.[5] To formulate a political economy, however, one needs more than a description of the area of study; one needs a method to apply to practical matters. A comparison of Smith and Hamilton contributes to this goal in two ways. By returning to the issues and debates that ultimately led to the fracturing of the original eighteenth-century political economy into political science and economics, the comparison helps us to understand how these two disciplines came to exist in their current state of unnatural and unproductive isolation from one another. In this respect, my study is an exercise in the history of political economy aimed at clarifying the nature of Smith's attempt to establish a *science* of political economy. Even though Smith remained a political economist, we will see that he decisively prepared the way for the emergence of an independent science of economics and, furthermore, that the difficulties that inhere in this later project were already present in Smith's political economy.

But a description of the topical area of inquiry and a history of that inquiry, however revealing, do not constitute a method of political economy. What does a comparison of Smith and Hamilton have to offer specifically in this regard? My study of Smith and Hamilton combines history, economic history, politics, and political philosophy, but it is aptly summarized as a study of economic statesmanship. The chief conclusion of the study is that the *example* of Hamilton's words and deeds provides a more useful guide for a liberal statesman than does the economic *model* yielded by Smith's science of political economy. The conclusion that the example of an outstanding statesman is more useful than the model constructed by an outstanding theoretician points to the need to rethink the relationship between theory and practice in economic affairs and leads to a suggestion that the study of economic statesmanship itself might come to form a significant part of any new political economy.

How does political economy conceived of as the study of statesmanship differ from political economy or economics conceived of as social science? The study of statesmanship, including economic statesmanship, is neither scientific, as, say, public-choice theory claims to be, nor radical, as, say, Marxist political economy explicitly defines itself. In the first place, the study of statesmanship implies a certain skepticism at the possibility of theorizing about economic affairs—something we will see was characteristic of Hamilton himself. The study of economic statesmanship does not have as its end the formulation of universal laws of behavior. Its focus is the actions of particular statesmen acting in particular circumstances. This focus makes the study of statesmanship conservative in one important respect. It accepts the statesman's moral orientation as more or less fixed, rather than searching for either an amoral objective standard, such as "facts," or for some transcendent moral standard. The former kind of search is demonstrably a delusion; the latter belongs to the realm of political philosophy.[6] In the case of studying Hamilton's economic statesmanship, the aim is simply to begin to clarify the *liberal* statesman's role with regard to stewardship of the economy. The study of statesmanship, however, is not value free. It not only acknowledges the normative dimension of all action but also seeks to illuminate that dimension as fully as possible, even if this requires calling in the aid of political philosophy. With respect to Hamilton, we must inquire into the compatibility of the means he chose with the end he had in mind. To do this we must attain a certain philosophic clarity about the nature of the liberal political order that Hamilton hoped to help establish.

To borrow some terminology from Donald McCloskey's work on the rhetoric of economics, the study of economic statesmanship aims at restoring the "active voice" to economic inquiry. McCloskey has shown how the devotion of neoclassical economists to neutrality and the universality of economic laws has led to the supplanting of the active voice by the "passive voice" in economic inquiry.[7] The passive voice—for example, "markets are cleared when there are no obstacles to free exchange"—removes human agency from the workings of the economy. Furthermore, as McCloskey emphasizes, the passive voice allows an author to use the authority of science as a rhetorical device because it hides the author's connection to the claims and assertions he or she advances. I should add that a return to the active voice does not imply a heroic political economy that tells tales of statesmen for the purpose of inciting emulation. Nor does it imply government activism of the kind seen in the United States since the New Deal. The study of statesmanship requires only that the focus of the study be the decisions of statesmen. The question of the choice of means depends upon the circumstances and the end in view. The attentive reader will notice a number of similarities between John Maynard Keynes's critique of classical and neoclassical economics and that presented in these pages. There is, however, an important difference. The great good sense that Keynes showed in his critique of economics was accompanied by a complete abandonment of sense with regard to politics. Though more subtle and high-minded than the efforts of the left-liberal planners who followed him, his attempt to imbue liberal capitalism with a spirit of idealism could only end, as it has, with a massive expansion of ineffective and soul-destroying bureaucracy.[8]

The remainder of this introduction contains a brief review of the state of Smith and Hamilton scholarship and presents an outline of the argument to come.

SMITH AND HAMILTON SCHOLARSHIP

In order to compare Smith and Hamilton, I will refer frequently and sometimes at length to the vast but distinct scholarly literatures on them. The tendency of recent scholarship to revise traditional assessments makes such references all the more necessary, because it has undermined the grounds of even the conventional, perfunctory Smith–Hamilton comparison. This is especially true of Smith scholarship, but scholarly views of Hamilton have also been affected by the broader historiographic upheavals in the study of early-modern political thought.

Smith scholars, roughly speaking, fall into two camps. In the first are those who see Smith as one of the founders of modern political economy. Modern economists, for example, generally accept Smith's *An Inquiry into the Nature and Causes of the Wealth of Nations,* which was first published in 1776, as one of the founding works of their discipline, though few, perhaps, have read it. Still, their view does accord with the judgment of most of the great classical economists who, as a group, were much more widely read than later generations of economists.[9] The precise nature of Smith's contribution to the foundation of economics, however, has long been a subject of considerable controversy. Two features of his writings have made the job of unearthing his original contributions to economics extremely difficult. Smith, it is now widely recognized, was not generous in acknowledging his debts to earlier thinkers. Furthermore, he presented a somewhat tendentious history of economic thought in the *Wealth of Nations* that proved to be enormously influential but that exaggerated the break between his theories and earlier ones.[10] Both Walter Bagehot and Joseph Schumpeter went so far as to argue that Smith's original theoretical contributions were few and unimportant. Instead, they identified his main accomplishment as popularizing the idea of free trade among political elites.[11] On one point, however, there is considerable agreement. Smith was the first political economist to construct a reasonably coherent system that was successful in capturing the public mind.[12]

The most-sophisticated versions of the view of Smith as the founder of modern political economy attempt to take into account Smith's other great work, the *Theory of Moral Sentiments,* which was first published in 1759. According to an influential statement by Joseph Cropsey, "Smith is of interest for his share in the deflection of political philosophy towards economics and for his famous elaboration of the principles of free enterprise or liberal capitalism." Peter Minowitz has called this the "deflection thesis." Cropsey's view of Smith was not narrowly economistic. While placing Smith's political economy in the context of the broader philosophical project of modernity, he distinguished Smith from, say, John Locke (and, by implication, from today's neoclassical economists), on the grounds that "Smith's teaching contains that formulation of capitalist doctrine in which many of the fundamental issues are recognizably those on which post-capitalism contests the field." For Cropsey, Smith was a complex and intriguing figure because he anticipated something like the Marxian moral critique of capitalism but nevertheless endorsed liberal capitalism.[13]

Criticism of the "liberal-capitalist perspective," as Donald Winch has termed views such as Cropsey's, served as the launching point for a second camp of Smith scholars. These revisionist scholars argue that it was a distortion to place Smith at the head of what is really a nineteenth-century intellectual movement. Smith's true niche was the eighteenth century—a time when economics had yet to eclipse both politics and virtue. The revisionists divide on the question of whether Smith belongs in the civic humanist tradition, in the classical republican tradition, in the natural jurisprudential tradition, or in some other tradition. They are, however, united in the view that Smith reserved a significant place for the figure of the classical "legislator." We will see that although the revisionists are correct in seeing a continuing role for politics and even for the legislator, they fail to see that Smith's legislator is fundamentally new. The form is similar to the classical legislator, but the substance is modern.[14]

As John Marshall was, perhaps, the first to observe, the exact character of Hamilton's political opinions has always been the subject of controversy.[15] In the public mind, Hamilton's stature as a statesman has long been recognized, but almost always with reservations. Over the years many scholars and citizens have questioned his allegiance to the republican cause. This is, perhaps, why he has consistently fared better in the judgments of foreigners than in those of his own countrymen.[16] Among scholars today, Marshall's observation still holds. Two views predominate. On the one side are those who see Hamilton as an American Walpole bent on modernizing American society. On the other side are those who see Hamilton as attached to doctrines, chiefly mercantilism and classical republicanism, that were rapidly being made obsolete by the new political order emerging in the United States.[17]

These approaches overlook the extent to which both Hamilton *and* his great rivals, Jefferson and Madison, were committed to modernization. Jefferson pointed to the true source of the disagreement in his "Second Inaugural Address." After discussing the obstacles to enlightenment among the Indians, Jefferson remarked that *"they, too, have their anti-philosophers* who find an interest in keeping things in their present state, who dread the reformation and exert all their faculties to maintain the ascendancy of habit over the duty of improving our reason, and of obeying its mandates."[18] To Jefferson, Hamilton belonged to the "anti-philosophers" because he held a different opinion of the place of reason and habit in the operations of society. I will show that just as Hamilton was suspicious of Jeffersonian Republican theorizing in politics, he was also skeptical of the claims of Smith's science of political economy.

Turning from general scholarship to some specific comparisons of Smith and Hamilton, the interesting ones are those that emphasize the forward-looking aspects of Hamilton's economic program as first secretary of the U.S. Treasury. These emphasize that Hamilton was, as Shannon Stimson has noted, "an heir, not a predecessor of Adam Smith."[19] Forrest McDonald, for example, has pointed to Hamilton's advanced ideas on finance and economic development, whereas Hiram Caton has stressed Hamilton's appreciation of the pivotal role of technology in the modern economy. Both scholars fault Smith for having failed to recognize the essential character of capitalist economic development.[20] Stanley Elkins and Eric McKitrick reached a similar conclusion, but by a different route. They have argued that Hamilton's thinking on economic development remained closer to David Hume's, in that both of them shied away from Smith's universalism and ahistoricism.[21]

I develop these insights and, in addition, pay particular attention to Hamilton's methodological remarks on theorizing about political and economic matters. As Gerald Stourzh has noted, Hamilton's career coincided with the emergence of the social sciences, including economics.[22] His response to Smith is of interest because it constitutes one of the first reactions to the new Smithian political economy by a thoughtful practitioner.[23] In this regard, Hamilton's case is more interesting than, say, William Pitt's, whose public praise of Smith in 1790 seems to have been important for establishing the influence of Smith's theory of free trade in England, because Hamilton was considering the case of an infant nation rather than a military and economic superpower.[24] Furthermore, Hamilton's response is significant because it was uninfluenced and, therefore, untainted by the great authority that the science of political economy attained in the nineteenth century. For there is considerable truth in Keynes's remark that Ricardo, Smith's great successor and follower, "conquered England just as completely as the Holy Inquisition conquered Spain."[25]

PLAN OF THE ARGUMENT

Chapter 1 aims to make clear Smith's view of economic statesmanship. It begins by considering his account of the relationship between philosophy and politics. Smith refined the insight of thinkers such as Locke, Montesquieu, and

Hume, who saw the spread of commerce as a way of curbing the harshness of politics. His contribution was twofold. First, he attempted to demonstrate conclusively that the pursuit of economic self-interest by individuals and nations is not necessarily a zero-sum game. Second, he anticipated that his system of political economy would reconcile the public good, moderate politics, *and* private ambition. In this regard, scholars have failed to pay sufficient attention to the role that Smith gave to the "spirit of system" as a means of channeling political ambition. The *Theory of Moral Sentiments* explains the role of the spirit of system in fueling economic acquisitiveness. This discussion is famous because of Smith's mention of the "invisible hand" that directs acquisitiveness to the benefit of society. But Smith presents a parallel discussion of the role of the spirit of system in political life that would seem to be of equal importance. Here, however, it is the speculator in politics, the philosopher, who constructs the system that fuels political ambition. Smith's analysis of the spirit of system is the key to understanding his revision of the idea of the legislator.

Chapter 2 deals with Smith's science of political economy. Smith treated political economy as both a philosophical and a practical pursuit. The latter he termed "political economy, considered as a branch of the science of a legislator." The system of natural liberty elaborated in the *Wealth of Nations* linked both pursuits. The foundation of the system of natural liberty was the "desire to better our condition." This force provided the principle of motion for his system. To it, he added a unit of measurement: the notion of "labor commanded" as the *real* measure of value. The notion that the wealth of nations is unambiguously quantifiable was critical for the establishment of a truly scientific political economy. It allowed Smith to proceed deductively in his elaboration of the system of natural liberty in books I–III of the *Wealth of Nations*. Books IV–V of the *Wealth of Nations* attempt to show how this system is applicable to a world of independent nations in which reason and humanity do not necessarily prevail. This transition represents the shift from science to art, or from what today would be called economics (theoretical and applied) to public policy. Smith believed that, subject to a very small number of exceptions, statesmen could use his system as a general rule or model, to use the contemporary term.

Chapter 3 considers Hamilton's economic statesmanship. By the time Hamilton became the treasury secretary, Smithian political economy had gained many influential adherents in the United States. Thus, when choosing policies, Hamilton was forced to consider Smith's views in some detail. Hamilton seems to have sensed not only the problems involved in a rash application of Smith's system of political economy but also the difficulties inherent in Smith's systematizing project itself. He departed from Smith in three ways.

First, Hamilton knew of but rejected Smith's hope of moderating the harshness of politics by relying on the influence of a humane and liberal "system." Hamilton's political creed was a moderate version of the modern natural-rights teaching. Furthermore, he thought that constitutional government provided the best hope of realizing his political principles in practice, because it made possible a "wise administration."

Second, Hamilton denied that extended chains of deductive reasoning are applicable to political and economic affairs. What is "geometrically true" is often "practically false," he remarked. Hamilton usually looked to "enlightened statesmen" and to the general policy of nations rather than to "theorists of political economy" for guidance. Practical decisions require that "all nice and abstract distinctions should give way to plainer interests and to more obvious and simple rules of conduct."

Third, Hamilton did not believe that the desire to better our condition was a natural and spontaneous growth. As a result, he formulated a plan for the commercialization of the United States. Without such economic management, he thought the natural course of things might lead to indolence or speculation, rather than to what he termed a "general spirit of improvement." The financial side of Hamilton's program aimed at establishing a national financial system. On the whole, he was successful in obtaining the support of Congress for implementation of his plan. Hamilton's departures from Smith in this area are far more important than is usually recognized. They reveal a profound difference over the nature of capitalist economic growth. Hamilton emphasized the speculative, dynamic, and, therefore, volatile nature of capitalist enterprise, whereas Smith emphasized the "uniform, constant, and uninterrupted desire of every man to better his condition." Furthermore, Hamilton's understanding of the financial aspects of American capitalism is particularly important for the purposes of distinguishing it from its more statist European counterparts.

For a multitude of reasons, Congress did not act upon Hamilton's famous *Report on Manufactures,* which recommended state encouragement of manufactures. It is important, however, to realize that the report was in many important respects a theoretical document rather than a practical one. It was designed to establish the importance of manufacturing for the nation's future by clearing away certain confusions that had arisen from the writings of political economists such as Smith.

In terms of the contemporary debate, my argument has a number of practical implications. It points toward a kind of constitutional economics quite different from that of the public-choice school. In terms of economic policy, it suggests the need to rehabilitate the idea of an "American system" that matches economic policy with the political culture of the nation. This change in policy reflects the need to supplement Smith's economics of exchange with an economics that takes into account choice and uncertainty. Finally, my argument highlights anew the old idea that the United States was the first new nation and for that reason still serves as a model for developing countries.

SMITH'S
POLITICS
RECONSIDERED

THE PROBLEM OF SMITH'S POLITICS

AS I NOTED, TWO VIEWS OF SMITH'S POLITICS have emerged. The first, or liberal-capitalist, view maintains that Smith deflected political and moral philosophy toward political economy. The result of this deflection was a depreciation or even eclipse of politics and a corresponding emancipation of economics from political control. The second, or revisionist, view argues that the liberal-capitalist perspective on Smith overlooks the breadth and depth of his politics. Revisionists point to several areas of state discretion and initiative. First, they claim that Smith left considerable discretion as to the pace and manner in which his political and economic recommendations ought to be implemented. Second, they point to the role that Smith gave to the state in political, economic, and moral affairs even after the system of natural liberty was implemented. Third, and most generally, revisionists argue that the liberal-capitalist perspective falsely portrays Smith as an economic determinist who finds little or no place for politics. The centerpiece of their argument in this regard is a rejection of the notion that Smith saw a necessary connection between the progress of freedom and the progress of commerce. As a result, a space is created for politics and, sometimes, for a legislator to shape society.

I believe that these two interpretations reflect two real and important strands of Smith's thought, strands that might seem to be in tension: on one hand, a certain kind of conservatism and, on the other, a certain kind of activism. This chapter and the next develop these two strands in detail. Here I will merely limn the broad contours of Smith's seemingly paradoxical accomplishment. Some elements of Smith display a cautious, evolutionary, and conservative approach to politics. He is rightly regarded as one of the originators of the idea of "spontaneous order": the notion that the social arrangements "under which we live are of such a high order of complexity that they invariably take their form not from deliberate calculation, but as the unintended consequence of countless individual actions, many of which may be the result of instinct and habit."[1] The emphasis on spontaneous order, especially in the economic realm, is compatible with a kind of political passivity and might be seen as a depreciation of politics. Yet other elements of Smith's thought seem to leave the door open for considerable government activism. He not only outlined a broad and novel scheme of public policy but also established certain normative standards for politics that called into question the existing social order.

Some remarks by Smith's friend and student Dugald Stewart are useful for clarifying Smith's position. These remarks seem to have been an attempt to distance Smith's writings from partisan interpretations, whether Whig, Tory, or liberal republican.[2] Stewart claimed first that Smith aimed at the "improvement of society not by delineating plans of new constitutions, but enlightening the policy of actual legislators. Such speculations . . . have no tendency to unhinge established institutions, or to inflame the passions of the multitude." Smith's recommendations were so slow and gradual in their operation that they could "warm the imaginations" only of "the speculative few" (*Account* IV.6). Furthermore, Stewart claimed that Smith was "abundantly aware of the danger to be apprehended from a rash application of political theories" (*Account* IV.18). He quoted Smith to the effect that decisions as to how to apply the theory of free trade must be left to the "wisdom and prudence of future legislators" (*WN* IV.vii.c.44). Helpful as Stewart's remarks are, they leave much unanswered and raise more questions. Immediately, they force us to ask about the nature of policies that reconcile change and stability. This was surely a political novelty. Furthermore, one wonders about the legislator. What is there in these policies to warm his imagination? Is it simply the improvement of society? Most important, perhaps, is that Stewart's remarks draw attention away from Smith's innovative approach to the very question of the relationship between theory and practice. As we will see, this was a philosophical innovation in itself and constituted a significant intrusion of theory into practice.[3]

Smith's application of the strategy of indirection and unanticipated consequences to politics is the key to reconciling the two strands of Smith's political thought—"spontaneous order" and the "legislator." Smith remarks many times that all human actions have multiple meanings, in that every action may be viewed from a number of perspectives: of the actor, of spectators in general, of the informed and impartial spectator, of society as a whole, of the philosopher, of nature, and, perhaps, of god. Much of Smith's moral and political philosophy consists of his reflections on the significance of and interdependence among these perspectives. One product of these reflections is the strategy of making use of indirection and unanticipated consequences to accomplish social and political objectives. Smith's political economy, for example, shows how individuals motivated solely by self-interest might contribute to the common good. Smith's political thought, I will argue, relies heavily on a similar strategy. Once recognized, the nature and magnitude of Smith's paradoxical accomplishment becomes clear.

Smith was particularly concerned with alleviating the tendency toward fanaticism and brutality in political life. The *Theory of Moral Sentiments*, more so than the *Wealth of Nations*, provides a rich account of both philosophers and political men that reveals the moral dilemmas and pitfalls inherent in political life. We will see that Smith's endeavor resembles Plato's description in the *Republic* of the education of the guardian class. Plato's Socrates set out an education in music and gymnastics to tame the natural ferocity of the ruling class. Smith had a similar end in mind but chose a different means. His approach was novel, because he relied on the humane tendencies of his system of political economy to curb the harshness of political life. Smith refined Montesquieu's insight in the *Spirit of the Laws* that the spread of commerce had begun to cure Europe of Machiavellianism because commerce teaches us to follow our interests and not our passions.[4] Smith's elaboration of the way in which a "spirit of system" directs the energies of the politically ambitious was his most original contribution. I will suggest that Smith's intention and, to a certain extent, the result of his writings were nicely captured by Walter Bagehot. Smith, Bagehot stated, put "certain broad conclusions into the minds of hard-headed men."[5] To understand this element of Smith is to begin to understand the distinctiveness of a Pitt, a Jefferson, or a Madison, not to mention a Reagan, a Thatcher, or a Gingrich. I conclude, then, that Albert Hirschman's influential thesis that places Smith beyond the great tradition of theorizing about the role of commerce in checking the ambition of statesmen is incorrect.[6] On the contrary, Smith's efforts constitute the last and perhaps most-sophisticated stage in this line of thinking.

Reflection on the relationship between philosophy and politics is critical for our comparison with Hamilton. In *The Federalist*, Hamilton responded to the arguments of certain "visionary or designing men" who contended that "perpetual peace" is possible among a number of independent and neighboring states, especially if they are commercial republics. Hamilton questioned whether it was really in the interest of nations to adopt a "benevolent and philosophic spirit" and asked whether ancient and modern history had not been enough to show "the folly and extravagance of those idle theories which have amused us with promises of an exemption from the imperfections, weaknesses, and evils incident to society in every shape?"[7] As we will see, Hamilton's rebuttal to these "reveries" is applicable to a number of Smith's more important arguments. Although it is not clear that Hamilton had read Smith at the time of *The Federalist*, it is apparent that when he did do so, he did not revise the expression of his views. A disagreement about the scope that can be given to a benevolent and philosophic spirit in politics, especially international politics, constitutes one of the sharpest differences between the two men.

A full account of Smith's politics will require an extensive consideration of his political economy. This will come in chapter 3. For now, I will make a somewhat artificial distinction between Smith's politics and his political economy. This and subsequent sections in chapter 1 raise several broad questions about the practical intent of Smith's writings. The *Wealth of Nations* was written, at least in part, to influence statesmen. We must ask, what did Smith think of statesmen? Furthermore, in what ways and to what extent did he think that philosophers influence politics and political men? The answers to these questions will help establish the context for Smith's account of economic statesmanship in the *Wealth of Nations*. Because these are also very broad questions, they will lead us to reflect, somewhat tentatively, on Smith's thought as a whole.

Before turning to Smith on philosophy and politics, however, I must first comment on how to read his enigmatic corpus. He seems to have contrived matters so that his thought as a whole would remain elusive. He took elaborate measures to ensure that his actual publications, along with his good reputation as a man and a teacher, were the only testimonies to his life's work. His published works, however, though great in substance and great in length, are silent on many important issues. Beyond this, his published writings form at best an uneasy whole; something that has led generations of Smith scholars to puzzle over the seeming inconsistencies and tensions between the *Wealth of Nations* and the *Theory of Moral Sentiments*.

READING ADAM SMITH

In order to restore the depth and complexity they see missing from the liberal-capitalist perspective on Smith, revisionist scholars have followed two strategies: first, they have made Smith's moral and political writings the focus of their studies; and second, they have paid greater attention to the historical context in which Smith wrote, to "historicity." Both of these approaches have something to offer, but they are not without serious problems. Although the focus on Smith's moral and political writings is useful, at some point his economic writings must be addressed. More importantly, if the liberal-capitalist perspective risks reading later thought into Smith, the new scholarship risks the geographical and historical provincialization of him in his historical context. The attempt to place him in his eighteenth-century context is fatally flawed if it limits itself to asking, as Winch did, "what it would be conceivable for Smith, or someone fairly like him, to maintain, rather than what later generations would like him to have maintained."[8] Historicity in this sense is a dogmatic, hermeneutical principle that tends to read out of Smith the universalistic, transhistorical, and epochal claims of both of his major works.

As Minowitz has observed, Winch stumbled into an "epistemological no man's land." He suggests instead placing Smith's texts in the limelight and paying careful attention to his "pervasive employment of rhetoric."[9] Two features of Smith's rhetoric deserve mention: his extreme caution and his awareness of the rhetorical power of modern natural science. When reading Smith it is important to bear in mind his extraordinary caution. Smith was hesitant about letter writing, and he saw to it that his unpublished papers were destroyed before his death.[10] He disapproved of his friend Hume's courting of controversy, refusing after Hume's death to publish his *Dialogues Concerning Natural Religion*. It seems more than likely that this abundant caution found its way into his writings. Some remarks in the *Theory of Moral Sentiments* about the "prudent man" are helpful for understanding the nature of Smith's caution and how it might have affected his writings. Smith recommends to all men the example of the prudent man. Although "the prudent man is always sincere," Smith remarks, "he does not always think himself bound, when not properly called upon, to tell the whole truth." The prudent man provides a better example than "has frequently been done by men of much more splendid talents and virtues . . . [who] have too often distinguished themselves by the most improper and even insolent contempt of all the ordinary decorums of life and conversation" (*TMS* VI.1.8,10). Smith includes a number of writers and philosophers among his list of bad examples: Socrates, Aristippus, Swift, and Voltaire. He might have mentioned his friend Hume. To say that Smith wrote cautiously does not mean that he wrote esoterically. Smith ridiculed the notion of what he called the "double doctrine"; that is, writing in such a way as to convey esoteric and exoteric levels of meaning (*Physics* 3, note). It means simply that, when reading Smith, one should be alert to the possibility that he was saying something new but doing so in a way that was respectful of the maxims and standards of his time.[11]

What were the concrete manifestations of Smith's caution? Minowitz stresses the way in which his caution influenced his writings on moral and religious matters.[12] Emma Rothschild emphasizes the more general problem of a political reformer facing conservative opposition.[13] To these perspectives on Smith, I would add another general consideration: his caution is probably the reason for his frequent practice of giving new meanings to old words. His caution here, however, is more for the purpose of insinuation than out of a fear of persecution by secular or religious authority. His use of the term *republic* is a good and clear example.[14] He sometimes speaks of republics and republican manners in the manner of Montesquieu or a classical republican (e.g., *WN* IV.vii.b.51; *WN* V.ii.k.80). But Smith also speaks of the "great mercantile republic," which is not, strictly speaking, a nation or a form of government but an economic community of consumers and producers. Among its citizens or subjects are capitalists who, he remarks, are not properly the citizens of any country (*WN* IV.i.28; *WN* V.ii.f.6). In this, as well as in many other important cases, the result is a certain amount of probably deliberate ambiguity in Smith's writings that allows him to introduce the new in the guise of the old.

Smith's awareness of the rhetorical power of modern natural science provides a second clue for understanding how to read his works. The extraordinary success of Newton's physics, in particular, provided a number of important lessons. In the first place, it brought to light new possibilities concerning the relationship between science and society. Smith's posthumously published *History of Astronomy*, the subtitle of which is *The Principles which Lead and Direct Philosophical*

Inquiries, makes clear Newton's importance.[15] His purpose in this essay was to examine "all the different systems of nature" solely with a view to considering "how far each of them was fitted to soothe the imagination, and to render the theatre of nature more coherent, and therefore a more magnificent spectacle than it would otherwise have appeared to be" (*Astronomy* II.12). Put otherwise, Smith's concern here was not with the principles that constitute scientific truth but with those that provide the motivation for scientific activity and account for the popular success of scientific theories. A theory or "system" of nature "is an imaginary machine invented to connect together in the fancy those different movements and effects which are in reality performed" (*Astronomy* IV.19). The popular success of a system depends on the ease with which the system can account for the phenomena under investigation. This in turn is a function of the coherence, explanatory power, and simplicity of the system as a whole.[16] Smith adds that the popular appeal of any system depends crucially on its ability to make use of connecting principles which are in some way familiar to mankind. Taken together, these features of a system of nature remove the unease or surprise that nature sometimes causes us. One system is likely to be superseded by another if the established system becomes too cumbersome and if an alternative system can explain the phenomena more simply and just as comprehensively. Smith argues that the classical view of the universe was replaced when, after a point, it simply became too complicated.

According to Smith, it was "the school of Socrates . . . from Plato and Aristotle, that philosophy first received that form, which introduced her, if one may say so, to the general acquaintance of the world" (*Astronomy* III.6). The school of Socrates, however, like all schools until the time of the Enlightenment, remained merely a sect that attracted a small but devoted following. It was the victory of Newton's physics that showed Smith the potential of a system founded upon a familiar principle:

> The superior genius and sagacity of Sir Isaac Newton . . . made the most happy, and, we may now say, the greatest and most admirable improvement that was ever made in philosophy, when he discovered, that he could join together the movements of the Planets by so familiar a principle of connection, which completely removed all the difficulties the imagination had hitherto felt in attending to them. (*Astronomy* IV.67)

That familiar principle was, of course, the "earthly" principle of gravity, which Newton simply extended to the heavens. "The gravity of matter is," Smith explains, "of all its qualities, after its inertness, that which is most familiar to us." Newton's success showed the way to and the potential for truly popular enlightenment by providing a rhetorical model that could be used by all sciences, including the moral and political ones. In his *Lectures on Rhetoric,* Smith recommends the Newtonian method of didactic rhetoric as the proper form for scientific discourse. It proceeds by laying "down certain principles known or proved in the beginning, from whence we account for the several Phenomena, connecting all together by the same Chain." Smith regarded this method as the "most philosophical, and in every science whether of moral or natural philosophy etc., is vastly more ingenious and for that reason more engaging" than the Aristotelian method, which did not employ an easily accessible mode of presentation (*LRBL* II.133–34). Using this method, Newton acquired "the most universal empire that was ever established in philosophy" by gaining "the general and complete approbation of mankind" (*Astronomy* IV.76).[17]

Although it is clear that Smith drew on the rhetoric of Newtonian physics, it is less clear how much he drew on its substance, especially its reliance on mathematics, quantification, and experiment. Deborah Redman suggests that Smith drew solely on the form of Newton's physics, whereas he adopted a distinctly Scottish approach to social inquiry, which used psychology and introspection. Redman charges that later political economists who followed Smith took the form for the substance.[18] The result is today's mathematical economics. Granting that Newton's method could not be applied wholesale to political economy, the examination of Smith's political economy in chapter 2 will make clear that Smith drew extensively on the substance as well as the form of Newton's physics.

PHILOSOPHY, POLITICS, AND THE GENESIS OF SMITH'S POLITICAL ECONOMY

Philosophers

Smith's account of civilized society reveals an important dichotomy between types of human beings—the speculative man, or philosopher, and the political man. It is a contrast between the man of the most exquisite humanity and greatest breadth of vision, on one hand, and, on the other, the man of superior self-command and political skill.[19] The dichotomy emerges in the following way. The understanding and character of a human being are formed in the course of his or her ordinary "employment" in life. This influence accounts for the greatest part—or, perhaps, all—of the differences we observe among human beings (*WN* I.ii.4–5). And certainly the "understandings of the greater part of men are necessarily formed by their ordinary employments" (*WN* V.i.f.50). Furthermore, the progress of society is accompanied by and, to a large extent, caused by an ever-increasing division of labor. With the progress of society, however, the great body of the people are threatened with losing their moral, martial, and intellectual virtues as a result of the dehumanizing effects of the division of labor. Members of "barbarous" societies, in contrast, possess rustic intelligence and martial vigor. Furthermore, every man "is in some measure a statesman, and can form a tolerable judgement of the interest of society, and the conduct of those who govern it" (*WN* V.i.f.51).

Ironically, Smith sees the deterioration in the great body of the people of a civilized society occurring at a time when, for a few, society presents an unprecedented variety of objects for study and contemplation. "The contemplation of so great a variety of objects necessarily exercises their minds in endless comparisons and combinations, and renders their understandings, in an extraordinary degree, both acute and comprehensive" (*WN* V.i.f.51).[20] Through the thoughts of the philosopher, society achieves an awareness of its own workings that it did not possess previously. Smith often refers to this perspective on society as a "cool," "abstract," or "philosophical light" that, while it yields vital insights into human life, is seldom, if ever, the perspective of the actual participants (e.g., *TMS* II.iii.intro.5; *TMS* III.5.9; *TMS* IV.i.9; *TMS* IV.ii.2; *TMS* VII.iii.1.2). For the philosopher, then, civilized society is a privileged moment. He is, in a sense, the culmination or end point of civilized society. Smith, however, does not see the philosopher as the peak of society. He states emphatically that the "most sublime speculation of the contemplative philosopher can scarce compensate the neglect of the smallest active duty" (*TMS* VI.ii.3.6). Philosophy has no priority over other goods or ways of life. The philosopher and the philosophic way of life are last, not highest.

What of the philosopher's moral qualities? Smith's philosopher lives an essentially private life. He "is company to a philosopher only; the member of a club, to his own little knot of companions" (*TMS* I.ii.2.6). The philosopher is, perhaps above all, a humane man who wishes the best for mankind. "In the mild sunshine of undisturbed tranquility, in the calm retirement of undissipated and philosophical pleasure, the soft virtue of humanity flourishes the most and is capable of the highest improvement." But because "in such situations, the greatest and noblest exertions of self-command have little exercise," he will likely be unsuited for political life (*TMS* III.3.37). Self-command is the "manly" capacity of mastering our immediate inclinations for the sake of gaining the approval of others. Humanity requires little self-command. It is the "virtue of a woman" (*TMS* IV.ii.10–11).[21]

Although Smith's philosopher is an observer of, rather than a direct participant in, the business of life, he may have an important indirect influence on society, in that his reflections on the apparent discontinuities and incoherences of nature yield knowledge that is useful to society. One could say that, for Smith, this service constitutes the philosopher's defense or apology before society for his peculiar activity. This provision of useful knowledge goes beyond the production of commercially useful inventions to include moral philosophy, which Smith also classifies as "useful."[22] But in the *Wealth of Nations,* Smith observes that "unless those few [philosophers] . . . happen to be placed in some very particular situations, their great abilities, though honourable to themselves, may contribute very little to the good government or happiness of their society" (*WN* V.i.f.51). What are these situations in which philosophers might influence society and politics? Before attempting to answer this question, we must complete our comparison of Smith's views of philosophers and political men.

Political Men

The political man stands at what is, in at least one important respect, the polar opposite to the philosopher. Political life requires the capacity for self-command in the highest degree. A private life of philosophy (or commerce, for that matter) is sufficient for attaining a certain degree of self-command, but the higher degrees of self-command requisite for great undertakings are possible only for those who have been continually exposed to the searing scrutiny of public life. There is, we will see, a profound tension between the possibilities inherent in Smith's account of political life and the strict demands of Smithian morality.

The best place to begin for understanding the tension between politics and morality is Smith's account in the *Theory of Moral Sentiments* of the virtue of prudence. It is there that we see most clearly Smith's ambivalence toward political life. Departing from the Aristotelian tradition, which made prudence an indispensable intellectual virtue for both private and political life, Smith defines prudence as the "care of the health, of the fortune, of the rank and reputation of the individual, the objects upon which his comfort and happiness in this life are supposed principally to depend" (*TMS* VI.i.5). He acknowledges his departure from Aristotle when he speaks soon afterward of the "superior prudence" of the "great general, of the great statesman, of the great legislator." Prudence is in these cases "*combined* with many greater and more splendid virtues, with valour, with extensive and strong benevolence, with sacred regard to the rules of justice, and all these supported by a proper degree of self-command" (*TMS* VI.i.15, emphasis added). This "superior prudence" is, then, a composite virtue.

Simple prudence, in contrast, is something of a double-edged sword. Smith deals with three cases: acts that are prudent and virtuous; those that are imprudent and base; and, lastly, those that are prudent and base. Acts of the first kind, he says, are universally admired; those of the second are universally disapproved; but those of the third meet with a mixed reception and are frequently admired. The "violence and injustice of great conquerors," for example, "are often regarded with foolish wonder and admiration" and "often pass for deeds of the most heroic magnanimity" (*TMS* VI.i.16). In what is an important concession to Machiavelli, Smith grants that it is human nature to admire results, even morally questionable ones, particularly when those results are obtained by bold and decisive action.[23] This kind of violence is a particular problem at times when there is no regular administration of justice, but the temptation to act in such a way is almost always before political men, even in more settled times. Moreover, self-command, like prudence, has its darker side. Great acts of self-command in the cause of injustice are, Smith notes, as useful for attracting the wonder and admiration of the world as are those made in the cause of justice (*TMS* VI.iii.12).

The man possessed of "superior prudence" corresponds to Smith's description of the man of the most perfect virtue "who, to all the soft, the amiable, and the gentle virtues joins all the great, the awful, and the respectable, must surely be the natural and proper object of our highest love and admiration" (*TMS* III.3.35). Such a man is most prudent in his personal life and the greatest benefactor of others. The man who is most fitted by "nature" to receive both sets of virtues is the man of the most "exquisite humanity," "who feels most for the joys and sorrows of others" and, as a consequence, will be the most sensitive to how he is viewed by others (*TMS* III.3.36). A natural disposition toward the virtues does not, however, necessarily lead to their acquisition. As I have already noted, our moral capacities are formed by the influence of society on our original passions. Furthermore, the place one occupies in society, along with the kind of society in which one lives, are the major determinants of character.[24] The man who lives a private life seldom has the opportunity to "exercise and practice" under the conditions necessary for acquiring the highest degrees of self-command. Smith explains that such a man "may have lived too much in ease and tranquility. He may never have been exposed to the violence of faction, or to the hardships and hazards of war. He may never have experienced the insolence of his superiors, the jealous and malignant envy of his equals, or the pilfering injustice of his inferiors" (*TMS* III.3.36).

The public man, by contrast, lives "under the boisterous and stormy sky of war and faction, of public tumult and confusion," where "the sturdy severity of self-command prospers the most, and can be the most successfully cultivated" (*TMS* III.3.37). Although the "great schools of self-command" are war and faction, "in such situations, the strongest suggestions of humanity must frequently be stifled or neglected; and every such neglect tends to weaken the principle of humanity." Smith adds that "it is upon this account that we so frequently find in the world . . . men of the most perfect self-command . . . who, at the same time, seem to be hardened against all sense either of justice or humanity" (*TMS* III.3.37). Thus, the virtues of humanity and justice thrive under a set of conditions very different from those that promote self-command.

The Permanence of Politics

The actual conflict, as opposed to the potential harmony, between humanity and self-command is an enduring problem. Both the structure of political life and the character of those who enter into politics perpetuate this conflict. Smith observes that our natural sentiments and our reason lead us to conceive of the idea of "universal benevolence": we are unable "to form the idea of any innocent and sensible being whose happiness we should not desire, or to whose misery, when distinctly brought home to the imagination, we should not have some degree of aversion" (*TMS* VI.ii.3.1). The constitution of human nature is, however, such that in practice we are unable to extend this benevolent disposition much beyond our own circle—our "society." Society is a compound of various little "systems" that radiate outward from the individual to encompass family, neighborhood, class or rank, and, finally, the society or nation as a whole. These systems are held together by mutual need and by "affection," which "is in reality nothing but habitual sympathy" (*TMS* VI.ii.1.7). The nation, for Smith, is a natural and necessary part of the world, but when looked at from a strictly moral perspective it is problematic. Nature, it seems, leads men down paths that drastically curtail their benevolence and even justice. The "love of our own country" and the "love of mankind" are distinct and sometimes contradictory sentiments. The "love of our own nation often disposes us to view, with the most malignant jealousy and envy, the prosperity and aggrandizement of any other neighbouring nation. . . . [A]nd the mean principle of national prejudice is often founded upon the noble one of the love of our own country" (*TMS* VI.ii.2.3). The lack of a "common superior" among independent nations means that they must "live in continual dread and suspicion of one another" (*TMS* VI.ii.2.3). For this reason the law of nations is seldom observed. In fact, this law itself is "laid down without regard to the plainest and most obvious rules of justice" (*TMS* III.3.42).

Notwithstanding the above, Smith is of the opinion that that "wisdom which contrived the system of human affections, as well as that of every other part of nature, seems to have judged that the interest of the great society of mankind would be best promoted by directing the principal attention of each individual to that particular portion of it which was most within the sphere both of his abilities and of his understanding" (*TMS* VI.ii.2.4). From an abstract, moral perspective, however, "the great society of mankind" remains the truly natural whole.[25] There is, in short, a conflict between Smith's moral standard—mankind—and his account of the foundation and operation of society. This conflict is most apparent in the life of the statesman who must lead his society against other societies. In times of civil unrest, he may even have to lead his own part of society against other parts. In such circumstances it is impossible for him to adopt the philosophic perspective of a partisan of mankind. The demands of society, to which Smith refers in one place as "the peculiar care and darling of Nature," take precedence, presumably so that nature can accomplish through indirect means her great and overriding ends of preserving and propagating the species (*TMS* II.ii.3.4; also *TMS* II.i.5 and *TMS* IV.i.10).

In the *Theory of Moral Sentiments*, where Smith discusses the politically ambitious in more general terms, he observes that under "all governments," even monarchies, most of the high offices and the "whole detail of administration" are committed to those who have risen from the middling and inferior ranks simply on the basis of their talent and industry.[26] A man of this sort craves distinction above all else. "He even looks forward with satisfaction to the prospect of foreign war, or civil dissension; and, with secret transport and delight, sees through all the confusion and bloodshed which attend them, the probability of those wished for occasions presenting themselves, in which he may draw upon himself the attention and admiration of mankind" (*TMS* I.iii.2.5). Thus private ambition, social station, and the order of nature conspire to perpetuate the potential for political and social turmoil.

The general problem of the character of the politically ambitious was exemplified in the disastrous quarrel over the fate of Britain's American empire. On both sides of the Atlantic, the politically ambitious were ambitious chiefly to increase their own importance. British pride proscribed giving up the empire. Moreover, to "the undiscerning eye of giddy ambition," Smith lamented, "it naturally presents itself amidst the confused scramble of politics and war, as a very dazzling object to fight for" (*WN* IV.vii.c.85). Similarly, the "ambitious and high spirited men"—the "natural aristocracy"—of the colonies had, despite what

Smith believed to a dubious cause, "chosen to draw the sword in defence of their own importance" (*WN* IV.vii.c.74).

It is no surprise, then, that Smith's overall account of political life is bleak. Just as every barbarian in the rude state of society is to some degree a statesman, every statesman in a civilized society remains to some degree a barbarian, even if he lives among philosophers. This is particularly true of the *Wealth of Nations,* in which criticisms of political life are seldom balanced by expressions of hope for a more virtuous politics. Smith sometimes puts the problem in extreme terms. Although he notes that government might be rid of the pernicious influence of merchants, he writes that the "violence and injustice of the rulers of mankind is an ancient evil, for which, I am afraid, the nature of human affairs can scarce admit of a remedy" (*WN* IV.iii.c.9).[27]

What remedy, then, was there for the "confused scramble of politics and war"? A major part of Smith's solution is to teach nations and statesmen that it is in their interest to pursue the just, generous, and liberal system of natural liberty that he discovered. Yet, as we will see, on the basis of Smith's own analysis this solution was insufficient. The rational pursuit of interest or power is not the sole or even primary human motivation. A clue to Smith's fuller solution is evident in the one instance in the *Wealth of Nations* when he flatters a certain kind of political man. He contrasts "the science of a legislator, whose deliberations ought to be governed by general principles that are always the same," with "that insidious and crafty animal, vulgarly called a statesman or politician, whose councils are directed by the momentary fluctuations of affairs" (*WN* IV.ii.39). The dignity of the Smithian legislator derives from the fact that he takes his bearings from a system that sets out "general principles." Before taking up Smith's remedy, we must take up the one that was proposed by liberal philosophers before him and embraced by Hamilton—constitutionalism.

Smith's Constitutionalism

State and Constitution

Though the notion that politically ambitious individuals are a threat to decent politics was not new, Smith's solution to the problem was novel. He departed not only from the ancient philosophers but also from those early-modern philosophers who conceived of the liberal project, such as Locke. His departures from the kind of Lockean constitutionalism that was so critical for the American Founders are particularly striking. Knud Haakonssen's account of Smith on constitutions stresses the tension between Smith's theory of the state or sovereignty—which Haakonssen describes as one of "absolute sovereignty"—and his theory of constitutions. Because Smith subordinates the latter to the former, Haakonssen concludes that he "did not allow room for constitutionalism—either for the 'Ancient Constitution,' consent, and right of resistance of whig lore, or for any premonitions of a written constitution."[28] Haakonssen is essentially correct, but I would like to explore the tension between state and constitution a little further before affirming his conclusion. In the first place, Smith remains a kind of constitutionalist in a normative sense in two important respects. He advocates respect for the established constitution of the state, and, furthermore, he emphasizes the internal structure of government as a key to good government. To be sure, Smith unceremoniously debunks the various partisan interpretations of the English constitution, but as a practical matter he shows almost complete deference to it in both of his published writings, despite its inherent flaws and the additional stresses placed on it by its embrace of the mercantile system.[29] Again we confront the problem of how Smith reconciled change and stability. The answer, we will find, lies beyond his constitutional thought in his account of the spirit of system. An account of Smith's constitutional thought is important though because it serves to highlight a crucial difference between him and Hamilton.

As I have already noted, when reading Smith one must always be careful of his practice of investing old words with uncommon and sometimes new meanings. There are similar complications in Smith's use of the word *constitution*. Here the difficulty is not so much that one word is used in two ways but that his idea of a constitution contains the germ of another idea that stands in tension with it. The problem is evident at the outset of his discussion of constitutions, in his distinction between the constitution, on one hand, and the "state or sovereignty," on the other. At times the two seem identical, but at other times they are distinct, with the latter the clear superior.

Smith equates *state* with the words *sovereignty, commonwealth, country,* and *nation* (*TMS* VI.ii.2.2–4,11,18). A state is a kind of whole composed of parts. The parts are the independent orders and societies that are somehow contained within the state. The state is a whole because the parts are linked by ties of interest and affection. It is, says Smith, the "greatest society upon whose happiness or misery, our good or bad conduct can have much influence. It is accordingly, by nature, most strongly recommended to us" (*TMS* VI.ii.2.2). The state is an intermediate grouping lying between, on one hand, the society of nations in which few, if any, natural bonds of affection exist and, on the other, the smaller societies of families and friends that are tied together by very strong natural bonds. Smith believes that "the wisdom of every state or commonwealth endeavours . . . to employ the force of the society to restrain those who are subject to its authority, from hurting or disturbing the happiness of one another" (*TMS* VI.ii.intro.2). The standard for state action is the public good. Although Smith seems to identify the public good with the good of the greatest number (cf. *TMS* VI.ii.2.2), he does not have in mind a strict utilitarian calculus, simply some general idea of that peace, stability, and prosperity of the state as a whole which necessarily affects every member of the state.

The "constitution" of the state is, Smith explains, "the particular distribution which has been made of [the] respective powers, privileges, and immunities" of the various orders and societies (*TMS* VI.ii.2.8). Although Smith does not state it explicitly, a constitution specifies where the sovereign power is customarily placed. The stability of any constitution depends partly upon the extent to which each of the different orders and societies that compose the state is capable of protecting its own prerogatives and partly upon each order and society keeping its ambitions within certain accepted bounds. Smith claims that the maintenance of an exact administration of justice is the key to maintaining the latter.

Every member of the state would, Smith says, in principle grant that the good of the whole is more important than that of any part, but it "may often . . . be hard to convince him that the prosperity and preservation of the state require any diminution of the powers, privileges, and immunities of his own particular order or society" (*TMS* VI.ii.2.10). The internal forces holding each of the different parts of society together are particularly strong. Each member of each order or society feels his "own interest, his own vanity, the interest and vanity of many of his friends and companions, are commonly a good deal connected with it. He is ambitious to extend its privileges and immunities. He is zealous to defend them against the encroachments of every other order or society" (*TMS* VI.ii.2.7). In addition to these forces of interest and vanity, Smith adds the "wisdom of nature," which is evident in the strong bonds of affection that families, friends, companions, and neighbors exhibit (*TMS* VI.ii.1.4). Such partisanship is beneficial in one important respect, because it "checks the spirit of innovation," thereby helping to preserve the "established balance" of the constitution (*TMS* VI.ii.2.10). The difficulty that emerges, however, is this: the constitution of the state places the power of sovereignty in a particular set of hands. What is it that keeps the sovereign power attached to the public good; that is, to the needs of the state?

The Formal Constitution

As a response to the problem just identified, I want to suggest that there are two sides to Smith's constitutionalism. For the sake of clarity, and for reasons which I hope will become apparent, I will label these two sides the *formal* elements and the *effectual* elements of his constitutionalism.[30] What I am calling the formal constitution of a state is found in Smith's account of the "principles" that he believes underlie all governments. It is these principles that secure the allegiance of subjects to the state and that account for the stability of a particular constitution.

Smith followed Hume in rejecting the contractualist account of the origin of government on the grounds that it was empirically false.[31] In the *Lectures on Jurisprudence,* Smith offered three essentially Humean arguments against the contractualist account. "In the first place, the doctrine of an original contract is peculiar to Great Britain, yet government takes place where it was never thought of, which is even the case with the greater part of the people of this country" (*LJB* 15). Second, whatever contracts were, in fact, entered into at the beginning of society are always considered binding on posterity, even though later generations had no part in making these contracts. Finally, the actual conduct of all governments belies the existence of such a contract. For example, treason is a crime of extreme proportions, whereas the breach of any sort of contract is never deemed to be so (*LJB* 15–18).

In place of a social contract, Smith looks at the variety of governments that have appeared throughout history, in order to find their common principles. Two factors, he argues in the *Theory of Moral Sentiments,* bind the parts of the state into a whole: "first a certain respect and reverence for that constitution or form of government which is actually established; and, secondly, an earnest desire to render the conditions of our fellow citizens as safe, respectable, and happy as we can" (*TMS* VI.ii.2.11). He explains the first of these two factors in the *Theory of Moral Sentiments,* but he addresses both fully in the *Lectures on Jurisprudence,* where they are described as the "opinions" of "authority" and "utility," respectively (*LJA* V.119–22; *LJB* 12–14).[32] In what follows, I draw on both accounts.

With regard to authority, Smith explains in the *Theory of Moral Sentiments* that there is a natural disposition in men "to go along with all the passions of the rich and powerful" and that upon this "is founded the distinction of ranks, and the order of society" (*TMS* I.iii.2.3). Sympathy with the rich and the powerful creates a natural deference before those of superior age and, especially, before those of superior birth and fortune. This deference is so essential to the stability of society that nature seems to have given it a power over men's minds greater than that of "enlightened" reason. Smith observes that "even when the order of society seems to require that we should oppose [the rich and the powerful] we can hardly bring ourselves to do it. That kings are the servants of the people, to be obeyed, resisted, or punished, as the public conveniency may require, is the doctrine of reason and philosophy; but it is not the doctrine of Nature" (*TMS* I.iii.2.3). The "visible" qualities of birth, age, and fortune hold more sway in human affairs than do "invisible" qualities, such as wisdom and virtue (*TMS* VI.ii.1.20; *WN* V.i.b.5).

"Utility" is the second opinion "which induces men to obey the magistrate." Smith does not have private utility in mind. "It is," he explains in the *Lectures on Jurisprudence,* "the sense of public utility, more than of private, which influences men to obedience. It may sometimes be for my interest to disobey, and to wish government over-turned. But I am sensible that other men are of a different opinion from me and would not assist me in the enterprize. I therefore submit to its decision for the good of the whole" (*LJB* 14). By utility, then, he seems to mean the sense that our own interest is connected to that of the community and therefore inseparable from that broader interest. We act on this opinion without necessarily calculating precisely what is in our own private interest.

The two opinions operate differently under different forms of government. Authority prevails in monarchies, whereas utility prevails in republics; but each of the opinions is present to some degree in all governments. Even in a despotism, for example, there must be some sense among some people—the palace guard, perhaps—that the government is for their collective benefit. Similarly, although it would be dangerous for authority to attach itself to individuals in democratic republics, it is nevertheless important that authority attach itself to offices of state in such goverments (*LJA* V.122).

Under "free governments," such as Great Britain, where the government has a democratic or representative part, the two opinions manifest themselves in the parties that naturally form. Authority is at the basis of the Tory party; utility is at the basis of the Whig party. Tories "pretend" that the monarchy is a divine institution; Whigs believe in the notion of an original contract that "can hardly be supposed to have ever been the case" (*LJA* V.114,123–24). The parties are manifestations of two natural dispositions: the "bustling spirited active folks, who can't brook oppression" find their home in the Whig party, whereas the "calm, contented folks of no great spirit and abundant fortunes" join the Tory camp (*LJA* V.124).[33]

In normal times, the forces of authority and utility are sufficient to secure the allegiance of subjects and thereby hold the different parts of the state together. In times of public disorder, however, the forces of attraction within these subsidiary groupings operate more strongly than do those that hold together society as a whole. The various little systems exhibit a tendency to break away from the controlling galaxy, the state. As Smith explains matters, under such circumstances the stability of a state to some degree resembles the stability of a balance of power among various independent nations. When public tranquility rests upon a mere balance of power, it is very easily disturbed.

It is important to observe that Smith's analysis of the principles or forces holding the state together provides only a limited basis for formulating law and policy. In the first place, one must remember that the perception of injustice will have a great deal to do with the stage of development that a society has reached. What from the point of view of a civilized society might seem the most extreme inhumanity might be regarded as the normal state of affairs in an earlier stage of society.[34] Furthermore, the principles of utility and authority themselves give little guidance as to what standards of justice ought to be established. The Whig contract argument, Smith believed, was really a confused attempt to articulate the utility argument. If a state is tranquil and prosperous as a whole, then the laws and policies in place are good ones and are approved of by those who live under them. But the utility principle tells us little about, for example, what changes would be needed to improve the state or what measures might be necessary to avoid an impending disaster. The notion of authority, in contrast, does provide some guidance for governing. In monarchies and aristocracies, especially, the "arts" of perpetuating deference to "authority" or, one might say, the arts of ruling are those of image making (cf. *TMS* I.iii.2.4). But here too it must be noted that knowing how to command is a matter very different from knowing what commands to give or the actual business of government.

The rejection of the contractualist account of government has a number of important further implications which grow out of Smith's belief that there are constitutions but no constituting acts, such as foundings or constitutional conventions. A comparison with the social-contract theories of Hobbes and Locke is very useful for bringing out these implications.[35] Smith agrees with Locke and differs from Hobbes by allowing that the sovereign power might be criticized on normative grounds by a subject. But, like Hobbes and unlike Locke, Smith makes the public or popular interest the sovereign concern of the state, while claiming that the public itself is not necessarily sovereign. The question that Locke raised about Hobbes might also be raised about Smith: what security is there that the sovereign will indeed pursue the public interest?

Smith differs from both Hobbes and Locke in that their contract theories show precisely who ought to be the sovereign. Hobbes made sovereign the person or persons authorized by the majority of persons party to the social contract. Locke made the legislative power the supreme power and left it to the majority of persons party to the social contract to decide in whose hands it should be placed. Smith, in contrast, seems content simply to leave the current or actual sovereign in possession of the sovereign power. In light of this observation, one is tempted to say that Smith argues for a doctrine of sovereignty that asserts the need for sovereignty but that he does so without specifying who ought to possess the sovereign power. If so, then Smith's constitutional theory involves a danger not far below the surface of encouraging a continuous power struggle. This observation raises, in turn, the question of how this power struggle is to be managed so that power and wisdom will coincide to achieve the public interest.

Forms of Government

The discussion in the previous section leads us to the observation that, for Smith, the issue of forms of government is subordinate to considerations of the underlying principles of government. Forms of government are just that—formalities that cover the true springs of society and government. That said, Smith's account of forms has certain important implications that bear on our general subject.

In the first place, Smith's general neutrality toward forms is important for the larger subject we are considering, in that it clears away one obstacle to combining government activism and political conservatism. If Smith's political economy is not tied to any particular form of government, then it is more likely that it will be useful to a wide variety of governments. More precisely, his political economy shows that although it is in the interest of the state to provide for a large degree of civil liberty, there is no reason why such an expansion of liberty should entail any change in the degree or kind of political liberty present in society.

In another way, however, Smith's account of forms brings us back to the problem of activism and constitutional conservatism, because his historical account of forms of government makes clearer the long-term political consequences of social and economic change. The possibility thus arises of deliberately managing political change using economic means. The post-Smithian statesman is in a position to be a skillful and farseeing political artisan. As a result, a version of the question of the best or ideal form of government enters through the back door.

The *Lectures on Jurisprudence* identify two basic forms of government: monarchies and republics, with republics being of two sorts, aristocratic or democratic. The form of a government is identified by locating the sovereign power. If it is with, say, the people, then we have a democratic republic. This typology of regimes is, however, quickly overshadowed by Smith's account of the evolution of government from its earliest beginnings to the emergence of modern Britain.[36] His history makes clear the manner in which the progress of commerce has affected forms of government.

On the subject of the best regime, however, Smith gives little guidance. Yet from his passing remarks, especially from his praise of the "system of liberty" that evolved in Great Britain, it is possible to discern three clear positions. First, Smith implicitly rejects democratic republicanism. This can be inferred from his comments on the laboring class that will necessarily form the majority in every commercial society. With regard to the public interest, he observes that "the labourer . . . is incapable either of comprehending that interest, or of understanding its connection with his own. His condition leaves him no time to receive the necessary information and his education and habits are commonly such as to render him unfit to judge even though he was fully informed" (WN I.xi.p.9). Second, Smith thought that a powerful aristocracy is always a threat to liberty. Indeed, he remarks that "the nobility are the greatest opposers and oppressors of liberty that we can imagine" (LJA IV.165). It is true that Smith does not display any great antipathy toward the English landed gentlemen. But we must remember, of course, that these "lords" had been stripped of the power their feudal and allodial ancestors possessed. The third inference follows from the first two: some form of monarchy is essential as a unifying element to the society, not only because of the monarch's clear interest in maintaining the state but also because of his ability to "manage" the various factions in society.[37] For Smith, a powerful and hereditary monarchy would seem to be an essential feature of every stable society.

The "Effectual" Constitution

In order to find answers to our concerns regarding Smith's balancing of constitutional conservatism and government activism, we must turn from principles and forms to a consideration of the internal workings of government. We are led in this direction for several reasons. First, although Smith stresses the need for a sovereign, he does not specify who ought to be sovereign. This difficulty is heightened by Smith's belief that political and social transformations follow from economic change. Taken together, these observations would lead one to anticipate a constant struggle for sovereign power. Finally, and most importantly, despite Smith's claim that the public interest is sovereign, he establishes no mechanism for ensuring that the public interest is the concern of the actual sovereign.

Thus the "formal" constitution of the state, though essential to the stability of the state, does not seem to have much to do with the actual business of government. Behind the formal constitution of every state lies what I have termed the "effectual" constitution or, perhaps, simply the administration. This is particularly the case in societies that have reached a high degree of complexity. To consider this suggestion we must discuss, first, Smith's understanding of the separation of powers and, second, his account of the administration of the actual business of government.

Separation of Powers: Smith discusses the separation of powers using categories derived from Locke and Montesquieu. He describes the growth of the various powers—legislative, judicial, executive, and federal—from their first manifestations in primitive societies to their developed forms in a civilized society. His most forceful recommendation is for the separation of the judicial and executive power. It is essential that these two powers be placed in separate sets of hands. Without this separation, an impartial administration of justice is impossible, because the executive will administer justice according to his whim. Yet Smith's history of government shows that this separation comes about largely as a result of the natural course of things. The sheer volume of judicial business in a large society means that the executive must create a separate class of judges (*WN* V.i.b.24–25). Even where the separation is not guaranteed—say, by life tenure for judges—the bulk of judicial decisions will be made impartially because the executive will be a partisan in only a limited number of cases. Thus Smith observes that, under Cromwell, the Tudors, and even the worst of the Roman emperors, the administration of justice was more or less regular (*LJA* IV.96–98,164–66).

With respect to the legislative power, Smith notes that "at the first establishment of judges there are no laws; every one trusts to the natural feeling of justice he has in his own breast and expects to find in others." The "growth of the judicial power was what gave occasion to the institution of a legislative power, as that first made them think of restraining the power of judicial officers" (*LJA* V.110–11). Thus legislative power, and therefore laws, come into existence only when a need is felt to limit the power of the judiciary. It is of considerable interest that Smith makes no similar case for the necessity of a separate legislative power, perhaps thereby leaving open the possibility that society might exist without a distinct legislative power.

Administration: The other aspect of the effectual constitution concerns those who actually exercise the powers conferred by the constitution in the daily administration of government. Smith believed that, in general, those who were members of the "ruling" classes by birth or fortune were unsuitable for political office. Louis XIV, for example, was regarded as "the most perfect model of a great prince," but he had not one jot of political skill (*TMS* I.iii.2.4). As a result,

> In all governments . . . even in monarchies, the highest offices are generally possessed, and the whole detail of administration conducted, by men who were educated in the middle and inferior ranks of life, who have been carried forward by their own industry and abilities, though loaded with the jealousy, and opposed with the resentment, of all those who were born their superiors, and to whom the great, after having regarded them first with contempt and afterwards with envy, are at last contented to truckle with the same abject meanness with which they desire the rest of mankind should behave to themselves. (*TMS* I.iii.2.5)

It is this class of men Smith calls the "natural aristocracy" (*WN* IV.vii.c.74; cf. *WN* V.i.a.41). Such men, he believes, are interested in public affairs "chiefly on account of the importance which it gives them."

We are returned to the problem with which we began—how to control politically ambitious people. What has become clear is that Smith depreciated the importance of the constitutional solution proposed by Locke. Smith even departed from the representational ideas expounded by Hobbes. What did he replace them with? To answer this question we must turn with greater care to Smith's account of the natural aristocracy, especially of the character and motives of those who seek or hold political office. They are the class who will at the very least shape policy by supplying advice. In some cases the whole business of government will be handed over to them.

THE SPIRIT OF SYSTEM

Speculation and Politics

Smith addresses the relationship between political speculation and politics briefly but suggestively in the central part 4 of the *Theory of Moral Sentiments*. entitled "Of the Effect of Utility upon the Sentiment of Approbation."[38] Chapter 1 of part 4 deals with the "secret motives" behind private and public endeavor, and it is in this context that Smith introduces the metaphor of the "invisible hand." Chapter 2 deals with the extent to which utility is an original principle of approbation. For present purposes, the most important passages are those in chapter 1 that deal with the "spirit of system." Although scholars have scrutinized the connection between the spirit of system and Smith's mention of the invisible hand, far less attention has been paid to his discussion of politics. This neglect is surprising, because Smith's discussion of the place of the spirit of system in politics reveals a great deal about his understanding both of political men and of how philosophy might influence politics. Indeed, because it explicitly parallels the discussion of the invisible hand, one must wonder whether it is not of equal importance.

Smith explains the principle of the spirit of system as follows.[39] Although we approve of a particular activity or object because of its utility to ourselves or others, it is often the case that this activity or object, which is "the means for attaining any convenience or pleasure," comes to be valued more than the end that it is intended to produce (*TMS* IV.i.3). For example, "[a] watch . . . that falls above two minutes in a day, is despised by one curious in watches. He sells it perhaps for a couple of guineas, and purchases another at fifty, which will not lose above a minute a fortnight" (*TMS* IV.i.5). When looked at from the point of view of the utility of watches, this is a foolish decision, because the two watches accomplish essentially the same purpose. Yet, Smith adds, human beings do not usually look at things in this "abstract and philosophical light." "It is the ingenious and artful adjustment of those means to the end for which they were intended, that is the principal source of [our] admiration" (*TMS* IV.i.8).

Smith emphasizes that this principle is not only applicable to trivial things but is "often the secret motive of the most serious and important pursuits of both private and public life" (*TMS* IV.i.7). The motive is secret in the sense that it is not explicit or stated. With respect to economic pursuits, we come to value the things that produce happiness more than happiness itself. When we observe the rich and the great, we marvel not at the actual happiness of the rich and the great but at their command of greater means to happiness. Our admiration sparks our own sense of vanity, which in turn fuels our acquisitiveness. The un-intended but beneficial results of this "deception" by nature—the invisible hand—are greater industry, an ever-expanding surplus of production, and the multiplication of the species.

In the political realm, Smith explains that

> when the patriot exerts himself for the improvement of any part of the public po-lice, his conduct does not always arise from pure sympathy with the happiness of those who are to reap the benefit of it. . . . The perfection of police, the extension of trade and manufactures, are noble and magnificent objects. We take pleasure in beholding the perfection of so beautiful and so grand a system, and we are uneasy till we remove any obstruction that can in the least disturb or encumber the regu-larity of its motions. (*TMS* IV.i.11)

As with economic pursuits, the end or the utility of the thing, in this case law and policy, is the only relevant criterion when viewed abstractly and philosophi-cally. Yet we do not always act with a view to this end, because "from a certain spirit of system . . . from a certain love of art and contrivance, we sometimes seem to value the means more than the end, and to be eager to promote the hap-piness of our fellow creatures, rather from a view to perfect and improve a cer-tain beautiful and orderly system than from any immediate sense or feeling of what they either suffer or enjoy" (*TMS* IV.i.11).

This observation leads Smith to contrast the man of humanity who lacks public spirit with the man of public spirit who lacks humanity. He remarks that it often will be to no avail to appeal to the humane man who lacks "public virtue"[40] by speaking of the "interest" of his country. "You will be more likely to persuade," he explains, "if you describe the great system of public police which procures these advantages . . . and all the several wheels of the machine of gov-ernment be made to move with more harmony and smoothness, without grating on one another, or mutually retarding one another's motions" (*TMS* IV.i.11). Although Smith says nothing that might lead one to believe that such an injec-tion of public spirit would be lasting in a man who has no public spirit to begin with, he next observes that "nothing tends so much to promote public spirit as the study of politics" (*TMS* IV.i.11). As Winch has justly observed, we have in these passages "the strategy of persuasion that lies behind the *Wealth of Nations*" and which provides "the basis of Smith's case for bringing science to bear on the conduct of the legislator."[41]

Yet Smith's emphasis on the role of a spirit of system is highly problematic.

In the first place, his discussion of the spirit of system in part 4 of the *Theory of Moral Sentiments* does not deal with the most interesting case of what to do about the men of great public spirit who lack humanity, such as Peter the Great, "the celebrated legislator of Muscovy" (*TMS* IV.i.11; cf. *WN* V.1.a.40). Later in the *Theory of Moral Sentiments,* however, Smith does take up the question.[42] He begins with the moderation of the man "whose public spirit is prompted altogether by humanity and benevolence" (*TMS* VI.ii.2.16). When such a man "cannot conquer the rooted prejudices of the people by reason and persuasion, he will not attempt to subdue them by force, but will religiously observe what by Cicero is justly called the divine maxim of Plato, never to use violence to his country, no more than his parents" (*TMS* VI.ii.2.16). He will, like Solon, "endeavour to establish the best that the people can bear." The "man of system," in contrast, "is apt to be very wise in his own conceit" (*TMS* VI.ii.2.16–17).

> [He] seems to imagine that he can arrange the different members of a great society with as much ease as the hand arranges the different pieces upon a chess board. He does not consider that the pieces upon the chess board have no other principle of motion besides that which the hand impresses upon them; but that in the great chess board of society, every single piece has a principle of motion of its own, altogether different from that which the legislature might chuse to impress upon it. (*TMS* VI.ii.2.17)

Here we glimpse an important element of the psychological basis of Smith's "spirit of system." It grows out of a desire to lead and direct other human beings in the most comprehensive manner imaginable. As Smith indicates, this kind of management of human beings is characteristic of founders and legislators. One might even say that it is a desire to imitate god—the architect and conductor of the universe.[43]

How can Smith's praise of political studies be reconciled with his rather dire warnings about the dangers of a spirit of system? We must not, of course, forget that Smith himself was the inventor and popularizer of a system: the "system of natural liberty." The difficulty with the spirit of system, as Smith describes it, is that it leads to a spiral of violence. Leaders begin by pursuing a policy that is inherently violent, in that it attempts to force society out of its natural course. Furthermore, they realize that spectacular acts of violence prove to be useful for keeping followers in awe. In contrast, Smith's political economy, I will suggest, is a system that avoids the dangers of systems. It teaches how the interests of the state can be achieved through moderate, though systematic, measures that satisfy private ambitions of the highest order. First, Smith's political economy dispenses with the need for violent policy, because it is a system in harmony with the natural motions of society and individuals. Second, instead of requiring acts of spectacular violence to keep followers in awe, it proposes to occupy them with the systematic pursuit of wealth under the discipline of competition. In addition to this moderation, it satisfies the desires of those who wish to lead and direct by placing them at the head of a great social machine.[44] From a strict moral standpoint this situation might be judged defective, in that humanity and benevolence enter into the actions of the Smithian legislator as unintended consequences of the spirit of system. But for Smith it was, perhaps, more important that government be effective and humane than that it be truly virtuous.

Public Enlightenment

In considering Smith's account of the relationship between speculation and politics, Smith's related recommendations in the *Wealth of Nations* for educational reform deserve more attention than they have received from scholars. "I have thought," Smith wrote to a friend, "a great deal upon this subject, and have enquired very carefully into the constitution and history of the principal universities of Europe."[45] The importance of Smith's recommendations grow out of his belief that the university, properly understood, is the transmission mechanism between those who discover ideas about laws and policy—philosophers—and those who use ideas—political men. Moreover, Smith's campaigns against the mercantile system and, less overtly, religious intolerance were battles against the prevalence of certain pernicious opinions as much as or more than they were political battles with particular ruling classes or groups. His thoughts on university reform indicate how philosophers might be placed in a situation in which they might have an influence on government and society. They form a complement to his views on the influence of a spirit of system on political men.

Smith proposed two kinds of reforms. First, the curriculum should be reconstituted to follow the model of the classical division of the sciences—natural philosophy, moral philosophy, and logic. Smith's object, however, was not the restoration of classical learning. The reformed universities were to teach modern natural science and moral philosophy. His object was to orient learning toward the education of those he termed "gentlemen and men of the world," rather than of ecclesiastics (*WN* V.i.f.32).[46] He believed that religion had subverted the teaching of useful knowledge by subordinating learning to the concerns of the next life, rather than to the "real business of the world." Smith's own writing and teaching fit neatly into this scheme. He taught many subjects: natural theology, rhetoric, ethics, and jurisprudence. The latter two he characterized as the useful and important branches of moral philosophy (*TMS* VII.iv.34; *WN* V.i.f.30). As it was, he published only two works: one on ethics, and one on "that part of jurisprudence which concerns police, revenue and arms."[47] His proposed work on government would have completed his study of jurisprudence. Clearly, he followed the program he recommended, one that addressed "the real business of the world." Furthermore, one must surmise that Smith would have hoped that his science of political economy would find its way into a new university curriculum.

Smith's second proposal was for the financial reform of the universities.[48] He argued that the system of public endowments had taken away the incentives for diligence on the part of teachers and, also, the necessity of teaching useful knowledge. Instead, such things as "the cobweb science of ontology" dominated the curriculum (*WN* V.1.f.5,29,34,46). Education, he suggested, should be put on a fee-for-service basis. He observed that those "parts of education . . . for the teaching of which there are no public institutions, are generally the best taught" (*WN* V.1.f.16). As evidence, he cited the healthy state of women's education, the public schools, the unendowed universities, and the philosophical schools of classical Greece. Smith's reasoning was based on a general rule: "In every profession, the exertion of the greater part of those who exercise it, is always in proportion to the necessity they are under of making that exertion" (*WN* V.1.f.4). Smith made one major and rather startling exception to this broad scheme of commercialization. Despite his general opposition to licensing systems, he recommended that the institution of "some sort of probation, even in the higher and more difficult sciences, to be undergone by *every* person before he is permitted to exercise *any* liberal profession, or before he could be received as a candidate for *any* honourable office of trust or profit" (*WN* V.1.g.14, emphasis added). If government created the demand, Smith was confident that teachers would be forthcoming.

The immediate context of Smith's remarks was a discussion of the dangers of religious zealotry among the common people. He was especially concerned with common people's fascination with ascetic religious leaders. Smith thought that an educated elite was an "easy and effectual" remedy for this tendency: "Science is the great antidote to the poison of enthusiasm and superstition; and where all the superior ranks of the people were secured from it, the inferior ranks could not be much exposed to it" (*WN* V.1.g.14).[49] This is one of the most intriguing cases in which the "wisdom of the state," government intervention, must supplement the "wisdom of nature," the natural course of things. Smith argues that society by itself produces and disseminates certain types of useful knowledge—for example, inventions with commercial applications. The clearest reason for his departure from this general rule is the strength of religious passions. He warns that "the authority of religion is superior to every other authority. The fears which it suggests conquer all other fears" (*WN* V.1.g.17). Civilization, it seems, will always be in a state of tension with religious passions.

Smith's proposed reforms would have a wide impact. He may have hoped that educating those who were to hold public office in the elements of enlightened statecraft would help preserve and extend civilization. It is important to be clear on what this means for Smith. He does not purport to have discovered an architectonic science of human things. He does not hold out a possibility like Plato's notion of a society oriented toward the good and ruled by a philosopher. Rather, he means to find the appropriate place for philosophy within the system of society, thus completing it. Philosophy, in this view, remains a part of the society, not its organizing principle.

Conclusion

The foregoing account modifies current views of Smith in two respects. First, Smith has been criticized for not extending his economic analysis to the realm of politics.[50] It should be clear now that, for Smith, the problem of dealing with the politically ambitious was inherent in political life. It is not appropriate to attribute the motive of economic self-interest to the politically ambitious. Nor is it adequate to expand the idea of self-interest to encompass the rational pursuit of votes or power. The most important kind of political ambition is both somewhat less rational (in the sense of calculating) and dramatically more ambitious. In contrast to Plato and Aristotle, Smith discounted the possibility of a morally educated elite. Instead, the humane influence of philosophy would be injected into politics by the indirect means of elaborating a humane system of law and policy. The appeal of this system to political men lay not in its humanity but in its delineation of a grand scheme of governance that satisfied high political ambition. Smith's systematic politics attempts to establish an alternative to both the Machiavellian politics and the religious politics of earlier times.

Second, one of the key criticisms of revisionist scholars has been that Smith's political economy must be sharply distinguished from that of later political economists. This claim is questionable if it is meant to imply that Smith did not look forward to a dramatic elevation in the importance of economics. It may be sustained in at least one respect, however. Smith presumed a permanent gulf between philosophers and political men. Contemporary mainstream economists, in contrast, occupy a kind of halfway house between Smith's philosopher and Smith's statesman. On one hand, they are detached from political life in that they are somewhat isolated from its passions. Moreover, they utilize an avowedly positivist methodology. On the other hand, they are attached to political life in that they both advise politicians and, increasingly, seek to explain their behavior. One might ask whether they have succeeded in creating a synthesis that Smith thought rare if not impossible or have failed to do justice to the demands of either way of life.

We are now in a position to discuss the aspects of Smith's thought that have preoccupied revisionist Smith scholars. In the next two sections I turn to the issues of natural justice and history, with the specific purpose of showing why Smith thought it was possible to blend activism and conservatism in a system that avoids the dangers of systems.

NATURAL JUSTICE AND POLITICS

To describe the nature of Smith's system that avoids the danger of systems, we must consider both his politics and his economics. This section considers the understanding of justice that provides the key normative standard for his politics. One goal of the discussion is to bring out what might be called the libertarian side of Smith, which revisionist scholars have obscured in their attempt to link Smith to the classical republican tradition. Another goal is to show that, although it is the normative standard for Smith the philosopher, justice is not necessarily or even likely to be the standard for the legislator. It is simply the standard the legislator ought to follow. Again Smith uses a strategy of indirection. Rather than showing the choiceworthiness of justice itself, he simply delineates the nature of justice and tries to show the benefits of following just policies. The next section deals with Smith's philosophy of history. As we will see, he believed commerce to be a progressive force in history. Most importantly, the spread of commerce brings justice within the reach of politics. We will see that this unintended consequence of economic progress is critical for understanding his endorsement of commercial society. It is also important for grasping Hamilton's suggestion that the theory of free trade involves an attempt to inject a "benevolent and philosophic spirit" into politics.

The Status of Smith's Lectures on Jurisprudence

Before turning to Smith's account of justice, we must attend briefly to the scholarly debate over the status of the two sets of student notes known as Smith's *Lectures on Jurisprudence.* Although these are not among Smith's published writings, they contain an extensive discussion of justice. Many scholars, particularly Haakonssen, have used the *Lectures on Jurisprudence* not only to flesh out the understanding of justice found in Smith's published works but also to argue for the continuity between Smith and the natural-law tradition that began with Grotius. The use of the *Lectures on Jurisprudence* as a guide to Smith's thinking in the area of justice is not without difficulties. Vivienne Brown has presented the most thorough challenge to this approach. First, she argues that the *Lectures on Jurisprudence* show "a reduced dependence on the traditional forms of argument of natural jurisprudence with its moral privileging of nature as reason by which all agents may know what is just." Smith instead makes external rules and positive law the core of justice. Second, the *Lectures on Jurisprudence* display a "more sociological and historical approach to justice and changing forms of property than had previously been apparent in the natural law writings." Third, the *Lectures on Jurisprudence* themselves display an incoherence on the critical question of the nature of rights, including the right to property. The 1762–1763 lectures seem to argue that most rights are natural, whereas the 1766 lectures seem to argue the reverse, that most rights are acquired, with natural rights being an exception. Brown sees this as symptomatic of a greater issue, the lack of discursive unity in Smith's writings. In the postmodernist vein, she dispenses with the assumption of authorial unity when reading Smith.[51]

Taking up Brown's points in reverse order, there has always been something problematic about using the *Lectures on Jurisprudence* as a guide to those elements of Smith's thought that are not elaborated elsewhere. Brown uses the differences between the two sets of notes to break up the "discursive unity" of Smith's writings, but there are simpler explanations. The *Lectures on Jurisprudence* are student notes, not transcripts of what Smith said. Furthermore, it seems that although Smith used the lectures to introduce his own theories, he tried to show the continuities between his ideas and earlier ideas about justice. It would not be surprising if a certain degree of confusion entered into the student notes as Smith shifted between the earlier philosophical accounts of justice and his own. Nor would it be surprising if Smith varied his account from year to year, as he felt the need to stress one earlier school of thought rather than another. With respect to Brown's specific example, it is much less important than what is clear and obvious in both the lectures and in the *Theory of Moral Sentiments;* namely, that Smith replaces traditional natural-law understandings of justice with his spectator theory of morality, thus making the natural–acquired distinction superfluous. It is of interest to note that the term *natural rights* does not appear in Smith's published writings, which suggests that he had moved beyond the concept. Smith's spectator theory of morality holds that we base our moral judgments not on a rule of reason but on the imagined judgment of an informed and impartial spectator.

One cannot argue with Brown's observation on the "sociological and historical" character of the *Lectures on Jurisprudence.* Again, however, her anxiety to show Smith's lack of discursive unity leads her to mistake its importance. She claims that it is in tension with the individualistic and universalistic focus of the *Theory of Moral Sentiments.* It should be noted first, however, that the historical and sociological emphasis is completely consistent with the account of the rise of civilization in the *Wealth of Nations.* Furthermore, with respect to the approach to morality taken in the *Theory of Moral Sentiments,* Smith himself saw no inconsistency between it and a historical approach. Indeed, near the end of that work he states his intention to apply just such an approach to the subject of justice!

This brings us to Brown's first argument, which claims that Smith's justice is essentially positivistic, a characteristic she believes is reinforced by the historical focus of the *Lectures on Jurisprudence.* Here, too, Brown's postmodern presuppositions lead to exaggeration. It is true that, for Smith, the rules of justice are general rules that guide our behavior, but this is far from making justice positivistic. It is one thing to say that justice is not the highest virtue, as Smith does; it is another to say that justice is not a real virtue. In a word, Brown fails to do justice to Smith's account of how our original and instinctive moral sentiments are transformed through experience into more complex but nevertheless moral responses to the variety of situations in which we find ourselves. On balance and subject to the qualifications mentioned above, it is perfectly legitimate to use the *Lectures on Jurisprudence* to make inferences about Smith. In particular, as Haakonssen points out and as we will discuss in subsequent sections, the *Lectures on Jurisprudence* are important for understanding the normative standard that the legislator ought to follow. Brown reads the significance of the legislator out of Smith, to the point that she seems to deprive not only his moral philosophy but even his political economy of any public-policy significance.[52] That said, Smith's account of the practical embodiment of the general rules of justice in law is not without complications. The most significant is the tension between our natural sentiments of justice and the demands of politics. We have already touched on this issue in the argument that there is a tension between Smith's cosmopolitan moral standpoint and politics.

Natural Justice, Justice, and Jurisprudence

"Society," said Smith, "may subsist among different men, as among different merchants, from a sense of its utility, without any mutual love or affection" (*TMS* II.ii.3.2). For society to exist on this basis requires a sense of justice, "the main pillar that upholds the whole edifice [of society]" (*TMS* II.ii.3.4).[53] Although society may operate through a "mercenary exchange of good offices," the sense of justice that secures those exchanges originally is not the result of calculation but, rather, grows out of our natural moral sentiments. Smith thought that virtues have a natural basis in human passions, and he regarded justice as the virtue having the strongest foundation in the human "constitution." The foundation for justice is the "sacred and necessary law of retaliation," which "nature has stamped upon the human heart, in the strongest and most indelible characters" and for which we have an "immediate and instinctive approbation" (*TMS* II.i.2.5).[54] It is not an interest in the preservation of society that originally arouses our indignation at injuries done to others. We feel for individuals because they are our fellow creatures, not, originally, because they are our fellow citizens. The "great law" of our nature that prompts resentment when we suffer injury or see others suffering injury is a sign of the "oeconomy of nature"; that is, of nature's reliance on passions rather than on reason (cf. *TMS* II.i.5.10).

Smith distinguishes two kinds of virtues: those that others may demand of us by force (negative virtue), and those that cannot be exacted by force (positive virtue) even though failure to practice them is blamable. Following from this distinction, he observes that a "remarkable distinction" exists between justice and all other virtues, in that justice is the only virtue that may be "extorted by force." No other virtue receives the degree of support that nature gives to justice. The "violation of justice is injury: it does real and positive hurt to some particular persons, from motives which are naturally disapproved of. It is, therefore, the proper object of resentment, and of punishment, which is the natural consequence of resentment" (*TMS* II.ii.1.5). Resentment is the desire to punish in proportion to a particular wrong. An excess of resentment is revenge.

In contrast, breaches of the positive virtues do not lead to "a real positive hurt." They deserve only blame or hatred. Not only does nature ensure that human beings resent injustice and sympathize with those who suffer injustice, it further supports justice by placing in the human heart a strong sense of remorse. A man who has committed an injustice soon reflects on his act and "is grieved at the thought of it; regrets the unhappy effects of his own conduct, and feels at the same time that they have rendered him the proper object of the resentment and indignation of mankind, and of what is the natural consequence of resentment, vengeance and punishment." Smith describes the feeling of remorse as "the most dreadful" that "can enter the human breast" (*TMS* II.ii.2.3). Without it, men would, "like wild beasts, be at all times ready to fly upon him; and a man would enter an assembly of men as he enters a den of lions" (*TMS* II.ii.3.4).

Justice is unlike the other virtues in one further respect: the rules of justice can and must be laid down with precision. Although moral judgment has its basis in our original passions, the "bulk of mankind" will rely for moral guidance on certain general rules that have been established and refined over a long period of time. A general rule is a rule of thumb that indicates a reasonably certain path toward gaining the approbation of others. Society's adherence to these rules fortifies individual consciences against the temptations of immediate passions, especially the selfish passions. With regard to most of the virtues, the general rules are "in many respects loose and inaccurate, admit of many exceptions, and require so many modifications, that it is scarce possible to regulate our conduct entirely by a regard to them" (*TMS* III.6.9). In contrast, the "rules of justice are accurate in the highest degree, and admit of no exceptions or modifications but such as may be ascertained as accurately as the rules themselves, and which generally, indeed, flow from the very same principles with them" (*TMS* III.6.10). The contrast between the rules of composition and the rules of grammar is similar, in that the rules of composition are not susceptible to a precise formulation, whereas the rules of grammar can be stated precisely and noncontroversially (*TMS* III.6.11).

The centrality of the passion of resentment to justice would seem to be the reason that the rules of justice must be strictly observed. What constitutes an injury must be clear. If the passion of resentment is unleashed without cause, then injustice is committed in the name of justice. Furthermore, strict adherence to the rules of justice keeps the passion of resentment from degenerating into the furious passion of revenge. Justice is absolutely necessary to society, but a lack of clarity about justice or an excess of justice, so to speak, might destroy society by giving rise to a spiral of violence.

Justice and Liberty

Because society would be at an end without justice, the "wisdom of every state or commonwealth endeavours, as well as it can, to employ the force of the society to restrain those who are subject to its authority from hurting or disturbing the happiness of one another" (*TMS* VI.ii.intro.2). The *Wealth of Nations* describes an "exact administration of justice" as the second duty, after defense, of a sovereign and, in the 1762–1763 lectures on jurisprudence, is said to be the "first and chief design of civil government" (*WN* IV.ix.50; *LJA* I.1,9). What are the rules of justice? In general, they aim at preventing "real and positive hurt" to others. "The most sacred laws of justice," however, "are the laws which guard the life and person of our neighbour; the next are those which guard his property and possessions; and last of all come those which guard what are called his personal rights, or what is due to him from the promises of others" (*TMS* II.ii.2.2). The *Lectures on Jurisprudence* describe and give rationales for an array of rights that, if protected, would constitute a liberal, commercial society. Regarding the justifiable limits on the freedom of the individual, Smith remarks that in "the race for wealth, and honours, and preferments, he may run as hard as he can, and strain every nerve and every muscle in order to outstrip all his competitors. But if he should justle, or throw down any of them, the indulgence of the spectators is at an end. It is a violation of fair play that they cannot admit of" (*TMS* II.ii.2.1). Smith's limitation of justice to commutative justice is based on the negative principle of doing no harm to others. In this regard, it departs clearly from the Platonic, Aristotelian, and Stoic conceptions of justice.

The rights to economic liberty and to property deserve special attention because they are so central to Smith's political economy. Consider first the right to economic liberty. English legal tradition had long guaranteed certain economic freedoms and maintained a presumption against grants of monopolies. These freedoms were not absolute, however. Freedom of trade was thought to be compatible with commercial regulation. Even the presumption against monopolies extended only to "ordinary trades" and, more generally, was subject to exceptions for the common good.[55] Smith's account of economic liberty in the *Lectures on Jurisprudence* and in the *Wealth of Nations* substantially broadens this liberty. Moreover, he gives it a novel theoretical basis.

Early in both sets of lectures Smith distinguishes three ways in which a person may be injured: as a man; as a member of a family; and as a member of a state. A man may be injured in his person, his reputation, or his property. With regard to his person, his body may be injured, or his liberty may be restrained. As to the latter, "the right to free commerce, and the right to freedom in marriage, etc. when infringed are all evidently encroachments on the right one has to the free use of his person and in a word to do what he has a mind to do when it does not prove detrimental to any other person" (*LJA* I.13). The right to *liberi commercii* he defines as "a right of trafficking with those who are willing to deal with him" (*LJA* I.12).

Smith treats the right to free commerce as an obvious or self-evident right. It is nevertheless remarkable just how little he has to say about the foundations of the right to economic liberty, even in his articulation of a system of natural liberty in the *Wealth of Nations*. What is the harm done by restricting free commerce that makes it self-evident? Smith presents two kinds of harm. The first is evident in his frequent claims that monopolies and other forms of exclusive privileges harm society by raising prices beyond their natural rates. This harm extends not only to consumers but even, where there are many monopolies, to the supposed beneficiaries of these privileges, in that they will often have to buy as well as sell at high prices. As I have noted, opposition to monopolies was an established part of the English legal tradition, but Smith implies that all regulation of trade has a monopolistic tendency and, therefore, is a source of harm. All regulation is harmful because it increases prices, which in the long run decreases the rate of economic growth. We will consider this argument in detail in chapter 2; here it is sufficient to note that Smith's argument follows from a rigid and systematic application of the following principle: "Every man is, no doubt, by nature, first and principally recommended to his own care; and as he is fitter to take care of himself, than any other person, it is right and fit that he should do so" (*TMS* II.ii.2.1). Regulations take from individuals decisions that they are best equipped to make. Although Smith stresses this kind of harm, one wonders whether it is self-evident enough to elicit an instinctive recognition of harm, depending, as it does, on the more or less remote consequences of policies. Smith implies, however, that there is a second, simpler and perhaps more instinctively understandable, kind of harm involved in economic regulation. Regulations prevent an individual from doing what he has a mind to do. When there is no prospect of harm to others, such regulations are violations of "natural liberty." They prevent him from following his innocent passions. The harm consists as much in the simple stop that is put to the pursuit of an innocent passion as it does in the denial of a tangible good, such as a cheaper commodity. One of Smith's other examples of freedom of the person is revealing. Freedom to marry does not ensure a good marriage, or a happy one, or even that the other party will consent when asked; it means only that one is free to pursue and to ask.

Smith granted that the right to property is not as self-evident and therefore requires some explanation. Whereas the impartial spectator's reaction to injury to a man's property is natural, property itself is a concept that has a historical development. As a result, the spectator's reaction to similar events will vary according to the level of social development. In a hunting society little private property of any sort exists. Theft goes unnoticed, because "there are but few opportunities of committing it, and these too cannot hurt the injured person in any considerable degree" (*LJA* I.33). As society develops, however, so do notions of property. The crucial event in the history of property, as Smith recounts it, is the move from the hunting to the shepherding way of life, because this transition introduces inequality of property into society and, with it, the need to protect the wealthy. More-refined notions of property evolve as society progresses.[56] For example, a person in an advanced society would be rightfully angry at the nonperformance of a contract he had made with another, even if he had never met that other person.[57] The way in which a right to property accrues by way of occupation helps to further clarify the point.[58] A man who picks up a previously unclaimed apple and takes it into his possession would have a reasonable expectation that he will be able to enjoy the use of the thing. If someone then takes the apple, those expectations would be disappointed; and the disappointed expectations, as much as the actual loss, would produce understandable resentment.[59]

Natural Justice and Politics

So far I have traced in Smith's account the emergence of the "sacred rules" of justice from our natural sense of justice. It appears, however, that when justice is considered in a political sense, it is not so natural.[60] When placed in a political context, acts otherwise blameless may sometimes become objects of disapprobation.[61] In this regard, Smith's consideration of those cases in which laws are made and punishments set solely with reference to the general interest of society is important. The most extreme cases are those of "civil police" or "military discipline." Smith describes as an example the fate of a sentinel put to death for falling asleep on duty. The sentinel "suffers death by the laws of war," a "just and proper" fate because when "the preservation of an individual is inconsistent with the safety of a multitude, nothing can be more just than that the many should be preferred to the one." Yet the "*natural* atrocity" of the act itself does not excite in us "any such resentment that would prompt us to take such dreadful revenge" (*TMS* II.ii.3.11, emphasis added). According to Smith, it is clear from this example that our approbation is founded on a different principle from that on which is based our approval of the punishment of, say, a murderer. Whereas the former requires an act of "firmness and resolution" to acknowledge the "interest of the many," the latter requires only that our natural sentiments run their course.

Two further examples indicate the way in which the impartial spectator always prefers the interest of society over that of the individual. They are taken from a class of laws that Smith terms "laws of police," as distinct from "laws of justice."[62] Consider first the institution of primogeniture, which Smith describes as "contrary to nature, to reason, and to justice" (*LJA* I.116). The "natural law of succession" is to divide family property equally among all the children (*WN* III.ii.3). The right of primogeniture once had a reasonable basis, however. After the fall of the Roman Empire, the lack of a central authority meant that "the security of a landed estate, . . . the protection which its owner could afford those who dwelt on it, depended upon its greatness. To divide it was to ruin it, and to expose every part of it to be oppressed and swallowed up by the incursions of its neighbours." Every great lord was "a sort of petty prince" (*WN* III.ii.3). With the progress of society, this institution ceases to be reasonable, though the pride of families might lead to its continuance, perhaps for several centuries.

The laws of marriage and divorce are "laws of police" that seem to be at all times necessary.[63] According to Smith, neither polygamy nor divorce, in their nature, violates natural justice, because neither inflicts any immediate harm. From the point of view of "police," however, there are very good reasons for laws that strictly regulate these activities (*LJB* 111–12). Polygamy, for example, introduces bitter rivalries of interest and love into society, and it is invariably found in despotic states (*LJB* 112–15). It also precludes the possibility of a hereditary nobility, which Smith sees as sometimes important to the defense of the state (*LJB* 116). He grants that when the ratio of men to women is particularly low, polygamy might be necessary, but against Montesquieu he argues that this is very unlikely because the natural laws of generation do not vary much across the globe (*LJA* III.35).[64]

Each of these three examples illustrates the priority of society over the individual. This priority clearly follows from Smith's account of society as the instrument for effecting the great ends of nature: the preservation of individuals, and the propagation of the species. For this reason, at times the impartial spectator will approve of violations of our natural sense of justice. The rationale for this type of law sheds light on a neglected but rather surprising passage in the *Theory of Moral Sentiments* concerning the duties of a "law-giver." The context is Smith's argument that among equals there is no right to enforce the positive virtues. A superior—for example, the civil magistrate—may, however, promote "the prosperity of the commonwealth, by establishing good discipline, and by discouraging every sort of vice and impropriety; he may prescribe rules therefore which not only prohibit mutual injuries among fellow citizens, but *command mutual good offices to a certain degree*" (*TMS* II.ii.1.8, emphasis added). When he speaks of the "prosperity of the commonwealth," he does not have in mind anything more than the continuance and growth of society. His specific examples are laws that oblige parents to support children and children to support parents. Furthermore, Smith is quick to add that of "all the duties of a lawgiver, however, this, perhaps, is that which it requires the greatest delicacy and reserve to execute with propriety and judgement. To neglect it altogether exposes the state to many disorders and shocking enormities, and to push it too far is destructive of all liberty, security and justice" (*TMS* II.ii.1.8).

Smith and the Natural-Rights Tradition

To conclude this section, it is helpful to draw a general comparison between Smith and Locke on natural rights. Such a comparison will pave the way for the discussion of Hamilton, who remained much closer to the Lockean version of the natural rights tradition. Locke begins with free and equal individuals in a state of nature. His theories of society and government seek to preserve the freedom and equality of that initial state while guarding against its inconveniences. That said, only in the state of nature is there "natural liberty," strictly speaking. In society, natural rights are modified according to circumstances and, to that extent, they are replaced by civil rights. These modifications result from deliberations by the community and are guided by the principle of majority rule. Natural rights, however, are inalienable, and, hence, the social contract is contingent on their continuing protection.

Smith did not claim to have discovered what justice is. That had been done by earlier philosophers and, perhaps, even by society itself. The objects of his philosophizing were twofold: first, to state precisely what the rules of justice are and, second, to answer certain important secondary questions, such as why we approve of justice and why we feel obliged to follow its commands. He departed from other early-modern accounts of justice in two respects. First, he reformulated the modern natural-rights tradition on the basis of his impartial-spectator theory of morality. Whereas Hobbes and Locke had spoken of man in a state of nature as possessing certain inalienable natural rights, Smith speaks simply of rights approved by an impartial spectator who acts as a kind of conscience, both for the individual and for society as a whole. Second, Smith sought to remove from rights theory what he saw as the excessive rationalism that characterized not only the theories of Hobbes and Locke but also Hume's theory of justice. Hume had, Smith believed, derived justice from a sense of utility that implied a degree of rationality which human beings do not possess, at least originally.

Smith, in contrast, takes a two-track approach. On one hand, he adopts a moral standard that is fundamentally apolitical and that provides general guidance for regulating relationships between equal individuals. This standard accounts for the libertarian side of Smith: we are free so long as we do no direct and immediate harm to others. On the other hand, Smith acknowledges the supremacy of the needs of society in the eyes of the impartial spectator, who must at times brace himself and recognize the need for laws that seem to violate our natural sentiments of justice. Smith is, in short, an uneasy utilitarian. It is in light of this uneasy utilitarianism that Smith's view of history and his system of natural liberty take on their full significance. In both cases, he shows that the gap between natural justice and the needs of society can be substantially narrowed if the right laws and policies are followed.

One must, however, go farther than either of these suggestions. If human psychology is the basis of our sense of justice, what accounts for the variety of conceptions of justice that have prevailed in the world at different times? What would account for the priority of the type of justice that prevails in commercial societies? Why, for example, did other societies so cherish honor? I suspect it was Smith's study of history that showed him the naturalness and immanence of commercial society and, hence, the priority of commutative justice. What factors led him to accept the judgment of history is a difficult question, discussion of which I will defer until we have considered more fully the connection between history, commerce, and civilization.

THE HORIZON OF PROGRESS

History and Smith's Politics

The evolutionary account of justice just discussed forms a part of Smith's larger story about the history of the progress of society. In this section I explore the connections between this larger story and Smith's history of justice. According to Winch, no "less than Hume, Smith is engaged in an experimental inquiry into the science of politics, making use of ordinary (i.e., not conjectural) historical material to provide evidence of regularity, or constant contingency, in a world of apparent diversity and change."[65] Chapter 2 takes up in detail Smith's analysis of the causes of economic progress. This section considers the connections between economic progress and change in other aspects of society. Smith is quite clear that economic forces, chiefly the desire of every man to better his condition, are among the "common causes" that influence the development of society.[66] Furthermore, all of Smith's writings contain indications that economic progress has a number of predictable effects on social and political life which are largely unanticipated by the historical actors. Scholars have, however, keenly disputed the precise connections between economic progress and progress in other aspects of society.

Proponents of the liberal-capitalist perspective tend to take Smith's emphasis on the role of economic forces as evidence of his depreciation of politics. Some have interpreted the emphasis on economics as an anticipation of Marx. Others have viewed it as an indication of a kind of political fatalism.[67] Perhaps the most intriguing suggestion remains that of Cropsey, who argued in *Polity and Economy* that Smith regarded "free government" (i.e., some form of republicanism) as naturally best. Furthermore, in the chapter entitled "The Problem of Smith's Intention," he concluded that Smith endorsed commercial society, despite its moral shortcomings, because commerce "generates freedom and civilization." In other words, Smith's "philosophy of history . . . dictated his general philosophy to him."[68] Cropsey believed that it was necessary to look for "Smith's intention" because he divined a deep tension between Smith's understanding of the moral order to which human beings aspire and the natural order their passions drive them to create. He suggested that it was Smith's preference for liberty which led him to endorse commercial society despite its moral shortcomings.

Revisionists respond that it is wrong to view Smith as an economic determinist who finds little or no place for politics. Duncan Forbes made the following points in response to Cropsey's argument. First, Smith did not believe that commerce or even justice requires the "freest republican government." Absolute monarchy, for example, is not necessarily incompatible with "free government" because free government requires only that civil liberty, not political liberty, be guaranteed. Forbes's second and more important argument is that Smith saw no necessary connection between economic progress, on one hand, and civilization and freedom, on the other. He suggests that one "cannot have freedom without commerce and manufactures, but opulence without freedom is the norm rather than the exception." Thus "liberty in the broader sense of the rule of law" is not "the natural and necessary result of economic progress." He points to the examples of China and India, which Smith presents as economically advanced, but backward with respect to liberty and justice. It was, however, the widespread persistence of slavery in the world that provided the most compelling evidence. Forbes suggests that Smith regarded this state of affairs as natural because the peaceful desire to improve one's condition is seldom a match for the Hobbesian "desire to dominate others and enforce [one's] will."[69] Haakonssen, who accepts Forbes's argument, concludes that it "was a mistake to call Smith's view of society and history 'economic' or 'materialist'" and that it is really "pluralistic and open-ended."[70] The open-ended nature of history means that there remains an independent role for politics and, sometimes, a decisive role for a legislator.

But this supposed opposition between political activism and economic determinism is really a false dichotomy. To begin with, as the history of Marxism tragically shows, even the most rigid economic determinism is quite compatible with the most fervent political activism. Smith's history of progress is not rigidly deterministic, however. He often identifies the natural with the necessary,[71] but this identification does not imply that the natural and necessary course of things is inevitable. Secular or religious authorities, for example, may thwart the natural course of things. Under such circumstances, nature will still exert itself, but it will do so less forcefully and therefore less clearly. In this section I want to make clear, first, the extent to which Smith thought that the spread of commerce was a force for progress toward civilization and freedom. This will pave the way for a consideration of the significance of this knowledge for politics and philosophy. The appearance that there is an opposition between political activism and the natural course of things grows out of a failure to recognize that philosophers and political men have different perspectives on the natural progress of society. As we will see, what appears as salutary constraint to the one might appear as an opportunity to the other.

Commerce and Politics

An interest in the course and pattern of historical change—the natural course of things—pervades Smith's writings.[72] The *Wealth of Nations* contains at least four perspectives on the natural course of things. First, Smith traces the rise of civilizations to the extension of the division of labor. Second, he considers the natural distribution of reward in a particular society or neighborhood. Third, he outlines the "natural progress of opulence," in which society moves through various kinds of investment activities, from agriculture through manufacturing to foreign trade. But Smith's broadest view of history follows the progress of society through four stages of economic development: hunting; pasturage; agriculture; and commerce. The search for comfort and security is present at each stage, but, as the struggle for bare self-preservation is gradually won, it is replaced by a more complex struggle for status. Smith is quite explicit in the *Theory of Moral Sentiments* that it is vanity—the desire for distinction—rather than the simple desire for self-preservation that leads to acquisitiveness (*TMS* I.iii.2.1). There are two levels to Smith's analysis. About the primary level there is little dispute. Smith identifies the desire of every man to better his condition, rather than government policy or the providence of god or nature, as the engine of economic progress. The debate is really about the secondary effects of economic progress on politics and society at large.

It seems clear that Cropsey exaggerated Smith's republicanism. In the first place, it is important to note that for Smith the natural course of things tends toward establishing absolute monarchies fortified by standing armies—"military monarchies." This tendency manifested itself in the ancient world, on the continent of Europe, and in Asia. "In England alone a different government has been established from the natural course of things" (*LJA* IV.168). The English system of liberty, with its representative institutions, was, in fact, the result of a great variety of accidents. More generally, the reader will recall from the previous section that Smith regarded justice as the essential pillar of society. His notion of justice does not, however, entail any need for political liberty. His account of the military monarchy that succeeded the Roman Republic makes this point clear. Imperial government meant the end of political liberty, but, for most Romans, it did not mean the end of civil liberty. Faction and intrigue sometimes reached frenzied proportions within the inner circle, but beyond it life went on much the same as before. Realizing the value of laws, the emperors had no interest in changing the administration of justice in private affairs. In fact, justice in private affairs was never administered better than under the worst emperors, Nero and Domitian (*LJB* 45).[73]

Cropsey's account of Smith's philosophy of history, however, is much closer to the truth than are those of his critics. The revisionist critique is wanting in two respects. First, it understates the extent to which Smith saw commerce as a progressive force in history. The critical point is that economic progress establishes a framework of society that makes it possible for the peaceful desire to better one's condition to hold in check the desire to dominate others. Second, the argument that, in the actual course of history, economic progress has not always led to the emergence of a fully free and civilized society misses the mark. Smith's history of progress was not rigidly deterministic. As a result, room remains for action on the part of the philosopher and the statesmen to bring the actual course of history more into conformity with the strictly natural course. Specifically, the philosopher is able to infer from the actual course of history what the truly natural course of history would be and, in addition, to present it in such a manner that it proves useful and appealing to statesmen. The real question concerns whether there are any natural obstacles to bringing the actual course of history into line with the strictly natural course. We will see that the only enduring obstacle is ignorance—something the philosopher is in a position to remedy. Each of these points deserves fuller development.

Smith shows that economic progress has three highly desirable secondary effects: first, it centralizes political power; second, it improves the administration of justice; and, third, it provides the psychological basis for a specific kind of moral improvement. These effects necessarily result in a certain level of civilization and freedom; and, what is more important, they make possible further expansions of both.

Centralizing Power: The centralization of political power is an almost certain consequence of economic progress. In small societies, economic progress has a democratizing effect, but small societies fall prey to large societies, and large societies are necessarily monarchical. A powerful, centralized monarchy is a necessary—though perhaps not sufficient—condition for the establishment of civil liberty.[74] The tendency toward centralization of political power is illustrated in Smith's famous account of how economic progress destroyed the power of the great barons and the clergy in Europe. Two kinds of powers emerged after the fall of the Roman Empire: the nobility, and the Catholic clergy. The European monarchs were completely overshadowed by regional lords. The lords governed their lands without regard to justice, but they made liberal use of their wealth in order to keep their subjects in a state of dependency that amounted to slavery. Commerce and manufactures, however, "gradually introduced order and good government, and with them, the liberty and security of individuals" (*WN* III.iv.4). Foreign commerce and manufactures "gradually furnished the great proprietors with something for which they could exchange the whole surplus of their lands, and which they could consume themselves without sharing it either with the tenants or retainers. . . . Thus for the gratification of the most childish, the meanest of all vanities, they gradually bartered away their whole power and authority" (*WN* III.iv.10). The resulting change in the balance of power among the different classes made possible the introduction of "regular government" into the countryside of Europe because it strengthened the hands of the monarchs, who found it in their interest to establish justice. Smith remarks that the contribution of the progress of commerce and manufactures to good government, "though it has been least observed, is by far the most important of all their effects" (III.iv.4).

Smith treats the Roman Catholic clergy as another species of nobility, though, perhaps, more powerful and more dangerous than ordinary nobles (*WN* V.i.g.22–25). The decline in the power of the clergy, which resulted from the same causes that weakened the lords, also contributed to the centralization of political power and to the extension of civil liberty. Like the lords, the Catholic clergy began to lose power over the common people when they curtailed their charitable works in order to have more money to spend on themselves. This shift loosened the tie of self-interest between the clergy and the people. Furthermore, as the clergy grew wealthy, they came to resemble mere "gentlemen." This resulted in a decline in their spiritual authority. The common people always adhere to the "strict" or "austere" moral code and, as a result, they are always moved by ascetic spiritual leaders. With the changed habits of the Catholic clergy, the people began to lose their religious awe, so the way was opened for new sects to emerge. The natural course of things tends toward a proliferation of small sects. Not only does this proliferation remove the threat to government from any one sect, but the ensuing competition for souls brings about a rationalization of religious doctrine. Each sect is so small that it must learn "candor and moderation" in order to survive. Had government policy not come to the aid of particular sects, Smith suggested that Great Britain might have as many as three thousand sects (*WN* V.i.g.8–12).

Separating Powers: Perhaps the most significant way in which economic progress promotes freedom and civilization is by bringing about an improvement in the administration of justice. Specifically, economic progress necessitates the separation of executive power and judicial power. As Nathan Rosenberg has emphasized, the separation of powers is really a form of division of labor, and in politics, as in industry, division of labor produces advantages.[75] The separation is essential for justice, because "[w]hen the judicial is united with the executive power, it is scarce possible that justice should not frequently be sacrificed to, what is vulgarly called, politics" (*WN* V.i.b.25). In the cases of Rome and modern Europe, the "separation of the judicial from the executive power seems originally to have arisen from the increasing business of the society, in consequence of its increasing improvement. The administration of justice became so laborious and so complicated a duty as to require the undivided attention of those to whom it was entrusted." Those holding the executive power were happy to relinquish this "burdensome" and "ignoble" part of government (*WN* V.i.b.24).

Fostering Commercial Virtues: The third contribution of economic progress to freedom and civilization is that it establishes the psychological basis for a kind of moral improvement, especially with regard to justice. Among "civilized nations, the virtues which are founded upon humanity are more cultivated than those which are founded upon self-denial and the command of the passions. . . . The abstinence from pleasures becomes less necessary, and the mind is more at liberty to unbend itself, and to indulge its natural inclinations in all those particular respects" (*TMS* V.2.8). Because passions operate under fewer restraints, civilization is characterized by a greater "naturalness." This is not to say that civilization leads to an overall increase in benevolence. Indeed, some of the more conspicuous forms of benevolence might decline, but sensitivity to breaches of certain virtues will be greater. With respect to justice, Smith observes that in "some countries, the rudeness and barbarism of the people hinder the natural sentiments of justice from arriving at the accuracy and precision which, in more civilized nations they naturally attain to" (*TMS* VII.iv.36).[76]

Smith closely follows Montesquieu when he describes the specific implications of the greater naturalness of commercial society. The commercialization of society creates a greater degree of self-reliance or independence. Every person becomes, in some measure, a merchant rather than live in a state of dependency on particular rich and powerful men. To earn a steady living, an individual must appeal to the economic self-interest of a multitude of other individuals. As a result, the virtues of punctuality, justice, and probity flourish, because they are the necessary prerequisites of commercial success. A commercial society is likely to have less crime, because "nothing tends so much to corrupt and enervate and debase the mind as dependency, and nothing gives such noble and generous notions of probity as freedom and independency." Commerce is one "great preventive of this custom" (that is, of dependency; *LJA* VI.6). The particular effects of foreign commerce should be noted. "The history of commerce," Montesquieu had said, "is that of communication among peoples."[77] This communication has a number of positive effects. Smith agreed that commerce tends to wear down habitual attachments to one's own country. Merchants, he says, are not really citizens of any country (*WN* V.ii.f.6). One might say that they are citizens of the "great mercantile republic." Furthermore, because commerce creates ties of mutual self-interest, it "ought naturally to be, among nations, as among individuals, a bond of union and friendship" (*WN* IV.iii.c.9). Smith sometimes refers to those nations that treat foreigners as enemies as "barbarous" (*LJA* V.91; *LJB* 88).

History and Liberty

With these observations in mind, let us return to the arguments made by Forbes about the connections among economic progress, civilization, and freedom. On the basis of the foregoing, I believe there are persuasive reasons for attributing to Smith the view that the relationship between economic progress and civilization is positive. One must first recognize that Smith uses the word *civilization* somewhat loosely. At times he means simply opulence, with its accompanying sophistication in the arts and sciences. He refers to the republics of ancient Greece and Italy and to the empires of China and India as civilized. At other times, he clearly means that civilization implies a high level of humanity and freedom, such as when he speaks of modern Europe. The question is really whether economic progress makes a contribution to freedom and humanity in societies like India and China. Smith's description of China is extensive and particularly bleak: poverty afflicts the majority; infanticide is widespread; and arbitrary rule prevails at all levels of government. It seems, however, that two factors explain the state of China. First, the rulers of China were ignorant of the value of laws (*LJA* iv.108). They were the descendants of the Tartars and simply continued the arbitrary ways of their ancestors. Second, China was an insular society that shunned foreign trade (*WN* IV.ix.40). This policy put limits on China's ability to grow. It also meant that China was deprived of communication with other nations, which might have brought knowledge of more-enlightened systems of policy. The important point is that China's lack of freedom was due not to something in the nature of man but to ignorance and a lack of commerce, specifically foreign commerce.

The issue of slavery is similar. Forbes is correct to draw attention to Smith's belief that opulence and republicanism tend to make the institution of slavery particularly harsh and to his remarkable statement that a "humane man would wish . . . if slavery has to be generally established that [freedom and opulence], being incompatible with the happiness of the greater part of mankind, were never to take place" (*LJA* III.111). But he is not correct when he says that slavery is "more natural" for Smith than for Montesquieu.[78] To the contrary, Montesquieu thought that despotism and even slavery were likely to prevail in many parts of the world, because "physical causes" such as climate had so shaped the souls of the inhabitants of those places that no alternative existed. True, "moral causes" might be deployed in the cause of liberty, but with respect to much of the world, Montesquieu does not give great cause for optimism.[79] Smith, on the other hand, points to the natural desire to dominate over others as the cause of slavery. This is not such an intractable problem. What is necessary is the introduction of institutions to hold that desire in check. Moreover, the desire to better one's condition is really a peaceful manifestation of the desire to dominate. Both have their basis in human vanity, but in the case of economic acquisitiveness, what Smith terms the "natural insolence of man" is held in check. Instead of dominating through force, individuals must dominate through persuasion, either through oratory or through appeals to the self-interest of the other person (*WN* I.ii.2; *WN* III.ii.10; *WN* V.i.g.19).

Smith's political economy shows that slavery is economically inefficient (*WN* III.ii.9). It is therefore not in the state's interest to maintain the practice. In the *Lectures on Jurisprudence,* Smith remarks on the difficulty and, perhaps, impossibility of abolishing slavery. These difficulties are especially great in democratic societies, but they are also present in monarchies. Smith's account of slavery in the *Wealth of Nations* is different in two respects, however. First, there is a significant change in Smith's account of the ending of slavery in Western Europe. After commenting on the obscurity that surrounds the causes of the abolition of slavery there, Smith gives his own account of it. In the *Lectures on Jurisprudence,* he had pointed to the strength and self-interest of two institutions as the causes: the clergy, and the monarchy. But in the *Wealth of Nations* he does not mention the strength of the clergy as a factor. Thus the causes were wholly secular. Second, though noting the role of pride in preserving slavery, Smith leaves open the question of whether it is possible to bring it to an end. In the *Wealth of Nations,* slavery appears as one example of the more general problem of pride that stands in the way of beneficial reform. The persistence of the institution of primogeniture and Britain's reluctance to give up its American empire were problems of the same kind (*WN* III.ii.2–4; *WN* IV.vii.c.66). Smith exposes the folly and injustice of these various policies, with the hope that an enlightened public official might act on his advice at an appropriate time. In this regard, the centralization of power that Smith saw as accompanying the progress of commerce might be conducive to the abolition of slavery by an enlightened state or statesman. To repeat, the most important point is that, for Smith, nothing in the nature of things stands in the way, as it did for Montesquieu.

More generally, Smith is more optimistic in the *Wealth of Nations* about the possibilities of overcoming the cycle of the rise and decline of nations. The *Lectures on Jurisprudence* chronicle how Greece and Rome rose out of poverty and barbarism, became soft as a result of the progress of commerce, and were eventually conquered by barbarian nations. This cyclical view of history is barely noticeable in the *Wealth of Nations.* On a number of occasions Smith refers to the usual span of human prosperity and to the mortality of human endeavors, including empires, but, unlike Greece and Rome, civilized nations now, chiefly because of the invention of firearms, possess distinct and, perhaps, insurmountable advantages over barbarous nations. If these modern nations perish, they will do so in a new way. Taken together, the differences between the two accounts of slavery and the cyclical view of history suggest that, by the time Smith wrote the *Wealth of Nations,* he had adopted a more optimistic position regarding prospects for the advancement of civilization, including freedom.[80]

If an intractable obstacle to the emergence of civilized society exists, it is religion, which has the greatest powers over men because the "fears which it suggests conquer all other fears" (*WN* V.i.g.17; also *WN* IV.v.b.40). Where superstition prevails, hope is slim that the liberty and security essential for commerce will exist. Yet one must not forget that Smith is an optimist on this front as well. The Catholic Church, he observes, was "*the most formidable combination* that ever was formed against the authority and security of civil government, as well as against the liberty, reason, and happiness of mankind." Nevertheless, what "all the wisdom and virtue of man could never have shaken . . . the natural course of things, first weakened, and afterwards in part destroyed, and is now likely, in the course of a few centuries more, perhaps, to crumble into ruins altogether" (*WN* V.i.g.24).

CONCLUSION

To conclude this chapter, it is appropriate to venture some speculative comments about Smith's history of progress. Although these comments might seem to distract from our main purpose of comparing Smith with Hamilton, they are relevant in the following way: Smith's rethinking of the relationship between history and liberty was critical for the emergence of the philosphy of history. He appears to make modern liberty a product of history itself. In Hamilton's view, modern liberty was the result of a project, conceived by philosophers and put into practice by enlightened statesmen.

Smith's history of progress has much in common with Max Weber's famous account of the rise of capitalism. Both point to the systematic, methodical, and rational character of modern society; and both reject the notion that philosophers and statesmen have given shape to the modern world. They differ, however, in three important respects. First, whereas Weber traces modernization to the secularization of the Protestant work ethic, Smith believed that the wholly secular desire to better our condition is the driving force behind progress. Weber made religion and religious leaders the primary force in human history because religion is the great sculptor of values. By positing a natural course of things, Smith seems to deny the final importance of religion in history.[81] Second, whereas Weber's account is particularistic, in that it is connected to the influence of the doctrines of Calvinism, Smith's is universalistic. It applies to ancient and modern society, as well as to western and nonwestern societies. A further implication is that Smith effectively abolishes the primacy of the distinction between ancients and moderns that was so prominent in political philosophy from Machiavelli to Rousseau. Indeed, Smith places all breaks—whether foundings, constitutional conventions, or intellectual revolutions—under the horizon of progress. Third, Smith does not express Weber's dark pessimism about life in a commercial society. His portrait of a fully commercial society is not without serious blemishes, but he nevertheless must qualify as one of commercial society's greatest advocates.

As I have noted, the question of the ultimate grounds of Smith's endorsement, his criteria for choice, remains unclear.[82] A full answer to this question would disclose why Smith thought that commercial society was the truly natural society. It would explain why Smith could regard as unnatural earlier societies which held that the life of honor was the highest. Here I can offer only a partial answer, which, though important for the purposes of this study, leaves perhaps the greater part of this puzzle unsolved. The natural course of things establishes a social structure in which enlightened rulers are forced to check their natural insolence and to rely on management and persuasion, rather than on force and violence, because they cannot or dare not do otherwise. Weber had said that capitalism was an "iron cage," but one must say that Smith saw it as an iron cage for rulers.[83]

Smith's foreshadowing of the philosophy of history forces us to wonder about Smith's own relationship to the historical movement he described with such great effect. It is, perhaps, possible to say that economic progress is a sufficient condition for the establishment of liberty and justice. A remark by Hume helps to clarify the point. Machiavelli, he noted, was "certainly a great genius," but he made many errors that proceeded, in great part, "from his having lived in too early an age of the world, to be a good judge of political truth." Hume observed, in particular, that trade "was never esteemed an affair of state till the last century

. . . though it now engages the chief attention, as well of ministers of state, as of speculative reasoners. The great opulence, grandeur, and military achievements of the two maritime powers seem first to have instructed mankind in the importance of an extensive commerce."[84] Smith was aware of the historical character of his own science. His political economy was an outgrowth of the economic progress of the previous centuries. It is the product of the great variety of objects that parade before the philosopher. Looked at in this light, the four-stages theory constitutes a comprehensive, secular, and universal history of progress. It is comprehensive because it embraces the social, economic, and political aspects of change and organizes them around a single cause; namely, the desire of every individual to better his or her condition. This cause is distinctive, in that it is spontaneous and substantially independent of the powers of both religion and government.

This suggestion that economic progress might be a sufficient condition for the establishment of liberty and justice raises a question rich in ambiguity. Did Smith see himself borne along by the tide of history? If so, then what is the status of his theorizing? Would it not be contingent; a perspective on history rather than a scientific theory? Or does he see himself as somehow outside history? If so, is he not a kind of intellectual founder who, like Newton, originates a certain view of the world that then constitutes the horizon for all who in his footsteps?[85]

CHAPTER TWO

THE POLITICAL ECONOMY *of* PROGRESS

POLITICAL ECONOMY AND STATESMANSHIP
IN THE *WEALTH OF NATIONS*

SMITH'S ACCOUNT OF THE WAY in which economic progress contributes to the emergence of a free and just society was highlighted in the previous chapter. As I have argued, the perspective Smith adopts in this analysis is chiefly that of the philosopher. He does give an account of how our original experiences of harm and benefit evolve into a sense of justice, but his account of the political and so-cial changes that have shaped that evolution is not from the perspective of the various actors in the historical drama. Of special interest is that, as Brown notes, the legislator does not cut a very large figure in Smith's *Lectures on Jurisprudence.*[1] Statesmen are acted upon by history; they do not shape it themselves. The driving force behind history is, rather, economic in nature—specifically, the desire of ev-ery man to better his condition.

The *Wealth of Nations* is, in one sense, an obviously more complex enterprise. Although it was written for readers like Smith himself, who cast a philosophical eye over the economic and political spheres, it was also a practical work aimed at shaping public policy. Adding to this complexity is the fact that it is both a warning and an invitation to statesmen. It concludes that, as a general rule, it is mere "folly" and "presumption" on the part of the statesman to attempt to di-rect the economic activities of society for the public good. But, as I suggested, this warning is compatible with the notion that the *Wealth of Nations* is an invi-tation because it sets forth a plan of government and policy that Smith thought would satisfy the highest political ambitions. Thus the work is a remarkable accomplishment: it blends philosophy and policy in a style that somehow combines invective and scientific analysis, didacticism and inquiry, and, perhaps most remarkable of all, tedium and enthusiasm.

I turn now to the substance of Smith's political economy with three purposes in mind: first, to point to the centrality of Smith's political economy for his politics; second, to explain the way in which his system is a system that avoids the danger of systems; and, third, to elaborate his understanding of the relationship between the science of political economy and the art of statesmanship. A summary of the basic doctrines of the *Wealth of Nations* is the best way to address the theme of political economy and statesmanship. The question of the relationship between the science of political economy and statesmanship is, perhaps, *the* theme of Smith's great work, in that he attempts to show the relevance of knowledge of the natural course of things, as revealed by philosophy and the science of political economy, to the statesman's art. It is, we will see, the key to understanding the other two issues.

We must first make clearer what kind of book the *Wealth of Nations* is. Smith's passing remarks in it indicate that he was somehow speaking to both theoretical men and political men. He sometimes speaks of the work as a whole as a "speculative"; that is, a philosophical work addressed to men like himself (*WN* V.iii.68; see also *WN* I.iv.18; *WN* I.v.22; *WN* II.ii.66; cf. *Account* IV.18). But on occasion he goes so far as to apologize, presumably to readers of a more practical bent, for the highly abstract character of certain parts of his argument (*WN* I.iv.18). More importantly, the work is practical in the sense that it is emphatically normative. Smith does not simply analyze and evaluate, he recommends, and on a range of topics much broader than the boldest of contemporary public-policy analysts would ever venture.

What kind of practical men does Smith aim to reach? Even though the *Wealth of Nations* presumes a general familiarity with commercial matters, it is clear that Smith was not writing for men engaged in commerce. He explicitly says that his theories have nothing to teach merchants. He can add nothing to their ruling maxim: buy cheap and sell dear. They know their interest (*WN* I.v.21; *WN* I.xi.p.10). Despite Smith's contention that the political prejudices against merchants are excessive, he seldom passes up an opportunity to play on and even expand those prejudices (consider, for example, *WN* I.xi.p.10; *WN* III.iv.17; *WN* IV.ii.21; *WN* IV.vii.c.63,75,103–4).[2] The practical men he addresses are those who recognize or might be taught to recognize the importance of commerce but who probably look down on it. Two groups suggest themselves. Both are kinds of natural aristocracies: first, country gentlemen, who, as Smith makes clear, generally do not know their own interest; and, second, politically ambitious men, who seek to make a name for themselves by participating in public affairs. The former class are specific to Great Britain and, perhaps, North America; the latter class are found in all societies. As I noted earlier, when reading Smith one must be careful not to provincialize his thought by interpreting its significance solely in light of the British experience.

A brief consideration of the title and the organization of the *Wealth of*

Nations confirms these suggestions about Smith's various audiences. It also indicates the intimate connection between the issue of Smith's audience and the theme of political economy and statesmanship. According to Smith, the proper title of the work, *An Inquiry into the Nature and Causes of the Wealth of Nations,* corresponds to one sense of "political economy," which he describes as "a very important science" (*WN* IV.ix.38). This use of the term *political economy,* which occurs in Smith's discussion of the Physiocrats, is similar to today's independent discipline of economics. The Physiocrats, Smith noted, dealt with not only political economy but also "every other branch of the system of civil government" (*WN* IV.ix.38). Smith's focus is narrower: the nature and causes of the wealth of nations. By declaring the independence of economic inquiry from politics, Smith paved the way for the emergence of scientific economics.

The prevailing eighteenth-century usage of political economy prior to Smith was captured by James Steuart, who observed that "[what] economy is in the family political economy is in a state" and, furthermore, that the "principal object of this science is to secure a certain fund of subsistence for all the inhabitants, to obviate every circumstance which may render it precarious." Steuart's definition is notable for the extensive and critical role it gave to the "statesman," a term he used broadly "to signify the legislature and supreme power, according to the form of government." "I constantly suppose a statesman at the head of government, systematically conducting every part of it." Steuart acknowledged that the statesman is not free to establish "what economy he pleases" or to overturn "at will" the established laws of society. Nevertheless, he must "judge of the expediency of different schemes of economy, and by degrees to *model the minds* of his subjects so as to induce them, from the allurement of private interests, to concur in the execution of *his plan.*" The "great art . . . of political economy" is to gauge the "spirit" of the people so that he can adopt the appropriate policies. This task cannot be brought under general or universal rules.[3]

Throughout the *Wealth of Nations,* however, Smith mixes older and newer usages of the term, a practice we must consider in order to grasp the significance of the work. He uses political economy in two ways. The first usage denotes the way in which political economy is a science in a strict or speculative sense; the second denotes the way in which it is a practical science—that is, in the sense that it is part of the science of the legislator or statesman.[4] These two senses correspond roughly to today's theoretical and applied economics, but in Smith's mind the gap is greater and the transition between the two more difficult.[5] It is likely that two reasons underlie this studied ambiguity. First, it appears that a political presentation of the science of political economy was necessary so that it might be accessible to practical men. A second and more important reason was that it was necessary to show that this science was relevant to practical political decisions. It was possible, after all, that the science of political economy was simply a matter of theoretical interest, as it was, say, for merchants.

A glance at the organization of the *Wealth of Nations* supports this line of reasoning. Book 1 deals with the issues of value, exchange, and distribution. For the most part, the argument assumes a given annual produce. Book 2 deals with the process of accumulation and the determinants of the rate of increase in annual produce. The first chapter of book 3 summarizes the principles of books 1 and 2 by presenting an account of the natural progress of opulence; and, in the final three chapters, Smith chronicles the way the "policy of Europe" had distorted the natural progress of opulence. In this section Smith's analysis is, for the most part, conducted in terms of subpolitical or transpolitical units—such as town or country, or geographic regions, or civilizations.

Books 4 and 5 deal with the practical application of these essentially theoretical principles. The introduction to book 4 signals the change in focus:

> Political economy, *considered as a branch of the science of a statesman or a legislator*, proposes two distinct objects; first, to provide a plentiful revenue or subsistence to the people, *or more properly to enable them to provide such a revenue or subsistence for themselves;* and secondly to supply the state or commonwealth with a revenue sufficient for the public services. It proposes to enrich both the people and the sovereign. (*WN* IV.intro, emphasis added)

The differences between this definition and Steuart's are subtle but, nevertheless, decisive. To begin with, Smith's definition implies that political economy may be considered in more than one sense and, furthermore, that the other senses are, in some ways, distinct from that in which it is relevant to the science of a legislator. Prior to book 4, as noted above, little attention is given to the connection between the science of political economy and political life. Smith does spell out the social transformation that resulted from the spread of commerce in book 3, chapters 2–4. The focus, however, is Europe as a whole, rather than the politics of an individual nation. There is, to be specific, no discussion of the way in which this theory is to serve political men who must make their decisions in light of the circumstances which confront independent nations. Though of limited interest to a statesman, an account of the rise and fall of civilizations might be of great interest to a philosopher. In book 4, Smith argues for the superiority of his system of natural liberty over that of its chief rivals, the mercantile system and the agricultural policy of the Physiocrats. Here, he attempts to show that his system is applicable, with few exceptions, to a world in which reason and humanity are not universal. The focus throughout is on the policies of independent nations. The critical connection between the theory and practice is his claim that one of the objectives of political economy "considered as a branch of the science of a statesman or a legislator" is "more properly to enable them to provide such a revenue or subsistence for themselves." This decisive change implies that the legislator is charged with providing the conditions that enable the people to provide a subsistence for themselves, not with providing subsistence itself. If government is able to limit itself to this task, it might quickly be able to cut itself free from the economy.

Book 5 deals with the expenses and revenues of the state. Smith goes beyond simply discussing the most efficient way of raising revenue and sets down, sometimes in great detail, the proper objects of state expenditure. The organization and relationship of books 4 and 5 is clear. Book 4 deals with the enrichment of the people, who are, in modern times, the chief source of the revenues the state requires to carry out its duties.

Another way of approaching the issue of the character of the *Wealth of Nations* is to reflect further on the precise meaning of the term *system* for him. Again we face the problem of his inventive use of terminology. If we take the analogy between systems and machines seriously, we see that a machine is composed of several parts that are linked by certain necessary operations. In a similar manner, a system is an assemblage of linked premises that tend to establish the truth of a proposition or set of propositions. Three meanings of system must be distinguished: first, a simply verbal or logical system, which may or may not correspond to reality; second, a system of policy, such as the mercantile system, that presumes an interdependence between government and society; and third, a system that is logical in character but that purports to correspond to reality because it has, in some way, been confirmed by experience. Smith's system of natural liberty falls into the third category. It is, as we will, see a logically consistent explanation of the nature and causes of the wealth of nations, and it claims to have empirical support. Ambiguity creeps into Smith's use of the term, in that he is also recommending it as a system of policy. What makes it different from the mercantile system is that it does not presuppose the constant and intimate interdependence of government and society. It is true, however, that any simple analogy between Smith's system and a machine breaks down after a point, because he was concerned not just with distribution of a given annual produce but with both the rate of growth of annual produce and, as we have seen, the secondary, noneconomic effects of economic growth. The analogy is no longer between the economy and a machine but between the economy and a living organism.

THE VERY IMPORTANT SCIENCE OF POLITICAL ECONOMY

In this section I set out the parts of Smith's system, and in subsequent sections I outline the necessary operations of those parts. We begin with Smith's account of the division of labor. This leads quickly to a discussion of self-interest, for that which gives rise to the division of labor and, therefore, that which underlies the progress of civilization turn out to be the same thing—self-interest, or, in Smith's more precise formulation, the desire to better our condition. Accompanying Smith's identification of self-interest as the force or principle that moves his system, we turn, as he did, to his account of labor as the real measure of exchangeable value. Smith's contention that such measure exists is critical for his project of describing the economy as a mechanism. If there is an unambiguous way to quantify the movement of the economy, we can determine which system of policy maximizes this movement.

Self-Interest as the Moving Principle

The *Wealth of Nations* opens with Smith inquiring about the cause of the relative prosperity of civilized nations. Why is it that "the accommodation of a European prince does not always so much exceed that of an industrious and frugal peasant, as the accommodation of the latter exceeds that of many an African king, the absolute master of the lives and liberties of ten thousand naked savages" (*WN* I.i.2)?[6] In civilized societies a general plenty coexists, not only with great inequality but also with great idleness on the part of some classes. Barbarous societies, in contrast, are "so miserably poor, that from mere want, they are frequently reduced, or, at least, think themselves reduced, to the necessity of sometimes directly destroying, and sometimes abandoning their infants, their old people, and those afflicted with lingering diseases, to perish with hunger, or to be devoured by wild beasts" (*WN* intro.4).

Smith thought that the cause of this enormous disparity was the division of labor. He delineates three ways in which the division of labor adds to "the productive powers of labour": first, by increasing the dexterity of workers; second, by saving time in moving between stages of the productive process; and, third, through the "invention of a great number of machines which facilitate and abridge labour, and enable one man to do the work of many" (*WN* I.i.5).[7] The division of labor does not arise because of natural differences. Indeed, the "difference between the most dissimilar characters, between a philosopher and a common street porter, for example, seems to arise not so much from nature, as from habit, custom, and education" (*WN* I.ii.4). This denial of the importance of natural differences has important consequences for the character of Smith's political economy. If individual differences are not important, then he is free to base his analysis on the movements of large classes of individuals and on their average or normal behaviors. The result is that Smith is able to envisage a world in which change occurs incrementally or at the margin, as today's economists say.[8]

If natural differences are ruled out, what is the origin of the division of labor? Smith denies that it is "originally the effect of any human wisdom, that foresees and intends that general opulence to which it gives occasion." It is, rather, "the necessary, though very slow and gradual consequence of a certain propensity in human nature which has in view no such extensive utility; the propensity to truck, barter, and exchange one thing for another" (*WN* I.ii.1). Notwithstanding its apparently fundamental importance, the propensity to exchange receives only the briefest treatment in the *Wealth of Nations*. Smith leaves it open whether "this propensity be one of the original principles in human nature, of which no further account can be given; or whether, as seems more probable, it be the necessary consequence of the faculties of reason and speech" (*WN* I.ii.2). He does say that the propensity to exchange distinguishes humankind from other animals. Animals lack speech and, therefore, lack the ability to make contracts. To obtain what they want, they must somehow gain the favor of others. Human beings have other means of persuasion available to them.

> It is not from the benevolence of the butcher, the brewer, or the baker, that we expect our dinner, but from their regard to their own interest. We address ourselves, not to their humanity but to their self-love, and never talk to them of our own necessities but of their own advantages. Nobody but a beggar chuses to depend chiefly upon the benevolence of his fellow citizens. (*WN* I.ii.2)

The propensity to exchange is a means to an end; namely, satisfying our wants or, as Smith usually puts it, our interest. In keeping with his economic history, Smith does not deal with what is obviously a third way of pursuing one's interest: force. Exchange represents a kind of peaceful and somewhat dignified mean between the extreme combinations of force and excessive pride, on one hand, and begging and lowliness, on the other.[9]

In primitive times, men specialized because they found it in their interest to produce a surplus of a particular good that could be traded for other goods. Specialization, of course, increases the total supply of goods, and, as a result, both individual and society are better off. In a civilized society, capitalists and managers imitate the wisdom of nature by dividing labor into particular enterprises. But it does not follow that human wisdom ought, as a rule, to be allowed to superintend the economic activity of society as a whole. Rather, Smith recommends that the propensity to exchange, guided by individual interest, be given free reign to act as the organizing principle of society.

What, then, does Smith mean by interest and self-interest? In the *Theory of Moral Sentiments* he uses the term *interest* in a multitude of ways, but in the *Wealth of Nations* it almost always means economic interest. At its simplest, interest means gain rather than loss. The merchant wants to buy as cheaply as possible and to sell as dearly as possible (cf. *WN* IV.vii.c.104). It is in the discussion of the motives for saving in book 2, chapter 3 that Smith gives his most complete account of what he means by interest. He explains that the principle that prompts us to save is the "desire of bettering our condition." This desire is "generally calm and dispassionate, comes with us from the womb, and never leaves us until we go into the grave." The "greater part of men" choose the "most vulgar and obvious" way of bettering their condition, which is to augment their fortunes through saving. The frugal man who saves is more generous, more truly charitable, in fact, than is the founder of a public charity, because his savings constitute a "perpetual allotment" for employing productive workers. This provision is "guarded . . . by a very powerful principle, the *plain and evident interest* of every individual to whom any share of it shall ever belong. No part of it can ever afterward be employed to maintain any but productive hands, without an *evident loss* to the person who thus perverts it from its proper destination" (*WN* II.iii.19). For Smith, interest, in this vulgar and obvious sense, is a form of acquisitiveness driven by the desire to better one's condition. In the short term, gains and losses are plainly measured in terms of money. As we will see, long-term gains are measured by purchasing power.

To a reader familiar with the concept of the "rational economic man," it is perhaps easy to envisage the way in which a calm and dispassionate desire could function as the principle of motion for a science of political economy modeled after Newtonian natural science. Yet it is important to remember that Smith did not consider his description of most men to be a construct or assumption that abstracts from other aspects of human nature. He thought he was describing actual men, not abstractions. Furthermore, he saw a kind of vanity as the basis of the desire to better one's condition (*TMS* I.iii.2.1). Beyond this, Smith links his discussion of the increase in the productive powers of labor with larger themes. Indeed, book 1, chapters 1–3, contain some of his broadest and boldest reflections on the progress of society. Smith's argument is remarkable, not just because he gives an economic history of the world—a feat in itself—but also, and more importantly, because he implies that the economic history of the world is the history of the world. Economic history is the key to understanding why rich nations differ from poor nations ones, why civilization emerged out of barbarism, and why civilized societies are composed of the most diverse kinds of characters—philosophers and street porters, for example. This economic history has a certain abstract quality, in that art, politics, and religion play little or no role. Again, however, we must realize that Smith's abstraction conceals a broad claim. Smith saw art, politics, and religion as less fundamental than economics.

Labor as the Measure of Value

Schumpeter charged that Smith's discussion of value turned political economy into the dead end that culminated in Marx's labor theory of value.[10] Smith, it is suggested, passed up an opportunity to elaborate a subjective theory of value of the kind developed by late-nineteenth-century economists. It has even been suggested that such a theory was available to Smith in the writings of Cantillon, Turgot, and others.[11] Why did Smith not take this route instead of setting off in search of an invariable standard of value? I will endeavor to make clear why Smith thought that such an approach was necessary to the task of establishing a science of political economy.

Smith moves, but without explaining the transition, from the discussion of the division of labor to a consideration of the origins and use of money. He explains that, for exchange to take place, each party must have something the other party wants but that it may not always happen that what one party has produced in surplus is desired by the other party at a particular time. It would soon become a practice to keep some commodity that was in wide and constant demand for the purpose of facilitating exchange. Although many commodities might be used as money, where trade is extensive, metals are for "irresistible reasons" adopted as money because metallic money is easily divisible, easily transportable, and extremely durable. In all "rich and commercial" nations, gold and silver are used as money. Money exchanges are, then, a species of barter: one commodity is exchanged for another which, because of its special characteristics, is commonly used as the medium of exchange.[12]

Smith expended so much labor explaining these apparently trivial points for an important reason: they are an essential part of his response to the mercantilists. He thought that the most-sophisticated formulations of mercantilism were those which resulted in a preoccupation with the balance of trade; that is, with the excess (or deficiency) of exports over imports. The positive balance of trade was thought desirable because it increased the nation's stock of precious metals. According to Smith, the foundation of the mercantilist position was an identification of wealth and money. He singled out Locke for special mention

(*WN* I.v.35; *WN* II.iv.9; *WN* IV.i.3). Earlier, in his 1762–1763 lectures on jurisprudence, Smith remarked that it was Thomas Mun who first arranged the mercantile views into a system and that Locke, though following Mun, "made it indeed have somewhat more of a philosophicall air and the appearance of probability by some amendments" (*LJA* VI.135).[13] In his influential economic essays, Locke gave three reasons why only money in the form of the precious metals can serve as the "universal commodity." First, most other "portable commodities" soon perish, either through consumption or wastage. Second, money is of a steady value. In the language of Locke's political economy, its "quantity" in proportion to its "vent" is roughly constant. The vent of money is always "sufficient, or more than enough," because it "answers all things" and because, therefore, everybody is "ready to receive money without bounds." It could, therefore, serve as a "pledge" for future purchasing power; that is to say, one can always find someone ready to exchange goods for money. Finally, the value of money, as distinct from jewels, varies directly with its quantity and is therefore suitable as a "counter." Money is the great object of trade, and where it is scarce, trade will decay. Locke did not regard paper money, even if sanctioned by government, as an adequate substitute for species money because of the uncertainties attached to its value.[14]

Although one would not know it from reading Smith, Locke did not simply identify money and wealth. As much as Smith, Locke was aware that those countries which possessed great mines were generally poor. Where money is not an incentive to industry, its good effects will not be seen. "It is death in Spain to export money," he observed, "and yet they, who furnish all the world with gold and silver, have least of it amongst themselves. Trade fetches it away from that lazy and indigent people, notwithstanding all their artificial and forced contrivances to keep it there."[15] Furthermore, what is important is the quantity of money in the nation relative to the total supply of money in the world. For the industry of a nation to go on increasing, there must be a continual increase in its supply of money, and this requires the maintenance of a favorable balance of trade. In this crucial respect, international trade is a zero-sum game. These views led Locke to recommend policies to increase the supply of active money by reducing hoarding and by maintaining a favorable balance of trade.

In light of the mercantilist argument, Smith's transition from a discussion of the division of labor to a concern with the nature of money is readily explainable. Having identified the true cause of the wealth of nations as the extension of the division of labor, Smith's first step in explaining the mechanism by which the division of labor is extended is to correct the understanding of money that led the mercantilists into the error of identifying money with wealth. Smith claims that this error grew out of the confusion of money with wealth that permeates ordinary speech. We commonly estimate a person's wealth in terms of the money value of his estate and income. We also speak of the value of commodities in terms of the quantity of money for which they are exchanged. Smith considers this way of speaking defective, because what we really mean by wealth is not a quantity of money but the purchasing power over goods and labor that the commodity confers. The mercantilist error was to infer from the common business practice of piling up money that this was also the appropriate policy for the state as a whole.

Smith's inquiry is founded upon an attempt to reach beyond the ordinary understanding of things by inventing a technical language for discussing the subject matter of political economy. After discussing the origins of money, he turns to the so-called paradox of value: why, for example, gold is useless but dear, whereas water is cheap but vital to life.[16] To explain the paradox, he distinguishes between value in use and value in exchange. Value in use refers to the "utility of some particular object," whereas value in exchange refers to the "power of purchasing other goods which the possession of that object conveys" (WN I.iv.13). Smith quickly drops any thought of inquiring into the utility of things and concentrates, instead, on value in exchange. As we will see, he believed that exchange value is scientifically measurable. The focus on exchange value allows him to abstract from considerations of the usefulness of things: something that varies from time to time, from place to place, and from person to person. Furthermore, an inquiry into the usefulness of things would have led quickly to a consideration of moral and political issues. Smith cannot forget completely about use value, however, because in the transition from theory to practice, he must take politics, in particular, into account. For example, Smith acknowledges that *judgments* must be made about the usefulness of military spending. We will consider this problem in subsequent sections. For now, let us follow the course of Smith's abstract argument.

Recall that the mercantilist starting point, at least in Smith's rendering of it, was that money is wealth. Smith begins by defining wealth or riches in such a way as to avoid any reference to money: "Every man must be rich or poor according to the degree in which he can afford to enjoy the necessaries, conveniences, and amusements of human life." This plausible suggestion is followed by what has turned out to be one of Smith's most controversial and confusing statements. He asserts that the "value of any commodity . . . to the person who possesses it, and who means not to use or consume it himself, but to exchange it for other commodities, *is equal to the quantity of labour which it enables him to purchase or command. Labour, therefore, is the real measure of the exchangeable value of all commodities*" (WN I.v.1, emphasis added). The point he is making is simple: the real or exchangeable value is equal to the amount of homogeneous or ordinary labor that possession of the commodity allows one to avoid. It measures the "power of purchasing other goods which the possession of that object conveys" (WN I.iv.13). Conversely, the "real price of everything, what everything really costs to the man who wants to acquire it, is the toil and trouble of acquiring it" (WN I.v.2). There is no suggestion here that cost is equal to the quantity of labor embodied in the commodity. This may have been true in a primitive society, in which each commodity was the result of the labor of one person only, but once the division of labor has firmly taken root, each commodity is the product of many different hands and many different kinds of resources. Put otherwise, the return to individual laborers is no measure of the exchangeable value of the commodity, because it does not take into account what must be paid to the capitalist and the landlord.

In what sense is labor the "ultimate and real standard by which the value of all commodities can at all times and places be estimated and compared"? Smith's answer is in essentially biological terms:

> Equal quantities of labour, at all times and places, may be said to be of equal value to the labourer. In his ordinary state of health, strength, and spirits; in the ordinary degree of his skill and dexterity, he must always lay down the same portion of his ease, his liberty, and his happiness. *The price which he pays must always be the same,* whatever may be the quantity of goods which he receives in return for it. (WN I.v.7, emphasis added)

There are various kinds of labor, of varying degrees of ingenuity and hardship, but Smith maintains that these may be reduced to quantities of ordinary labor by the "higgling and bargaining of the market" (*WN* I.v.4). This understanding of labor is a further extension of the notion that all talents are acquired. Because there are no significant natural differences among human beings, the differences in talent we see must be the results of education or, to be more precise, past labor.[17] By "ordinary labour" he has in mind some elemental form of expenditure of effort. In short, the pain of labor is a constant in a world of flux.

Smith grants that valuation in terms of labor commanded is an "abstract notion," not "so natural and so obvious" as valuation in terms of some other commodity, which would be to value it in terms of "a plain and palpable object." Of what does the superiority of the labor-commanded measure consist? In the first place, the values of all commodities in relation to each other are constantly changing. Thus, when the prices of two commodities are compared at two different times, it is impossible to tell in which particular commodity there has been a change unless there is some other commodity of fixed value in terms of which these two might be compared. As it turns out, money is the commodity by which the value of all other commodities is commonly measured. Money values, which are equivalent to the quantity or weight of the coin, are also in flux because gold and silver, "like every other commodity, vary in their value, are sometimes cheaper and sometimes dearer, sometimes of easier and sometimes of more difficult purchase" (*WN* I.v.7). At a particular time and place, money values will be in a certain proportion to real values, because the supply-and-demand conditions for the precious metals may be assumed to be constant. This is not, however, true at different times and places.

What role does the real measure of exchangeable value play in the *Wealth of Nations*? The scholarly consensus today has reduced Smith's account of the real measure of exchangeable value to something of a toothless tiger, largely irrelevant to his more important innovations.[18] Smith's only explicitly stated purpose in formulating a real measure of exchangeable value in book 1, chapter 5 is that such a measure is necessary for comparing the values of different commodities at different times and places. That much is clear. Furthermore, such comparisons are used in Smith's refutation of the mercantile position that increases in the quantity of money are equivalent to increases in the wealth of the nation. The use of labor as a measure of value, however, runs through Smith's entire critique of the mercantilists, and it is by considering its wider role in this critique that the full significance of the concept is revealed. Here, again, a comparison with Locke is useful.

Smith's revision of Locke and the mercantilists begins with his redefinition of the origins and use of money. It is completed by his formulation of the notion that labor commanded is the real measure of exchangeable value. Recall that, for Smith, money exchanges are a species of barter, in which one commodity is exchanged for another commodity, money, which is also the accepted instrument of commerce. The real value of money is measured by the amount of labor it can purchase. Money is desired not because it is a safe port in a storm but simply because it is useful for facilitating current transactions. One exchanges goods for money simply for the sake of purchasing other goods in the future. For Locke, the money transaction is the essence of exchange. The unlimited acquisition of money is our defense against the changeability of circumstances. Money gives us power over those circumstances, and, therefore, the acquisition of money is the essence of any exchange. We part with money so that we may obtain more of it. Smith, in contrast, makes money of instrumental importance only. We acquire money so that we can acquire other goods in the near future.

Smith regarded money as he did any other commodity. In the short period, money values reflect real values (that is, real exchangeable value in terms of labor commanded), but, over time, money, like all other commodities, varies in value. The prospect of alterations in the value of money did not enter into Smith's calculations, because transactions are made with only the short term in mind. We purchase money with goods for the sake of future transactions. Moreover, Smith maintains that although a merchant may have trouble selling his produce in the market because of a scarcity of money, this "accident" cannot happen to an entire society, because exchange can take place without money (WN IV.i.18). Smith's and Locke's accounts have in common the idea that economic society is a mechanism governed by what Locke termed "natural laws of value" and what Smith termed the "natural progress of opulence." In Locke's account, however, money plays the crucial role by providing the object that can be pursued without limit. The desire for money elicits industry and frugality and leads nations out of poverty and into opulence.

What replaces the desire for money in Smith's account? It is the desire to better our condition that acts as a constant and steady force prompting individuals to industry and frugality. In the process of "augmenting our fortune," the acquisition of money is merely instrumental. It remains true that all of the common transactions of economic life utilize money, but these values are nominal only. This nominal level is a reflection of a deeper level of significance, which is represented by their real values. In what way is labor commanded more real than money? Throughout the *Wealth of Nations*, Smith maintains that labor is the chief cause of value, almost as rigidly as he maintains that it is the measure of value. With respect to manufactures, he always speaks of labor as adding value.

He does not attribute any value added to fixed capital, such as machinery. When Smith speaks of the benefits of the division of labor, which include improvements in machinery, he always speaks of improvements in the "productive powers of labour." It is true that, with respect to agriculture, he sometimes speaks of the "spontaneous" products of nature, but he makes clear that these are so insignificant that societies forced to rely on them are "miserably poor" (WN II.iii.3, WN Intro.3).

The connection between labor as the source of value and labor as the measure of value is important. The link is Smith's assertion that real value is equivalent to cost or price, not, for example, use. For Smith, the real value of anything is, as we have seen, the "toil or trouble of acquiring it." Labor is the "first price" or "the original purchase money of all things" (WN I.v.2). Smith's language is distinctive and surely not accidental, in view of his attack on mercantilism. Labor is the transforming agent that converts the more-or-less useless products of nature into things somehow useful to man. The labor-commanded measure of real value measures the ability of a particular commodity to put labor into motion; that is, to sustain the "toil and trouble" of an ordinary laborer for a period of time. Thus the quantity of the transforming agent that any commodity is capable of putting into motion is the appropriate measure of value. Furthermore, ordinary labor is the basic building block of the more complex forms of labor and, of course, of machines, which represent the accumulated efforts of past labor. It is in this way that Smith replaces Locke's use of money as the measure of value. For Locke, the value of money varied with its quantity, whereas for Smith, the value of labor varies with its quantity.

In Defense of Smith

We are now in a position to say something conclusive about the role of labor as a measure of value. I would suggest that establishing the capacity to speak of the annual produce—or parts of it—in terms of fixed quantities is essential for Smith's project of establishing a science of political economy. To speak of quantities is to abstract from the evident truth that the annual produce is composed of different kinds of things that have different uses and, therefore, different use values. The mechanistic view is made plausible by Smith's belief that it is possible to speak in a precise and determinate way about the motion that is communicated to the economy. In Smith's system, the real value of any commodity is fixed in terms of labor commanded (which its nominal value reflects), and, when this commodity is exchanged, it will (if put to a productive use) communicate a fixed quantity of motion (measured by labor commanded) to the economy. Thus labor commanded adds a unit of measurement to the analytical tools of the Wealth of Nations. Smith's unit of measurement complements the principle of motion in his system, which is self-interest or the desire to better our condition. His analysis of the real economy is offered as a substitute for analysis of the economic society that we immediately perceive. Analysis in terms of the "real" aims to disclose the underlying order. Without such a measure, it would be impossible to speak of the economy as a mechanism. Labor commanded links past, present, and future economic activity in a way in which money does not. Furthermore, what must be done in terms of policy is to influence not the supply of money but the amount of labor that is set in motion.

In light of the severe criticisms that later economists heaped on Smith's theory of value, a word in defense of Smith's effort is in order. It is important also because I will later make the case that Hamilton's response to Smith is of more significance than are most of these later critiques. Smith was driven to look for an invariable measure of value because he sought a link between the present and the future—between all times and all places. Labor commanded served this purpose because it implied that the surface or money economy was not the real economy. The wealth of nations derives from the motion communicated to the economy by labor. The consequences of this point of view were enormous. It vindicated the virtues of saving and sober industriousness, the independence of the economy from government, and the mechanical nature of the economy. The mercantile system saw the money economy as fundamental. This perception led it to take monetary fluctuations seriously, whether they be in the balance of trade or due to hoarding or any other form of a scarcity of money. Perhaps most importantly, it seemed to invite government intervention in the economy. Smith's later critics, especially from the so-called marginal revolution onward, dispensed with labor as a measure of value replacing its "utility" while keeping the core of Smith's policy prescriptions. Furthermore, Smith's critics continued his neglect of the money economy, believing it to be a mere reflection of the deeper relationships of utility. Granting that Smith's ideas about the value-creating quality of labor are dubious at best, one must nevertheless wonder whether his critics did anything more than relocate or simply rename the source of the difficulty. Both theories posit a deeper stratum in the economy that determines economic activity. Both suggest that economic change is incremental. And, lastly, both describe an economy that operates mechanically. The question, though, is whether this rejection of the volatility of the money economy is justified. In conclusion, on Smith's behalf it must be noted that the later theory is less plausibly a system in the scientific sense, because it tried to include factors, such as entrepreneurship, which Smith considered outside the scope of scientific analysis.

THE NATURAL PROGRESS OF OPULENCE

The next step in Smith's argument is to show that the economic mechanism is a benevolent one. The critical burden of Smith's argument is to show that the economy free of government-imposed restraints will produce more wealth than any system of government regulation. Three concepts shape the argument: competition, saving, and investment. It culminates in Smith's description of the "natural progress of opulence."

Competition

The role of competition first becomes important in Smith's chapters on price. His discussion of natural price and market price is widely regarded as one of his great achievements because of its sophisticated analysis of supply and demand (*WN* I.vii). It is in this account that Smith gives the most explicit indications that he is borrowing from both the form and the substance of Newtonian physics. However, another analogy, that of the physiology of the human body, plays a great role in the *Wealth of Nations*. This analogy figures prominently in Smith's discussions of economic growth and economic policy. Thus, in addition to speaking of "forces," and of prices "gravitating towards," and of "constant tendencies," he speaks of economic society in terms of the "unknown principle of animal life" and of the health and recuperative powers of the human body (*WN* II.iii.31; *WN* IV.ix.28). Later in this chapter, I will take up the relationship between these two analogies.

In the earliest stages of society, every man was, so to speak, self-employed. As a result, when one commodity was exchanged for another, the exchange could only take place on the basis of the quantities of labor embodied in the commodities. This proportion served as the rule for exchange. In this state of society, the quantity of labor embodied in the commodity corresponded to the quantity of labor commanded (*WN* I.vi.1–4). But once society reaches a more advanced stage, this coincidence of labor commanded, or price, and labor embodied no longer holds. When stock has been accumulated by some individuals, they will seek to use it by employing others. The wages of those whom they employ are really advances or loans of subsistence goods that must be repaid with interest, or profit, to the owner of the stock once the commodity has been sold. Smith describes profits as a deduction from the value added by the laborer. Similarly, once land has been engrossed, a similar deduction from the value added by the laborer must be made for the payment of rent to the landlord. In an advanced society, the natural price of commodities is the sum of the components parts of price—wages, rent, and profits—when those component parts are at their natural rates (*WN* I.vi.7–9).

The natural wage level is set by a contract that is the outcome of bargaining between owners and employees. Wages will be higher when society is advancing rapidly and lower when it is stationary or declining. In the advancing stage, labor will be scarce, because demand is higher; in the stationary or declining stages the reverse will take place. Smith adopted an elastic definition of subsistence, one that, at times, includes more than what is required biologically to sustain the laborer and his family (*WN* V.ii.k.3). That said, he believed that, when wages rose above the biologically set minimum, there would be a tendency for the population to increase because of a declining infant-mortality rate. The supply of laborers—or, perhaps, the production of laborers—is, then, not the result of a deliberate calculation on the part of the lower classes to increase their birthrates but, rather, the effect of an increase in the quantity of available subsistence. This is in accord with Smith's belief that every animal multiplies in proportion to the available quantity of subsistence (*WN* I.xi.b.1). When society is in a declining state, wages will, for a time, fall below the level required to maintain the existing number of laborers. Wages will continue at this lower level until the population is brought into proportion with the quantity of available subsistence.

Profits are determined as a percentage of the total stock invested. In every neighborhood or society there exists an average or ordinary rate of profit. This ordinary or average rate, according to Smith, corresponds to the natural rate. Smith is quite clear that profits have nothing to do with the entrepreneurial functions of the owner or even the management of the workplace (*WN* I.vi.6). Although he does not enquire into the determinants of this natural rate, we may surmise that it is historically determined at a level that reflects the bargaining power of the various relevant parties. One of the striking features of Smith's analysis is his prediction of a long-term decline in profit rates, a result of the dry-ing up of investment opportunities as society becomes more highly capitalized and as competition for resources squeezes profit margins. Thus, "the rate of profit does not, like rent and wages, rise with the prosperity, and fall with the declension of the society. On the contrary, it is naturally low in rich, and high in poor countries, and it is always highest in countries which are going fastest too ruin" (*WN* I.xi.p.10).

Smith's presentation of rent is peculiarly difficult. Its chief complications, the analysis of rents in alternative uses of land and the determination of the rent of "corn" land, need not, however, detain us here. Smith presents the landlord as a kind of monopolist, reaping where he has not sown, who will extract from his tenants whatever they can afford to give. The activities of the landlord, unlike those of the merchant, are not, however, in conflict with the general interest of society. It is always in the interest of merchants and manufacturers—but not of society as a whole—to widen the market and to narrow competition. In con-trast, the progressive improvement in the productive powers of labor in agricul-ture and manufactures benefits the landlord directly, by increasing the real value of his rents, and indirectly, by decreasing the real price of the manufactures the landlord purchases from his revenue (*WN* I.xi.p.2–6).

Where competition is free—that is, where there is complete legal freedom to enter the market and there are no natural barriers to entry—the market price will be "continually gravitating" toward the "central" or "natural" price. If there is an excess of "effectual demand" and if, as a result, profits rise above their natu-ral rate, producers will be encouraged to produce this product, and the resulting increase in competition will drive the market price down toward the natural price. Where there is an excess of supply over effectual demand, the reverse will take place. Thus the "quantity of every commodity brought to market naturally suits itself to the effectual demand. It is the interest of all those who employ their land, labor, and stock, in bringing any commodity to the market, that the quantity should never exceed the effectual demand; and it is the interest of all other people that it never should fall short of that demand" (*WN* I.vii.12). In any society or neighborhood there will be a tendency for wages, profits, and rents to equalize in the various productive activities as individuals, following their interest, seek out the best uses for their land, labor, and capital.

Smith's analysis resembles a partial (as opposed to general) equilibrium analysis, in that he describes the adjustments which follow a disturbance of the equilibrium, "the center of repose and continuance," in a particular market (*WN* I.vii.15). He does not discuss the adjustments that might take place in all markets. He should not, however, be faulted for his failure to follow through in this part of his analysis.[19] Although Smith invoked the parallel between Newton's law of gravity and the principle of self-interest, he did not consider it necessary to enquire into the farthest implications of such disturbances of equilibrium. His concern was more important than the distribution of a given annual produce: the "natural progress of opulence," or, as we would say, economic growth. Competition is not simply a mechanism for maximizing and distributing output at a given level of resources and technology. It plays another, more vital role in Smith's analysis. The constant striving engendered by free competition maintains those habits that extend the division of labor, especially good management and frugality.

Accumulation and the Division of Labor

Smith's fundamental contention is that there is a natural progress of opulence that is more rapid than any which can be produced by government policy. Beginning with Smith, mainstream political economists increasingly came to believe that the growth issue was settled. Ricardo, for example, believed that the "principal problem in political economy" was to "determine the laws which regulate . . . distribution." This preoccupation on the part of theoretical political economists with questions of distribution was to last until the Great Depression. Keynes's concern with the level of employment represented a partial return to the issue of growth, but not until after World War II was the debate about growth reopened.[20] As I argued earlier, however, distribution was not Smith's principal concern. His discussion serves to highlight the role that competition plays in shaping economic activity. The more important issue was growth, or the wealth of nations.

Smith observes that, for the division of labor to become in any way extensive, there must be some prior accumulation of stock or capital. Without this, owners would be unable to purchase machines and materials and to sustain the labor necessary for the productive process. Thus "the accumulation of stock must, in the nature of things, be previous to the division of labour, so labour can be more and more subdivided in proportion only as stock is previously more and more accumulated" (*WN* II.intro.3). Accumulation is, then, the driving force behind the increasing productive powers of labor. Beyond this, the division of labor is constrained only by the extent of the market. The measure of the potential for accumulation is the surplus of annual produce over the part of it that goes to the reward of labor; namely, rent and profits. "If the society was to employ all the labour which it can annually purchase, as the quantity of labour would increase greatly every year, so the produce of every succeeding year would be of vastly

THE POLITICAL ECONOMY OF PROGRESS · 71

greater value than that of the foregoing" (*WN* I.vi.24). This does not happen, because "everywhere" much of the annual produce goes to the support of the "idle."

Accumulation results from parsimony. What an individual saves, he either invests himself or lends to others at interest. The borrower, in turn, is faced with a choice of investing or lending. This same idea can be extended to society as a whole, because the capital of a society "which is the same with that of all the individuals who compose it, can be increased only in the same manner" (*WN* II.iii.15). Parsimony "puts into motion an additional quantity of industry, which gives an additional value to the annual produce" (*WN* II.iii.17).

The process of saving, investment, and growth is automatic. Smith's anticipation of what came to be known as "Say's Law"—"supply creates its own demand"—is clearest in the following passage.[21]

> What is annually saved is as regularly consumed as what is annually spent, and nearly in the same time too; but it is consumed by a different set of people. That portion of his revenue which a rich man annually spends, is in most cases consumed by idle guests, and menial servants, who leave nothing behind them in return for their consumption. That portion which he annually saves, as for the sake of profit it is immediately employed as capital, is consumed in the same manner, and nearly in the same time too, but by a different set of people, by labourers, manufacturers, and artificers, who reproduce with a profit the value of their annual consumption. (*WN* II.iii.18)

As I noted earlier, Smith believed that it is "the desire of bettering our condition" which leads to saving and, furthermore, that in "the greater part of men, taking the whole course of their life at an average, the principle of frugality seems not only to predominate, but to predominate very greatly" (*WN* II.iii.28). For similar reasons he also believed that common prudence would prevail in the majority of men.

Smith's understanding of the role of money is crucial to the assertion that savings are more or less automatically transformed into investments. The purpose of money is simply to facilitate current transactions: "What is annually saved is as regularly consumed as what is annually spent, and nearly in the same time too." This means that savings do not result in any reduction in the purchasing power of the community as a whole and that, as a result, purchasing power will be sufficient to provide a market for all current output. It also means that hoarding is not a significant problem. Because money "will not be allowed to lie idle" and because the "interest of whoever possesses it, requires that it should be employed," savings will automatically give rise to investment (*WN* I.iii.23). Smith does not take seriously the danger of a "scarcity of money" that so concerned Locke and other mercantilists (*WN* IV.i.16). Those who lack the means to secure credit can always be found complaining of a scarcity or dearness of money. Where the complaint is general throughout an entire neighborhood, it is always the result of what Smith calls "over-trading," by which he means the imprudent extension of credit. This is the result of high spirits, which at times infect not only "projectors" but also sober men. When the inevitable bust hits, many men, sober and otherwise, are left chasing after money but without the means to command it; hence a general complaint of a scarcity of money (*WN* IV.i.16). As a consequence, he sees no need for the state to adopt measures that will ensure an adequate circulation of money. He does, however, see a need for the state to take steps to insure that the lending industry stays within the limits of sobriety. I discuss these limits later in this chapter.

Although prodigality and imprudence never characterize the majority of a society, they have been known to prevail in governments and, sometimes, to bring about their downfall. The mismanagement by governments is not always fatal, for the effects of the desire to better our condition are not easily stifled.

> The uniform, constant, and uninterrupted effort of every man to better his condition, the principle from which public and national, as well as private opulence is originally derived, is frequently powerful enough to maintain the natural course of things towards improvement, in spite of the extravagance of government, and of the greatest errors of administration. Like the unknown principle of animal life, it frequently restores health and vigour to the constitution, in spite, not only of the disease, but of the absurd prescriptions of the doctor. (*WN* II.iii.31; also *WN* IV.ix.28)

Smith's account of the rebirth of Western Europe after the collapse of the Roman Empire is one critical piece of evidence for this contention, in that prosperity returned despite the unsettled state of affairs and of what Smith thought to be the fallacious economic theories that prevailed.

In light of this statement, one can see how the analogies of the Newtonian worldview and that of the human body dovetail nicely to present a compelling account of the process of economic growth. Smith is interested not so much in the precise specification of equilibrium as in how the forces acting toward equilibrium contribute to the process of economic growth. The principle of motion on which Smith bases his system is the desire to better our condition, or interest that is channeled in the direction of frugality and good management by the discipline of competition. The habits of frugality and good management to which competition gives rise in the capitalist class and which emulation spreads to other classes of society in turn ensure that resources will be used efficiently and that saving will predominate over prodigality.

Even though the case of Spain indicates that the natural recuperative powers of society may not always be enough, Smith's understanding of the process of economic growth has an important bearing on the political teaching of the *Wealth of Nations.* If imperfections in society can be tolerated, it becomes less of an imperative for society's economic program to include a radical political agenda. Furthermore, Smith's argument conceals a far-reaching assertion: all the policies of the previous centuries to encourage economic growth had, in fact, had the opposite effect. The real cause of economic development was the generally unhindered operation of the desire to better our condition. Book 3 describes the way in which the "policy of Europe" had distorted the natural progress of opulence. This distortion acted as a brake on economic progress, but not to such a degree as to stifle completely the effects of the desire to better our condition. The policy chiefly responsible for this distortion was the encouragement of manufactures (and the resulting discouragement of agriculture).

Economic Growth

The truth of Smith's claim about the retrograde effects of the policy of Europe depends on the accuracy of his account of the natural progress of opulence. The account has two steps: first, the setting down of the relative social advantages of various forms of investment, and, second, a description of how private investment decisions naturally follow this socially desirable scale of investment priorities. Smith ranks the relative advantages for society of what he considers to be the four productive uses of capital—agriculture, manufacturing, wholesale trade, and retail trade—partly on the basis of the amount of labor they immediately employ and partly on the basis of the value the particular employment adds to the annual produce of the nation immediately and in the future. The value added to the annual produce is the measure of the potential for putting productive labor into motion in the future. The retailer employs only himself, and his contribution to the annual produce is measured by his profits. The wholesaler employs more men in his trade and adds to the annual produce the value of his profits and the wages of his workmen. The manufacturer often employs a great many men, and their labor adds to the value of the annual produce an amount equal to their wages plus the profits on the "wages, materials, and instruments" used in production.

According to Smith, it is agriculture that puts immediately into motion the greatest quantity of labor and, in addition, adds the greatest value to the annual produce of the nation: "of all the ways in which a capital can be employed, it is by far the most advantageous to the society" (WN II.v.12). The capital of the farmer puts into motion the labor of his servants and that of his "labouring cattle." In addition, "nature labours along with man"; and, as a result, investment in agriculture yields not only the wages of the servants and the profits of the master but also, almost always, a rent to the landlord, which is greater or smaller according to the fertility of the land. "No equal quantity of productive labour employed in manufactures can ever occasion so great a reproduction. In them nature does nothing; man does all; and the reproduction must always be in proportion to the strength of the agents that occasion it" (WN II.v.12).[22]

After establishing a scale of investment priorities for society, Smith's next step is to show how the natural course of things follows this scale. The natural course of things is the aggregate of individual decisions to save, consume, and invest. With respect to these individual decisions, "profit is the sole motive." The "different quantities of productive labour which it may put into motion and the different values which it may add to the annual produce of the land and labour of society, according as it is employed in one or other of those different ways" never enter into the thoughts of an investor (WN II.v.37). Nevertheless, the "natural inclinations of man" are such that the natural sequence of investment coincides with that which is socially most beneficial (*WN* III.i.3). Smith maintains that "[a]ccording to the natural course of things . . . the greater part of the capital of every growing society is, first, directed to agriculture, afterwards to manufactures, and last of all to foreign commerce. *This order of things is so very natural, that in every society that had any territory, it has always . . . been in some degree observed*" (*WN* III.i.8, emphasis added). How does this come about?

To understand this argument, we must recall Smith's claim that in a competitive market there will be a tendency for profits to equalize themselves across the various uses of capital. "Upon equal or nearly equal profits," Smith argues, "most men will chuse to employ their capitals rather in the improvement and cultivation of the land, than either in manufactures or in foreign trade" (*WN* III.i.3). Given equal profits, what determines the choice in favor of agriculture? Investments in agriculture are more secure than are those in foreign trade, where the owner's capital is at the mercy not only of "the winds and the waves" but also of "the more uncertain elements of human folly and injustice, by giving great credits in distant countries to men, with whose character and situation he can seldom be thoroughly acquainted" (*WN* III.i.3). Smith does not say that agriculture necessarily provides a more secure investment than do manufactures. The agricultural life has, however, other attractions:

> The beauty of the country . . . the pleasures of a country life, the tranquility of mind which it promises, and wherever the injustice of human laws does not disturb it, the independence which it really affords, have charms that more or less attract every body; and as to cultivate the ground was the original destination of man, so in every stage of his existence he seems to retain a predilection for this primitive employment. (*WN* III.i.3)

Smith also remarks on the relative moral superiority of the agricultural way of life. The agricultural life keeps men independent, enlivens their minds, keeps their bodies vigorous, and protects them from the immorality of city life. Furthermore, in a truly classical republican vein, Smith drew attention to the connections between agriculture and *amor patriae:* the farmer is tied to his land, whereas the merchant may make his home or take his money anywhere. Smith observes that human beings retain certain primitive yearnings that attract them not only to agriculture but also to hunting and fishing. In contrast to Rousseau, Smith does not elevate these yearnings to a position of preeminence. Smith replaces Rousseau's longing for the state of nature with a desire to establish a tranquility of mind. To accomplish this, he believed that the institutional apparatus of commercial society was both necessary and natural.[23]

Smith also argues for the priority of agriculture from a historical point of view. In any country with a significant extent of arable lands, it is natural that the subsistence of the people be the first object of industry. Once this subsistence is obtained, any surplus can be exchanged for other goods. Some manufactures are, however, necessary for conducting even the most rudimentary forms of agriculture. Smith conjectures that towns naturally have their origins in the grouping of these manufacturers. The growth in the surplus of agricultural production makes it possible for towns to increase their output of manufactured goods. "The great commerce of every civilized society, is that carried on between the inhabitants of the town and those of the country. . . . The country supplies the town with the means of subsistence, and the materials of manufacture. The town repays this supply by sending back a part of the manufactured produce to the inhabitants of the country" (*WN* III.i.1). Smith contends that had "human institutions, therefore, never disturbed the natural course of things, the progressive wealth and increase of the towns would, in every political society, be consequential, and in proportion to the improvement and cultivation of the territory or country" (*WN* III.i.4).

Manufactures, in turn, are to be preferred, upon equal or nearly equal profits, to foreign trade because the capital of the manufacturer "being at all times within his view and command, is more secure than that of the foreign merchant" (*WN* III.i.7). Citing the example of North America, Smith adds that it is not, economically speaking, desirable for a nation to use its own capital in the carrying trade if there are other uses to which it could be put; better to allow other nations to carry the nation's exports.

This account of the natural progress of opulence is the centerpiece of the *Wealth of Nations*. The three chapters that follow it consider the way in which the natural course of things was distorted in modern Europe. These chapters contain Smith's vindication of the proposition that the effects of the desire to better our condition, not government policy, were responsible for the great commercial progress of Europe. Smith's discussion is deceptive, because the bucolic simplicity of his description of the natural progress of opulence obscures its technical basis. There are four elements to this technical basis. First, as I noted earlier, the type of individualism that Smith identifies as the cause of economic progress is sober and cautious. This sobriety and caution are also evident in his description of the natural progress of opulence. Second, the assumption of the superior productivity of agriculture is crucial to the argument. Without it, Smith's entire account of the natural workings of economic society becomes questionable. If it is not the case, might not a preference for agriculture or any sluggishness in taking up manufactures be interpreted as backwardness? Third, Smith abstracts more or less completely from politics. The great commerce of every civilized society is that which is conducted between the town and the country. The distinction between town and country is an economic one, which is applicable to the world as a whole, "the great society of mankind," and perhaps more so than to any independent nation. The prescription for international free trade is implicit in Smith's account of the natural progress of opulence. The abstraction from politics is also evident in his description of the rise of cities. Cities arise from economic necessity. The account makes no mention of the multitude of other factors that might be thought central to the emergence of cities, such as defense or even the attractiveness of political life itself.

Finally, Smith's assumption of the naturalness of economic progress is critical to his argument. The most important claim, for our present purposes, is that the desire to better our condition is spontaneous. In the three chapters that follow book 3, chapter 1, Smith describes how commerce brought about a revolution in the political and economic affairs of Europe. Smith's account of the natural progress of opulence assumes that only liberty and security are necessary for the desire to better our condition to exert itself. Now, the aim of this desire is, as we have seen, something more than "necessary subsistence" (*WN* III.iii.12). Yet, in Smith's actual history of the rise of modern Europe, he stresses the crucial role that foreign trade played in spreading a taste for finer and more-improved manufactures (*WN* III.iii.16). In other words, the flourishing of the desire to better one's condition seems to have required what must be considered an artificial stimulus outside the natural course of things. In this case, the accuracy of Smith's conclusion—namely, that the natural progress of opulence has been distorted—depends upon the validity of his premise that the desire to better our condition is natural.

Smith's description of the natural progress of opulence may be described as a conjectural or theoretical history, as distinct from an actual history.[24] The account begins with certain assumptions about human nature and moves, by deduction, to establish a set of propositions that describe the course of the natural progress of opulence. The accuracy of these assumptions is never a theme in the *Wealth of Nations.* Instead, Smith refers to past and present events for proofs and demonstrations of his propositions. For example, the prosperity of the North American colonies is evidence of the superior productivity of agriculture, as well as of the potential for the use of paper money. These facts, he would argue, provide a confirmation of his premises. This is to an extent true, but the case of the rise of modern Europe indicates the problem. How do we know that some alternative explanation—perhaps the mercantilist interpretation—for the rise of modern Europe is not correct? Does Smith interpret the "facts" in light of his premises?

The Moral and the Philosophical Significance of the Natural Progress of Opulence

The question of the moral significance of the *Wealth of Nations* returns us to some of the themes of the previous chapter. As I observed there, raising the question of the goodness of commercial society takes us to the inner sanctum of Smith's mind. First, and most clearly, the natural progress of opulence is consistent with natural liberty; hence the nomenclature, "system of natural liberty."[25] The mercantile system, on the other hand, is a system of restraint. Much of the immense polemical force of the *Wealth of Nations* lies in this contrast: nature, liberty, and reason are arrayed against artifice, restraint, and prejudice. One might say that Smith deftly harnesses the rhetoric of the Whig spirit of liberty in the service of an expansion of a certain kind of civil rather than political liberty. Yet the injustice of the mercantile system is not so self-evident that it does not require explanation. The justice of natural liberty comes to sight negatively in light of the injustice that restraint inflicts on individuals. Smith describes two sorts of harm. First, preventing an individual from pursuing a particular trade results in loss. The precise extent of the pecuniary harm would, of course, be subject to some uncertainty. Furthermore, this kind of harm represents a denial of a positive good rather than the infliction of an injury—which is the most severe sort of harm, according to Smith. Second, restraint does, however, inflict an injury by impeding or preventing the natural motion of an individual or, what for most people is the same thing, the desire to better their condition by increasing their wealth. In addition to any physical restraint, there is the psychological damage or disruption to the mind's tranquility that results from impeding the desire to better our condition. Smith, for example, speaks of the mercantile restrictions on the North American colonies as a "violation of the most sacred rights of mankind" and as "impertinent badges of slavery"; but, at the same time, he believes that they did little, if any, economic harm to the colonies (WN IV.vii.b.44).

Other moral benefits flow from the commercialization of society, but they are less clear-cut. As I noted earlier, praise of the agrarian way of life is sustained throughout the Wealth of Nations. Where liberty and security exist, those who make their living off the land are superior morally and intellectually to those who live in the cities. They are also, perhaps, better citizens. In the natural progress of opulence the most productive form of economic activity coincides with the form that is most appealing from a moral point of view.

The natural progress of opulence is also appealing from the point of view of the morality of the system as whole. Smith indicates in various places that the commercialization of society involves a form of moral decline or corruption. In particular, the gentlemanly virtues of liberality and generosity give way to a sometimes mean-spirited quest for creature comforts. Yet these virtues live on in the system as a whole, which Smith often describes as not only "just" but also as "generous" and "liberal" (cf. WN I.viii.36; WN IV.v.b.39; WN IV.ix.24).[26] Its liberality and generosity seem to lie in the opportunity it gives to all for at least modest success. This opportunity is extended not merely to fellow citizens but to the whole world. The generosity and liberality of this system stands in contrast to what Smith considered to be the narrow-minded, national perspective of the mercantilists.

Justice and generosity enter into Smith's system in another way. I have noted his difference with the mercantilists on the question of wages. The natural progress of opulence, by maximizing the rate of increase in the annual produce, ensures that demand for labor will be high, and so will wages. Smith insists that it would be impossible to consider a society flourishing and happy when the great body of its people were miserable. It is true that the specter of a stationary state looms in the future. Smith contends that, as a nation becomes richer and more populous, competition among both laborers and capitalists becomes increasingly severe. As a result, the rewards going to each class will at some point be reduced to that which is just sufficient to maintain them. Profits will tend to zero and wages will fall to a level barely consistent with "common humanity." Yet the true stationary state is only a theoretical possibility. For Smith, China comes closest to having arrived at a stationary state, but China's economic advance has been limited by the "nature of its laws and institutions." In particular, Smith points to China's neglect of foreign trade and to its poor administration of justice, especially with regard to the common people (*WN* I.viii.24; *WN* IV.ix.40–41; *LJA* IV.108).[27] Furthermore, Smith was well aware that the age of globalism had arrived, and with it new markets, where trade might flourish to an unprecedented extent.

In any event, Smith claims that the system of natural liberty, even when it has reached a stationary state, secures the basic needs of all people. He implicitly calls into question the idea that there should be organized public or even private support of subsistence for the poor. In his discussion of the corn laws, he argues that dearths become famines only where there is mismanagement on the part of the state (*WN* IV.v.b.5). He seems to suggest that a society will only enter a declining phase if there is gross incompetence on the part of the state, as happened in India under the management of the East India Company (*WN* I.viii.26).[28]

The philosophical meaning of the natural progress of opulence is less ambiguous. By philosophical I mean only the perspective that Smith himself often adopts when he stops to consider things in an abstract or philosophical light. It might also be called the perspective of nature. Smith calls his system the "system of natural liberty." One might, then, expect a close connection between the ends of his system and the ends of nature simply. The great end of nature, we are frequently told, is the preservation and propagation of the species. It is helpful here to recall the remarkable passage in the *Theory of Moral Sentiments* that introduces the idea of the "invisible hand." The context is Smith's discussion of the way in which nature deceives us into pursuing worldly comfort.

> And it is well that nature imposes on us in this manner. It is this deception which rouses and keeps in continual motion the industry of mankind. . . . The earth by these labours of mankind has been obliged to redouble her fertility, and to maintain a greater multitude of inhabitants. It is to no purpose that the proud and unfeeling landlord views his extensive fields, and without a thought for the wants of his brethren, in imagination consumes himself the whole harvest that grows upon them. The homely and vulgar proverb, that the eye is larger than the belly, never was more fully verified than with regard to him. . . . The produce of the soil maintains at all times the number of inhabitants which it is capable of maintaining. The rich select from the heap what is most precious and agreeable. They consume little more than the poor, and in spite of their natural selfishness and rapacity, though they mean only their own conveniency, though the sole end which they propose from the labours of all the thousands they employ, be the gratification of their own vain and insatiable desires, they divide with the poor the produce of all their improvements. They are led by an invisible hand to make nearly the same distribution of the necessaries of life which would have been made had the earth been divided into equal portions among all its inhabitants; and thus, without intending it, advance the interest of society, and afford means to the multiplication of the species. (*TMS* IV.i.10)

According to Smith, nature operates on several levels, each of which is consistent with and subordinate to nature's deepest purposes. The hurried pursuit of wealth that dominates our lives, and generates civilization, also serves the—at first sight—more mundane purpose of distributing the necessaries of life more or less equally among the populace. Yet we must remember that nature's unequivocal end is the preservation and propagation of the species. Smith's procedure in the *Wealth of Nations* follows from his realization that nature operates on several levels. I have already indicated that his approach assumes a substratum to human life that is, in some ways, more real than the world we immediately perceive and seem to understand. This is the implication of his distinction between real and nominal value, which he admits is worthless in the ordinary transactions of life but which somehow holds the key to revealing the true operations of the society. How might this be?

Recall that Smith located the "real," or the unequivocally natural, in the "toil and trouble" or "cost" of acquisition. Thus the real measure of exchangeable value is expressed in terms of the power to put labor into motion, or, in other words, to sustain laborers while they work. The system of natural liberty, because it is the system that maximizes the rate of increase in the real exchangeable value of the annual produce, is also that which maximizes the demand for labor. The maximum demand for labor results in the fastest rate of growth of the population. Population growth, to repeat, is the outcome not of the deliberate actions of the state or of individuals but of the passion that unites the sexes and of a plentiful subsistence. "The most decisive mark of prosperity of any country is the increase in the number of its inhabitants" (*WN* I.viii.23). No state program to increase the population could improve upon this outcome.[29]

When viewed in this light, the naturalness of the system of natural liberty becomes most manifest. The human animal is not so different from the other animals; all multiply in proportion to the quantity of available subsistence. In the case of humans, though, the spontaneous productions of nature can provide only a miserable existence, and, as a result, the entire edifice of civilization is required to call forth the production of an easy subsistence. Perhaps only in the rapture of the philosopher's contemplation can the true beauty of the system that conduces to this end be perceived.

POLITICAL ECONOMY, CONSIDERED AS A
BRANCH OF THE SCIENCE OF A LEGISLATOR

From Nations to Nation

In this section I deal with Smith's view of the role of the state in the economy. Smith was not Marx or Lenin. He did not believe that the state would wither away. He left open two areas for state involvement. The first covers the responsibilities of the state under the system of natural liberty. These state responsibilities serve either to provide a framework in which the system of natural liberty may operate or to step in where the system of natural liberty is inadequate for achieving the public interest. Establishing a regular administration of justice is an example of the first kind of intervention. Building public roads, bridges, and canals is an example of the second. Both kinds of interventions are necessary supplements to the system of natural liberty. The second area of state responsibility involves making specific exceptions to the system of natural liberty itself. The most interesting circumstance in this area involves the question of how to implement the system where it has never existed or has not existed for a long time.

Smith's treatment of the role of the state brings to the fore the theme of political economy and statesmanship. As I have noted, the argument of the *Wealth of Nations* has both a philosophical dimension and a practical one. Students of the *Wealth of Nations* must be careful not to collapse either of its chief purposes into the other. These two dimensions are intertwined, however, and Smith moves—effortlessly, I might add—between his role as a polemicist and that of a scientist and philosopher. Disentangling the two is sometimes difficult, but each side of the work has a specific purpose. The theoretical enterprise is to set down the general principles that operate in a fully commercial society and to point to the forces that raise men out of barbarism and poverty and take them to civilization and opulence. The practical purpose of the work is to indicate the relevance of a science of political economy for statesmen.

Smith begins the specifically practical task of the work in book 4 of the *Wealth of Nations,* when he observes that political economy "considered as a branch of the science of a legislator" proposes two distinct objects: to enrich the people, and to enrich the sovereign (*WN* IV.intro.1). Political economy in the more emphatically political sense is concerned not with the wealth of nations but with the wealth of independent nations. The former is a global or cosmopolitan concern; the latter, a national or political concern.[30] Smith's task is to show that his account of the natural progress of opulence is relevant to the concerns of an independent nation.

Recent scholarship has tended to downplay Smith's commitment to what would today be called free-market economics.[31] Three arguments are advanced in support of this view. First, Smith left a considerable role for the state in certain specific areas.[32] Moreover, he recognized that, at times, exceptions to the system of natural liberty would have to be made—for example, to meet defense needs. Second, it is said that although Smith thought of free trade as theoretically the best arrangement, he was reconciled to the fact that it was an ideal or utopian proposal.[33] The influence of politics and the interest of humanity made it, practically speaking, impossible. Third, whatever Smith's position regarding these first two issues, some scholars argue that, because of his belief in the superior productivity of agriculture, the practical implications of his political economy would have been to curtail the manufacturing and commercial sectors and to expand the agricultural sector.[34] Taken together, these arguments suggest that Smith's political economy should not be confused with the political economy of the nineteenth- and twentieth-century advocates of liberal capitalism. But this view of Smith as backing away from free-market prescriptions, however welcome it is as a corrective to certain contemporary misappropriations of him, is difficult to square not only with what Smith himself says but also with the writings and actions of those who immediately embraced his political economy.

Political Economy and the Horizon of Progress

Before turning to the specifics of Smith's treatment of the role of the state, it is important to make clear a fundamental assumption that underlies his analysis and that distinguishes him from predecessors such as Locke, Steuart, and the Physiocrats. Smith constructs an horizon of progress under which the Smithian legislator operates. This assumption is crucial for Smith's understanding of the role of the state. The distinctiveness of his position regarding the role of the state is on display in the statement with which he introduces book 5, which deals with the duties of the state. He begins this remarkable statement by asserting that, once the various barriers to perfect liberty are removed, "the obvious and simple system of natural liberty establishes itself of its own accord." Thus he implies that, whereas the legal framework—the laws of justice—is established by government, the system of natural liberty establishes itself spontaneously. Once this has happened, he continues, the sovereign is "completely discharged" from the "duty of superintending the industry of private people, and of directing it towards the employments most suitable to the interests of the society." The sovereign is left with three important duties, ones that are "plain and intelligible to common understandings" (*WN* IV.ix.51).[35] It must be emphasized that this remarkable statement concerns not the workings of an abstract system but the operations of a society that participates in the world.

Smith's statement is somewhat deceptive.[36] First, as we will see, the sovereign has a number of duties that are not so plain and intelligible, because they depend on circumstances. Second, Smith says nothing about the difficulty involved in establishing the legal framework for the system of natural liberty. Third, he says nothing about the difficulty of executing the three tasks left for government; only that they are easily identified. I will return to these points. Nevertheless, Smith's silences regarding these matters reflect his belief that he has discovered an independent science of political economy, one which requires only a limited, incremental, and moderate political agenda. Smith, as Dugald Stewart put it—with perhaps only a little exaggeration—aimed at enlightening legislators "not by delineating plans of new constitutions, but by enlightening the policy of actual legislators."[37]

A comparison with the political radicalism of the Physiocrats provides an illuminating perspective on Smith's politics. Though aware of their eccentricities, Smith entertained a very high opinion of the Physiocrats, believing their doctrines to be "perhaps, the nearest approximation to the truth that has yet been published on the subject of political economy." He recommended their views as "well worth the consideration of every man who wishes to examine with attention the principles of that very important science" (*WN* IV.ix.38). Despite its theoretical errors, such as denying that manufacturing is a productive activity, the Physiocratic system was just, generous, and liberal, because it advocated the most perfect freedom of trade at home and with other nations. Practically speaking, then, it corresponded almost exactly to the policies of the system of natural liberty.[38]

The political program of the Physiocrats was, however, starkly at odds with the proposals of the *Wealth of Nations*.[39] The Physiocrats held the paradoxical position that, for society to be perfectly free, it had to be perfectly regimented by a "legal despotism." Thinking that natural laws exist which are "self-evident" to all men who have been freed from prejudice and superstition, the Physiocrats recommended a combination of popular enlightenment and enlightened despotism as the only way to avoid the calamities they saw as following from departures from the natural law. The Physiocratic position might appear to be an aberration in the evolution of liberal thought, but one must remember that in the seventeenth and eighteenth centuries the European monarchies were powerful forces for modernization. As Caton observes, Frederick the Great's Prussia was the archetype for this model of political and economic development.[40]

The ultimate reasons for Smith's departure from the Physiocrats' political program were rooted in his political economy. As I have explained, Smith identified the productive sector of the economy as the key to economic progress. The dynamic power of this sector is sufficiently great to carry a nation to substantial opulence even though large parts of the society are engaged in nonproductive pursuits. Moreover, Smith believed that the force that moves the productive sector, "the desire to better our condition," is a spontaneous growth that requires only freedom and security to exert itself. This view led him to take a moderate attitude toward the political and even economic imperfections in society.

Smith comments on François Quesnai, the leading Physiocrat and someone Smith admired so greatly that he considered dedicating the *Wealth of Nations* to him (*Account*, III.12), show that he recoiled at the Physiocratic proposal that society be remade by an enlightened absolute ruler.[41] Of Quesnai, Smith observes that

> [h]e seems not to have considered that in the political body, the natural effort which every man is continually making to better his own condition, is a principle of preservation capable of preventing and correcting, in many respects, the bad effects of a political economy, in some degree, both partial and oppressive. . . . In the political body, . . . the *wisdom of nature* has fortunately made ample provision for remedying many of the bad effects of the folly and injustice of man; in the same manner as it has done in the natural body, for remedying those of sloth and intemperance. (*WN* IV.ix.28, emphasis added; cf. *TMS* VI.ii.2.16–18)

The consequences that follow from this argument are most important. It is not so much that Smith is opposed to enlightened absolutism in principle, but, rather, that he objects to sudden and violent change, especially in the political order. The political order need not be perfect in order for society to progress. It may even progress while laboring under severe disabilities. Consider, in this regard, Smith's treatment of English country gentlemen. Smith was always quick to point out their lack of commercial and political sense, but he did not think they constituted a significant drag on economic progress (*WN* I.xi.p.8; *WN* III.ii.7; *WN* III.iv.3). It is Smith's political economy that gives him the political latitude to avoid the need for a revolutionary reshaping of society. The wisdom of nature is such that reform may be steady and deliberate, but it may be conducted without urgency. Furthermore, the desire to better one's condition does not have to be created or formed by the government. It is an independent and spontaneous growth, for which the government need only make way. Thus not only does Smith rule out a revolutionary reshaping of society, he also rules out a role for the statesman along the lines described by James Steuart. Steuart, the reader will recall, charged the statesman with introducing a new spirit into the nation. To Smith, such an attempt would be both unnecessary and presumptuous. Republican revolution of the kind Locke advocated would be even more dangerous. With this in mind, let us look more closely at the duties that Smith left to the state.

Duties of the Sovereign

The three duties of the sovereign stipulated by Smith—defense, justice, and certain public works and institutions—imply a fourth, that of taxation to finance the activities. It is appropriate to begin with taxation, because Smith saw the tax system not merely as critical for the functioning of the economy but as central to liberty itself.

Taxation: The chief source of the revenue of modern states is ultimately the wealth of the subjects of those states. Modern states cannot rely on the treasure troves of kings and princes to finance their activities. Smith's extensive analysis of taxation was a major effort to establish rational principles on which to base taxation policy. He wished to focus discussions of taxation on revenue questions— which taxes raise the most revenue with the fewest possible inconveniences?— rather than on designing a tax system to stimulate particular enterprises (or, for that matter, to redistribute wealth) (*WN* V.ii.k.32). His discussion of taxation extends to other aspects, including the costs of collection and the implications for civil liberties. The science of political economy is relevant in these areas, because it indicates the way in which revenues can be raised with the greatest ease and the least possible detriment to economic progress. It turns out that equal treatment is the basic principle of both political economy and justice (*WN* V.ii.b.3; *WN* V.ii.c.7). Smith's contention is that taxes should be levied in such a way as to cause the least deviation from the natural progress of opulence. Equality of taxation across different industries and income groups involves the least possible distortion, because it imposes an equal discouragement on all activities.

Smith believed that, as a general rule, the tax system should not be used to stimulate particular forms of economic activity. He made three exceptions, all minor. First, he recommends some small tax incentives and tax penalties to encourage (or discourage) certain forms of activity in the agricultural sector.[42] Second, he recommends that taxes be used as a substitute for sumptuary laws, even though such taxes usually involve some distortion of "the natural direction of national industry" (*WN* V.ii.k.63). Excise taxes, for example, are useful for checking the excessive consumption of alcohol (*WN* V.ii.k.50). More important, though, is the general role that he saw for taxation as a means of checking the consumption of luxuries. "Upon the sober and industrious poor, taxes upon [luxuries] act as sumptuary laws, and dispose them either to moderate, or refrain altogether from the use of superfluities which they can no longer easily afford" (*WN* V.ii.k.7). Smith's concern is not with the effect of the consumption of luxuries on the balance of trade but with the support of certain virtues. Third, Smith gives a mild endorsement to the principle of progressive taxation. He proposes, for example, that luxury carriages be subjected to higher highway tolls than those to which ordinary or business carriages are subjected. House rents are also a suitable subject for taxation because they fall most heavily on the rich. "It is not unreasonable," he writes, "that the rich should contribute to the publick expence, not only in proportion to their revenue, but something more than in that proportion" (*WN* V.ii.e.6). Without spelling out just how it might be accomplished, he recommends that the profits of firms that have a monopoly position in the market are more suitable targets for taxation than are industries that must compete (*WN* V.ii.k.54).

Smith's departures from the principle of equality are extremely limited. Moreover, the exceptions he makes for the most part apply to sectors of society that in a sense fall *outside* the system of natural liberty. He never claims, for example, that monopoly industries or country gentlemen feel the effects of the competitive system. His most striking use of taxation as a policy instrument is his effort to encourage frugality. It seems to contain an echo of the mercantilist preference for low wages as a spur to industry. This appearance must, however, be weighed against his claim that the system of natural liberty is the generous and liberal system. He is not recommending that the people be subjected to the sharp pinch of necessity. The liberal reward of labor is the great incentive for ordinary laborers to increase their industry. The chief support for industry and frugality comes from the discipline of competition, which is part of the system of natural liberty itself, not from a government policy to suppress wage levels.

Defense: Smith calls defense the first duty of the state (*WN* V.i.a.1). His discussion of defense in book 5 focuses on the necessity for a standing army in modern times. In barbarous societies, and even in shepherding and farming societies, the way of life is compatible with the life of a soldier. Matters are different in civilized societies. The "wisdom of the state" must see to it that a class of men continue to devote themselves to military careers, because in the natural course of things most men will become unfit for such a life (*WN* V.i.a. 14). The wisdom of nature is not sufficient because in a commercial society not enough men will attempt to better their condition by pursuing a military life. Management of the standing army involves developing a system of rewards and honors that keep the military subordinate to the civil authorities. Where a "natural aristocracy" (in this usage a "nobility and gentry") exists this is not difficult, because this class "has the greatest interest in the support of the civil authority." Although Smith says he is aware of the real dangers of a standing army, as well as of those dangers imagined by "[m]en of republican principles," he seems largely unconcerned. Indeed, he points to the advantages for liberty, remarking that a "degree of liberty which approaches to licentiousness can be tolerated only in countries where the sovereign is secured by a well-regulated standing army" (*WN* V.i.a.41).

Defense is clearly an important state responsibility. It is one of the chief examples in which the "wisdom of nature" must be supplemented by the "wisdom of the state." Yet the message of this discussion—and, even more so, the overall message of the *Wealth of Nations*—is that the system of natural liberty is the surest path to military strength. Wealth and technical sophistication are key elements in the defense of any modern nation (*WN* V.i.a.42–44). Here, Smith's response to the mercantilists is that the twin objectives of power and plenty are best achieved through a system of free trade at home and with other nations. Thus the wisdom of nature provides a framework in which the wisdom of the state operates.[43] Later in this section, we will consider the cases in which Smith believes there must be a departure from this general rule.

Justice: The second duty of the sovereign discussed in the *Wealth of Nations* is that of "protecting, as far as possible, every member of the society from the injustice or oppression of every other member of it, or the duty of establishing an exact administration of justice." As I noted, in Smith's view, justice is the fundamental pillar of all social life. In addition, it is the foundation of commercial prosperity, because it secures to individuals the fruits of their labors (*WN* V.iii.7). Smith's focus in book 5 of the *Wealth of Nations* is on the administration of justice, rather than on the rules of justice themselves. He favors, as I noted above, a separation of powers between the judicial and executive branches. Furthermore, he suggests that the cost of the legal system be defrayed principally by "court fees" paid by those bringing cases before the courts. Under such a system, competition between the various courts is likely to be productive of both cost efficiency and justice, because judges seeking business will try to dispense justice as quickly and impartially as possible.

It is striking that for all its bulk, the *Wealth of Nations* has little specific to say about the laws of justice in the economic sphere. What is clear and what Smith emphasizes again and again is that among the laws of justice are those that protect economic liberty. The system of natural liberty, in which there are no preferences or restraints and in which everyone is left "perfectly free to pursue his own interest in his own way," is a system of justice. Perhaps most interesting about Smith's treatment of justice are the situations in which he believes that natural or perfect liberty may be restrained at certain times or, in some cases, always.[44] The general principle used in these cases is made clear in Smith's discussion of banking regulation. Banking, he explains, must always be regulated in certain important respects (*WN* II.ii.106). For example, there should be restrictions on the issuing of paper for small sums, in order to discourage the entry of small lenders into the market. In addition, bank notes should be immediately convertible, in order to discourage the extension of credit beyond what is prudent. Smith approved of paper money issued by the state, as long as it was issued with "moderation." Perhaps his most surprising argument is that for a maximum rate of interest.[45] He argues that, without such a provision, lending will be skewed toward those "prodigals and projectors" who erroneously believe or fraudulently assert that they can afford to pay a higher rate of interest. Such lending directs funds away from sober and cautious men, who have a better appreciation of their ability to pay (*WN* II.iv.15). Smith grants that these regulations represent "violations" of "natural liberty," which it is "the proper business of law, not to infringe, but to support." But he reasons that, where the natural liberty of a few endangers the "security of a whole society," it is right and proper to place restraints in the law. These comments bring to light the utilitarian side of Smith's thought that is, as I have noted, in tension with his more libertarian side.

Two considerations cast these regulations in a slightly different light, more in keeping with Smith's political economy as a whole. First, with respect to the Ayr Bank—Smith's chief example of poor banking practices—the discussion is as much a caution about commercial ventures undertaken for "public spirited purposes" as it is a caution about the dangers of financial imprudence (*WN* II.ii.73). The Ayr Bank was established to remedy a problem that Smith denied could ever exist: namely, a scarcity of money. Second, the degree to which Smith seeks to discourage "projectors" and those engaged in "spirited undertakings" is again striking.[46] Human nature is prone to overrate its chances, especially when the prospective prizes are outside the normal run of things (*WN* I.x.b.27). The paradigmatic case is exploring for gold, which has an enormous but utterly irrational appeal for most men (*WN* IV.vii.a.18).

Public Works and Public Institutions: Smith charges the state with the maintenance of certain public works and public institutions. We have already considered Smith's far-reaching proposals for the reform of education. These recommendations are important examples of the "wisdom of the state." Two further points should be noted. First, many of these proposals do not involve continued active government intervention. At the most, they involve reforms that simply do away with ancient practices. In the area of religion, he recommends what amounts to deregulation, in order to allow the churches to compete for souls. Second, it is important to see the extent to which these proposals draw on the system of natural liberty. The university, for example, provides a kind of market for the exchange of useful knowledge between philosophers and practical men.

The maintenance of public works that facilitate either specific branches of commerce or commerce in general involves the state in a much more active way. With respect to the first, Smith recommends that the state give support to "hazardous trades." He has in mind here the protection of commerce in "barbarous and uncivilized nations." He proposes that the state give military support and temporary monopolies to merchants engaged in "dangerous and expensive experiments" (*WN* V.i.e.1–5,30). Such encouragement is warranted because the community as a whole gains greatly from these activities, which otherwise might not be undertaken. It would be wrong to see this as an endorsement of commercial imperialism, for, as Caton remarks, the *Wealth of Nations* is one of the great anti-imperial tracts.[47] His recommendation for the support of hazardous trades is not made in light of a belief that political and commercial rivalries are inseparably intertwined, as they were for Steuart and Locke. What Smith seems to have in mind is the encouragement and protection by civilized nations of the gradual globalization of commerce. This is, perhaps, the only occasion on which Smith advocates any significant support for "adventurers."[48]

Furthermore, certain public works—those that facilitate commerce in general but that would not be profitable for any single individual to undertake—are properly the responsibility of the state. This function is most important. Roads, canals, bridges, and so forth, are, says Smith, "the greatest of all improvements" (*WN* I.xi.b.5). The greater part of his discussion concerns how such projects should be financed. Where possible, he recommends that they be self-financing and administered by local and provincial governments.

The Wisdom of Future Legislators

Smith granted that there are a number of exceptions to the general rule of free trade which are not simply complementary to his system of natural liberty. In these areas, he seems to leave a degree of discretion to the statesman. Two questions must be borne in mind when considering his approach. First, to what extent is this discretion real? Although Smith recognizes the need for statesmen to act on the basis of the prevailing circumstances, he recommends they do this in light of the understanding of the natural course of things established in the *Wealth of Nations*. The second question goes to the heart of Smith's approach. He suggests a general rule, subject to exceptions. The great question here is whether the exceptions he marks out really have the character of exceptions or are so numerous or so grave as to call into question the validity of the general rule. In particular, I wish to draw attention to the way in which he deals with the problem of implementing his system of natural liberty in a world that is not characterized by universal freedom of trade and perpetual peace. The situation of a new nation that is weak and inexperienced is a particular case of this general problem.

Recall that Smith's case for international free trade was twofold. First, wealth consists not of money but of goods, and the measure of wealth is the purchasing power of the annual produce. The exchangeable value of the annual produce increases most rapidly where freedom of trade is the most perfect. This recommendation extends to foreign trade, for the only economic effect of foreign trade is the beneficial one of extending the market for the surplus produce of the nation. By so doing, foreign trade also removes the limit on the division of labor set by the size of the national market. The mercantile system's restraints constricted production by raising the price of domestic and imported goods and by diverting resources from more productive pursuits into less productive ones. Merchants and manufacturers were the only beneficiaries of this policy.

Smith's second argument for free trade was essentially moral.[49] International free trade promises benefits beyond an increase in the rate of economic progress. "The wealth of neighbouring nations," he observes, "though dangerous in war and politicks, is certainly advantageous in trade." In "a state of peace and commerce," the wealth of a neighboring nation allows it to purchase more of the surplus produce and at a greater price. The maxims of the mercantile system had, by obscuring this fact, sown dissension among the nations. "Commerce," Smith observes, "which ought naturally to be, among nations as among individuals, a bond of union and friendship, has become the most fertile source of discord and animosity" (WN IV.iii.c.9). A further implication of Smith's argument is that the progressive expansion of commerce throughout the globe is the surest means of bringing the various nations of the world into that state of equality which could establish a global balance of power. It was a means of stabilizing the global balance of power by making the weak strong.

How should an enlightened statesman, who, Smith acknowledged, must have his nation's interests in mind (TMS VI.ii.26), conduct himself in a world in which reason and humanity do not guide all nations? In book 4 Smith outlines two kinds of exceptions to the doctrine of free trade: in one class are a number of automatic exceptions; in the other, matters for deliberation.

Smith's oft-quoted maxim, "defence . . . is of much more importance than opulence," occurs in his discussion of the first automatic exception (WN IV.ii.30). This discussion represents an addendum to the discussion of defense as the first duty of the sovereign. Smith makes what appears to be a very broad exception. Where a particular commodity is necessary for defense, it must be protected from foreign competition, so that it will be available in emergencies. Smith's main example is the Act of Navigation (1651), which gave an "artificial" stimulus to the shipping industry (the "carrying trade") by giving it a monopoly in certain areas, including the North American trade.[50] A closer look at this specific example shows that in the case of Great Britain, at least, the defense exception might not be as consequential as it first appears. Smith argued that many provisions of the Act of Navigation were unwise and stemmed largely from a misunderstanding of the principles of political economy. First, the monopoly of the colony trade secured by the Act of Navigation was in reality an economic burden, because it had drawn trade away from more productive endeavors, such as trade with less distant Europe (WN IV.vii.c.22). Second, Dutch preeminence in the European carrying trade had not declined at all, even though its decline was one of the main objectives of the act (WN IV.ii.26). Third, because the monopoly on the colony trade retarded English commerce, it acted to decrease trade and, therefore, shipping. The advocates of the colony trade did not understand Great Britain's security interests, in part because they did not understand her true economic interests. Fourth, England was a great naval power *before* the advent of the Act of Navigation (WN IV.vii.c.23). Lastly, the coastal trade, especially in coal, was Great Britain's largest employer of sailors and ships (WN II.v.30).[51]

Furthermore, Smith's arguments are a response, rather than a concession, to the mercantilists' twin preoccupations of power and plenty. Whether he thought there was a sharp conflict between wealth and power in the case of Great Britain is open to question. It is, however, significant that he posed the defense-versus-opulence trade-off so sharply. He does not deny that power and plenty must be the objects of the nation's political economy. The mercantilists regarded the two concerns as so interconnected that they were seldom in conflict. Jacob Viner reminds us that "it was the anti-mercantilist, Adam Smith, who laid down the maxim that 'defense is more important than opulence.' A typical mercantilist might well have replied that defense is necessary to opulence and opulence to effective defense, even if momentarily the two ends might appear to be in conflict."[52] At bottom, Smith and the mercantilists differed in their assessments of the future. Smith believed that, as a general rule, increases in the annual produce increased the ability to acquire military power and were the most likely way to secure the nation. A mercantilist might respond that it is only so if war is a possibility only in the indefinite future. If it is more likely than this, a judgment now must be made about the appropriate level and type of military expenditure. Moreover, defense and opulence would then no longer be in conflict. Beyond this, commercial expansion through colonialism of the sort advocated by mercantilists does not figure in Smith's scheme. Commercial expansion, according to Smith, takes place in a smooth and incremental process that begins at home and extends to foreign trade only in its last phase. The diversion of expenditures into the carrying trade and defense necessarily retards this process; hence the sharp trade-off between defense and opulence.

A second automatic exception to the rule of free trade occurs when a tax is levied on a domestically produced good that must compete with imports. In this case it is proper that a comparable duty be placed on the imported good, because the tax on the imported good would restore the proportion between the price of domestic and foreign goods, thereby maintaining the natural balance of industry in the nation (*WN* IV.ii.31).

The second class of exceptions consists of matters that require deliberation (*WN* IV.ii.37). In the first case Smith discusses, the nation's exports are burdened with discriminatory treatment in a foreign country. Here, he says, it is a matter of deliberation whether this treatment should be met with retaliatory measures. He observes that although the spirit of revenge necessarily dictates retaliation, it may not be the wisest course of action. Only if the retaliation is likely to result in the removal of the restrictions is it the correct course. When it is unlikely to have this effect, to retaliate is to respond to an injury by injuring oneself further. With respect to such decisions, Smith remarks that

> To judge whether such retaliations are likely to have such an effect, does not, perhaps, belong so much to the science of the legislator, whose deliberations ought to be governed by general principles which are always the same, as to the skill of that insidious and crafty animal, vulgarly called a statesman or politician, whose councils are governed by the momentary fluctuations of affairs. (*WN* IV.ii.39)

By "momentary fluctuations of affairs," Smith clearly means considerations of war and politics. Thus he leaves open the possibility of a kind of commercial warfare in the cause of free trade. This argument is important because, as we will see, Madison and Jefferson advocated such a strategy against Great Britain.

Beyond the issue of the exception, Smith's remarks constitute a paradigmatic statement, in that they provide a general insight into his understanding of the way in which the science of political economy is relevant to politics.[53] He believed that some aspects of human affairs are governed by general principles, in a manner similar to the laws that govern the natural world. To be fully operative, however, these social laws, summarized in the description of the natural progress of opulence, require a legal framework established by positive law. The hierarchy implicit in Smith's analysis places the "legislator," guided by knowledge of the general course of things, above the "politician," who operates only in the area of exceptions to the general course of things. One must ask here, as with the question of war, whether this hierarchy can be maintained without assuming that there is in the historical process some general tendency toward the universal adoption of the system of natural liberty. In other words, if it is, for some reason, found that the world always operates within the exceptions marked out by Smith, then we must question the relevance of the system of natural liberty.

The other situation in which deliberation is required is when free trade is to be established in an industry or, perhaps, an entire society where it has never existed or has not existed for a long time (*WN* IV.ii.40). Smith cautions that equity with respect to those who have made large investments under existing laws, as well as humanity toward those who might be thrown out of work, requires that free trade be restored slowly and with adequate warning (*WN* IV.ii.44). When discussing the issue of free trade with the North American colonies, Smith argues that it must be left to the "wisdom of future statesmen and legislators" to decide the way in which perfect liberty of trade should be restored (*WN* IV.vii.c.44). More so than in the case of defense, it is a mistake, however, to exaggerate the extent to which Smith regarded this as a major obstacle to the introduction of free trade. In the case of Great Britain, he noted that many of its major exports were profitable without artificial incentives (*WN* IV.ii.41). Moreover, recent experience had suggested that large numbers of men who had become unemployed could be easily absorbed by other sectors of industry. Smith recounts that after the Seven Years' War (1756–1763), one hundred thousand men, all "accustomed to the use of arms" and "many to rapine and plunder," were, without convulsion or disorder, absorbed into the workforce (*WN* IV.ii.42). He concludes that, if there is perfect liberty of trade, the dislocations caused by large-scale retrenchments are not likely to be great.

The greatest obstacle to the restoration of free trade in Great Britain was political, rather than social or economic, in that a large number of powerful, vested interests had grown up as a result of the artificially large colony trade. These had reached such a size that they resembled an "overgrown standing army" that could intimidate a government. "To expect," he concludes, ". . . freedom of trade should ever be entirely restored *in Great Britain,* is as absurd as to expect an Oceana or Utopia should ever be established in it" (*WN* IV.ii.43, emphasis added). This statement should not be taken to mean that Smith considered free trade utopian. As we saw earlier, the political situation of Great Britain was unusual because of its representative institutions. The general tendency of the natural course of things is toward absolute monarchies fortified by standing armies. Under such governments, the "clamour and sophistry" of merchants would not constitute as important an obstacle to reform. The colony trade monopoly had introduced a disorder into the constitution of Great Britain that could only be removed at the risk of creating further disorder. The correct approach was, first of all, not add to the problem, and then to take remedial measures "slowly, gradually, and after a very long warning." Perhaps that is why Smith leaves this matter to the wisdom of future legislators and not to the sneaking arts of a politician.

The Smithian Legislator and Free Trade

Smith's comments on the constitutional problem of Great Britain recall his praise in the *Theory of Moral Sentiments* of the "greatest and noblest characters": the "legislator and reformer" of a great state who rises above partisanship and undertakes to reform the constitution of the state, fully aware of the dangers involved in a spirit of innovation. Smith contrasts this kind of statesman with the man of system who willfully and cruelly insists on establishing, at a stroke, his own ideal plan of government. His remarks here have a classical republican tone.[54] They would also seem to cut against the grain of the argument I have developed about his use of the spirit of system. The tension is less than might appear, however. First, the passages in question were added to the final 1790 addition of the *Theory of Moral Sentiments*. It is likely that Smith had in mind recent events in France, which threatened to destroy the old regime. This sort of change is a far cry from the kind of reforms implied in his political economy. Second, Smith was not making a new point. As we have seen, he had always been critical of "imperial and royal reformers" whose intent was to remake society (*TMS* VI.ii.2.18; *WN* IV.ix.28). Thus his later remarks are really elaborations, rather than qualifications. Third, Smith does not deny that statesman ought to be guided by some "general, and even systematical, idea of the perfection of policy and law" (*TMS* VI.ii.2.18). A legislator and reformer, insofar as he is influenced by Smith, would act with a knowledge of the natural course of things that points to the benefits of moderation and caution. Smith's system is, as I have observed, a system that avoids the dangers of system.

Does a gap between Smith and later free-market economists exist, as revisionist scholars claim? Smith's view of the role of the state surely differs from that of today's free-market economists. But this important fact should not distract us from Smith's central claim: the natural progress of opulence is the surest path to riches and power.

When confronting the reality that universal free trade and perpetual peace do not yet exist, Smith advocates a strategy based on general rules and limited exceptions. The economic difficulties of implementing free trade are minimized, and the political difficulties seem to apply chiefly to those nations with powerful representative institutions. But what of Smith's belief in the superior productivity of agriculture? Would it in effect convert the *Wealth of Nations* into an argument against the kind of industrial capitalism that was celebrated by later free-market economists? In the case of Europe, especially Great Britain, free trade would have meant an expansion of agriculture, but it is hardly likely that it would not have meant a curtailment of mercantile and manufacturing industries. Indeed, the superior productivity of agriculture might have stimulated these industries to a greater degree. In the case of North America, however, the end of the mercantile system would mean that agriculture would remain the predominant pursuit for many years. As to the question of whether Smith would have celebrated industrial capitalism, we have already seen that his endorsement of capitalism was not without qualifications, many of which concerned the effects of manufacturing. But, again, this should not distract us from the fact that, for whatever reason, Smith placed economic liberty above these other concerns. Thus, in the long term, he endorsed full-blown capitalism— everywhere.

THE SMITHIAN LEGISLATOR AND NORTH AMERICA

That the *Wealth of Nations* and the Declaration of Independence both appeared in 1776 has forever linked Smith to the American experience. The issue is whether there is anything more to this link than a historical accident. In what follows, I will point to the differences between Smith's account of commercial society and Hamilton's understanding of American capitalism. That said, it is important to recognize that, for Smith, the *Wealth of Nations* and North America were very closely linked. Several factors account for the particular place North America occupied in Smith's mind. The "colonial disturbances," as he called the American Revolution, were the burning political issue of the day. Smith took the opportunity to comment at length on them in the context of his general discussion of colonies in the *Wealth of Nations.* Furthermore, North America was, for Smith, both a demonstrable proof of his theory and the place where it was most likely that his ideas would have their chance.[55] Each of these concerns deserves a fuller treatment before taking up the comparison with Hamilton.

Smith's opinions on the "colonial disturbances" were widely read and may have had an influence on British policy toward North America.[56] Smith remained steadfast in his views on the issue. Although the *Wealth of Nations* was published shortly before the adoption of the Declaration of Independence, Smith made no significant changes to his treatment of the colonial disturbances in the six editions of the work that appeared between 1776 and his death in 1790. He gave no credence to the colonial complaints about taxation, but, nevertheless, his preferred option was for Great Britain to cut herself free from the colonies and thereby relieve herself of the arduous burden of defending them.[57] After a peaceful separation, he thought it likely that "the same sort of parental affection on the one side, and filial respect on the other, might revive between Great Britain and her colonies, which used to subsist between those of ancient Greece and the mother city from which they descended" (*WN* IV.vii.c.66). Despite the appeal of separation, he said he regarded the measure as implausible, even to the eyes of the "most visionary enthusiast." The "pride" of the British nation and, more importantly, the "interest" of its governing part were more than a match for considerations of the general interest (*WN* IV.vii.c.66). There may have been an element of rhetorical exaggeration in Smith's argument. Perhaps he held out greater hopes that Great Britain would put interest ahead of pride. In any case, his failure to acknowledge in any way the justice of the American claims with regard to taxation seems now thoroughly wrongheaded.

Smith's fall-back position was for the establishment of an imperial union that would grant to the colonies free trade and representation in the British Parliament. Two aspects of this scheme are worth mentioning. First, it held out a "new and more dazzling object of ambition" to the "ambitious and high-spirited men" of the colonies. Instead of the "paltry raffle of colony faction," they could hope for "some of the great prizes which sometimes come from the wheel of the great state lottery of British politicks" (*WN* IV.vii.c.74–76). These remarks are of interest because they underrate the attraction that the leading men of America, such as Hamilton, would find in being "statesman and legislators" engaged in founding a new nation (cf. *WN* IV.vii.c.75). The second point of note is that Smith was reasonably confident that North America would overwhelm Great Britain economically in the not-too-distant future. If representation were proportioned to taxation, the "seat of empire would then naturally remove itself to that part of the empire which contributed most to the general defence and support of the whole" (*WN* IV.vii.c.79).

Smith's opinion of the economic potential of North America is closely related to another of his positions. He regarded the rapid progress of the North American colonies as a critical proof of his theory of the natural progress of opulence. As I mentioned earlier, he believed that "the most decisive mark of the prosperity of any country is the increase of the number of its inhabitants" (*WN* I.viii.23). He observed that in the colonies the population doubled every twenty to twenty-five years, rather than every five hundred years, as in Europe. The rapid increase in population was a result of the high demand for labor, and this, in turn, was a result of the amount of funds devoted to the maintenance of productive labor. The reasons for American prosperity were clear to Smith. First, the Americans, he thought, had benefited from the institutions they derived from Great Britain. They were already a "civilized" people: understanding the value of laws, imbued with the habits of subordination necessary for government, and possessing a knowledge of the arts and sciences necessary for the conduct of agriculture (*WN* IV.vii.b.1–2). Second, American laws against the engrossing of land and against primogeniture were both particularly suited for the promotion of agriculture. Third, taxes were low and government cheap, a circumstance aided greatly by the colonies' failure to provide for their own defense. Finally, although the colonies were bound by the mercantile laws that protected British manufacturing, these laws had as yet done no harm to the colonies. Only in the future, when it became desirable for Americans to engage in manufacturing, would these "impertinent badges of slavery" become "really oppressive and insupportable" (*WN* IV.vii.b.44). The laws had not harmed the colonies because they confined Americans to agricultural pursuits. The rapid increases in population were ultimately traceable to this singular attention to agriculture.

At times Smith went beyond analysis and gave advice. Agriculture, he contended, is the "proper business of all new colonies," because the cheapness of land renders it more advantageous than any other activity (*WN* IV.vii.c.51). The devotion of the Americans to agriculture was bringing them quickly to a situation of "real wealth and greatness." New colonies produce large surpluses of agricultural products, which they can exchange for manufactured goods from other lands. Smith warned that, were the colonies to encourage manufactures, "they would retard instead of accelerating the further increase in the value of their annual produce, and would obstruct instead of promoting the progress of their country towards real wealth and greatness" (*WN* II.v.21). He added that the same reasoning would argue against any attempt by the Americans to monopolize their own foreign trade by subsidizing their merchant marine.

Conclusion

Perhaps more than anywhere else in the world, North America was a suitable testing ground for the system of natural liberty. It is not surprising that Smith found a ready audience in the new United States. In particular, his views nicely buttressed one of the deepest and most-enduring of American political currents— American exceptionalism. He seemed to provide a rational economic argument for American exceptionalism, one that could stand alongside the political and religious dimensions of American exceptionalism.

In Chapter 3, I turn to the political and economic statesmanship of Alexander Hamilton. There are two large issues that carry over from our consideration of Smith. The first is the gap in Smith's thinking on the question of founding. This gap was not an oversight on his part; nor was it simply a matter of his having not completed his projected work on government. His neglect of founding grew out of his revision of Whig political thought. Rather than positing an original contract that puts an end to the state of nature, Smith described the evolution of various forms of government. This gap is somewhat filled by the system of law and policy that he elaborated. That system of policy itself is the second issue dividing Smith and Hamilton. Smith both elaborated a system and saw the usefulness of the spirit of system. The question is whether he exaggerated the advantages of each.

HAMILTON *and the*
FOUNDATION *of the*
COMMERCIAL
REPUBLIC

HAMILTON AND THE "NEW SCHOOL"
OF POLITICAL ECONOMY

AFTER SUCH A LONG AND INTRICATE CONSIDERATION of Smith's political and economic thought, it is best to begin our consideration of Hamilton by concentrating on some of the major issues between the two men. This will make the descent into the details of Hamilton's term as treasury secretary a little easier to follow. The purpose of this chapter, then, is twofold. First, it is a provisional conclusion for the study as a whole, in that it considers Hamilton's overall response to the "new school" of political economy. Second, it introduces the discussion of Hamilton's term as treasury secretary that occupies the next three sections. These sections consider the response in action, so to speak, and emphasize Hamilton's disagreements with Smith. Later, in the conclusion of this study, I will provide a fuller comparison between Smith and Hamilton and bring their points of agreement more clearly into view. The fuller comparison will make possible some reflections on the contemporary practical relevance of the discussion of the issues that divided the two men. In this first section I focus chiefly on the difference between Smith and Hamilton as to the possibility and usefulness of theorizing about political matters, including economic affairs.

The critical issue for this section is Hamilton's claim that Smith's doctrine of free trade is true as a general rule but not as an exclusive one.[1] This judgment, which Hamilton advanced in an essay critical of the Jefferson administration's economic policies, sounds similar to Smith's suggestion that free trade should be the general rule, subject to a limited number of exceptions. If these two statements were, in fact, the same, the differences between Smith and Hamilton might only be apparent. Hamilton may have simply misunderstood Smith. Or he may have disagreed with other American followers of Smith, such as Thomas Jefferson and James Madison, on the practical question of how to apply Smith's theory to the American situation. We will see, however, that neither of these explanations is satisfactory. It is certainly likely that Hamilton learned from Smith, but important differences remained, and the decisive difference concerned the extent to which it is possible and useful to theorize about economic affairs.

To understand more precisely Hamilton's view of the relationship between economic theory and economic practice, we turn to some of his earliest writings on the subject of political economy. It seems that Hamilton first turned his mind to the serious study of economic matters in about 1779. The desperate state of American finances was the immediate impetus. The result of these studies was a series of letters and essays written over the course of approximately two years. In these writings, Hamilton made two important points about the methodology of political economy. First, there are important limitations on the usefulness of theorizing about the operations of society. These limitations were manifested in the defects of the theory of free trade. Second, given the limitations of theory, one must base law and policy on firmer foundations. Chiefly, Hamilton looked to the practice of enlightened statesmen and the general policy of nations for guidance. In the ensuing section, I consider the more general issue of the contrast between Hamilton's approach and that of modern social scientists, especially economists.

The Spirit of Geometry in Politics

In 1781 and early 1782 Hamilton published a series of essays under the title "The Continentalist." The main purpose of the series was to make the case for thinking continentally about the future of the United States. In particular, Hamilton urged an immediate increase in the powers of the national government. Surveying the state of postrevolutionary America, he lamented that Americans had begun the war with "very vague and confined notions of the practical business of government." Of those who had experience in government, many had taken the Tory side in the war; the remainder possessed "ideas adapted to the narrow coloneal sphere, in which they had been accustomed to move, not of that enlarged kind suited to the government of an INDEPENDENT NATION." This lack of both knowledge and experience had led to errors of administration so grave that they threatened the successful establishment of a "rational" and "durable" liberty. Compounding these errors were "many chimerical projects and utopian speculations" that had arisen in the political vacuum created by inexperience.[2] For example, the speculative drift in the political thought of the new nation fed the dangerous hope that it would be unnecessary to grant new and important powers to the national government. This theme of the dangers posed by political speculators would become a constant and central theme of

Hamilton's political thought. The centrality of this theme has been obscured by historians and political scientists who have emphasized Hamilton's alleged reliance on the manipulation of self-interest as the key for understanding him. One consequence has been a certain mischaracterization of the conflict between Hamilton and his chief rivals.

The nub of Hamilton's reservation about the role of the spirit of speculation in politics is evident in a long letter he penned in 1779. This somewhat hubristic letter by Washington's young (twenty-five-year-old) aide-de-camp, dealing with the problems of war finances, was certainly not his last word on economic affairs. The letter was, Hamilton said, the "product of some reading on the subjects of commerce and finance and of occasional reflexions on our particular situation." But, he added, a "want of leisure" had prevented him from perfecting his recommendations. Moreover, scholars have not been able to establish with certainty either the addressee of the letter or whether it was even sent. Nevertheless, it is of great interest to us because of the methodological remarks Hamilton made in the course of dealing with the problem of war finances.[3]

The reader will recall that Smith had made two criticisms of the use of systems. First, systems must be put to the test of experiment. In political economy, this means looking to the evidence provided by history. Second, systems should be implemented with caution, and care should be taken not to disturb society. As we saw, however, for Smith these caveats did not constitute a bar to the construction of the most elaborate and comprehensive systems. Hamilton's criticisms of the spirit of system went beyond Smith's, in that they called into question the value of systematizing itself. Hamilton pointed to two other general problems inherent in using extended chains of reasoning, such as those that are used for constructing systems of political economy. First, he drew attention to the element of enthusiasm that was likely to infect theoretical enterprises. "I am aware," he said, "how apt the imagination is to be heated in projects of this nature." Abstract, especially deductive, reasoning provides a false sense of certainty and, moreover— as Smith understood so clearly—possesses a considerable charm for the human mind. The second problem is inherent in the process of deductive reasoning itself. "A great source of error," Hamilton explained, "in disquisitions of this nature is the judging of events by abstract calculations, which though *geometrically true* are *practically false* as they relate to the concerns of beings governed more by passion and prejudice than by an enlightened sense of their interests. A degree of illusion mixes itself in all the affairs of society." Thus geometric, or deductive, reasoning is of limited utility, because it cannot take into account the complexity of economic reality. First principles or premises conceal within them a multitude of potential sources of error; and the farther one moves away from those first principles, the more likely it is that one will fall into error. In the area of political economy, it is the influence of the passions that makes it problematic to rely upon elaborate calculations about the operations of society, calculations which assume that those operations are determined by the actions of individuals moved by an enlightened sense of their own self-interest. Often individuals do not— and, perhaps, cannot—know what is truly in their self-interest. At other times, they know but are led astray from their true interests by their immediate passions and inclinations.[4]

Hamilton made these general points in a discussion of the depreciation of the market value of government-issued paper money during the revolution. The excessive issue of paper had resulted in a sharp decline in its market value. The puzzle was that the decline in value seemed disproportionately large when looked at simply in terms of the magnitude of the increase in the supply of paper money. The apparently excessive decline, he explained, was "derived from opinion, a want of confidence." The want of confidence went beyond the nation's finances and was, in fact, a crisis of confidence in the government itself. Furthermore, he added, "we deceive ourselves when we suppose the value will increase in proportion as the quantity is lessened. Opinion will operate here also; and a thousand circumstances may promote or counteract the principle."[5] In other words, because the depreciation was not simply a mechanical process, more was needed than a simple reversal of the policy that had led to the problem. We will have occasion to return to Hamilton's stress on the dependence of economic and, especially, financial matters on considerations of opinion and confidence. For now, it is sufficient to note that Hamilton believed that decisive action on the part of the national government was called for. Such action would help to restore the people's confidence, not only in their currency but also in the government and in the future of the nation. More generally, one task of government is to create a political and social context in which individuals are not only free to pursue their true self-interest but also likely, in fact, to do so.

If there was one clear influence on Hamilton at this early stage, it was David Hume's political and economic essays. The particular arguments of these essays exercised great influence on Hamilton throughout his career; although, as we will see, on some critical issues, such as public debts, he departed from Hume. Perhaps at least as important as the substance of Hume's arguments was Hamilton's admiration for the cautious and empirical manner in which Hume advanced his positions. Although Hume began his series of essays on commerce with a praise of "abstruse" thinkers, much of what Hamilton says about the methodology of political economy is really an elaboration and commentary on what he took to be Hume's method. In this regard, it is worthwhile to note that Hume differed conspicuously from Smith in that he wrote essays, rather than elaborating a comprehensive system. For Hamilton, the designation "theorist in political economy" was a neutral and sometimes critical one. It is of more than passing interest that Hamilton generally refers to Hume as celebrated, profound, solid, sensible, ingenious, or simply as "one of the ablest politicians"—but rarely, if ever, as a theorist of political economy.[6]

In addition to the influence of Hume, it is also important to note the congruence between Hamilton's ideas on the limitations of theory and those of Jacques Necker and James Steuart. Necker, who had won renown as France's finance minister, distilled the lessons of that experience in *De l'administration des finances de la France*. He contrasted the superficial but instantly attractive "spirit of system" with the truly important efforts of what he termed the work of "genius" combined with "good sense." The spirit of system gives the illusion of understanding by uniting within a small number of principles a seemingly wide array of phenomena. Genius combined with good sense, in contrast, produces real understanding by reflecting the complexity of reality, especially of the "nuances and exceptions" to "general ideas." Necker warned that "it is the imagination, encouraged by pride, which gives birth to the spirit of system." He believed genius to be a gift of nature, whereas good sense was born of experience. Furthermore, although only history can provide a true measure of genius, the spirit of system is "instantly able to surround itself with spectators, because it diminishes the work of the understanding, in relating vague ideas, all of which require precision; and because it has some words of raillery which, in the midst of the greatest obscurity, permit its disciples to easily recognize it."[7]

Similarly, Steuart, near the beginning of his *Principles of Political Economy,* warned that

> the vivacity of [an] author's genius is apt to prevent him from attending to the variety of circumstances which render uncertain every consequence, almost, which he can draw from his reasoning. To this I ascribe the habit of running into what the French call *Systèmes.* These are no more than a chain of contingent consequences, drawn from a few fundamental maxims, adopted, perhaps, rashly. Such systems are mere conceits; they mislead the understanding, and efface the path to truth.

Steuart savaged the "French theorists" Dutot and Jean Melon for failing to grasp the causes of France's financial problems because of their attachment to their pet systems. According to Steuart, "no *general* rule can be laid down in political matters: everything *there* must be considered according to the circumstances and spirit of the nations to which they relate." It is true that Steuart drew an analogy between society and a machine, but he believed that the machine required the supervision of a statesman in order for it to operate successfully. What Steuart called the "great art of political economy" was to first grasp the spirit, manners, and customs of the people and "afterwards to model these circumstances so as to be able to introduce a set of new and more useful institutions."[8]

The similarities with Hamilton are striking. But although it is obvious that Hamilton relied heavily on Steuart and Necker for guidance when he became treasury secretary, there is no evidence that he knew of their views at this early stage of his career. Necker's treatise was not published until 1784. With regard to Steuart, Hamilton may have had good reason to refrain from mentioning his name because of Steuart's association with Jacobitism and with an alleged antipathy toward liberty, but he gives no clear hint of having read Steuart before the late 1780s. Thus Hamilton seems to have arrived independently at his general approach. Furthermore, in one way his views deserve a certain priority, because he, more than Steuart and even Necker, was able to put them into action. Finally, it is worth noting Smith's opinion of these two men. He is said to have dismissed Necker as a "mere man of detail." About Steuart he wrote that "I flatter myself, that every false principle in [Steuart's book], will meet with a clear and distinct confutation in mine."[9]

In Hamilton's "Continentalist" essays, while discussing some particular matters of taxation policy, he repeated his caution about the role of general principles in political economy. The specific question at hand concerned the incidence of taxation: do duties ultimately fall on the consumer, the producer, or the middleman? The importance of the question stemmed from fears that, if national import duties were enacted, coastal states would benefit at the expense of inland states. Theory suggested that the consumer paid the duty, but, Hamilton argued, experience suggested that frequently the case was otherwise. He again cautioned that "[g]eneral principles in subjects of this nature ought always to be advanced with caution; in an experimental analysis there are found such a number of exceptions as tend to render them very doubtful." In this essay Hamilton went on to draw out one important implication of this realization: "in questions which affect the existence and collective happiness of these states, all nice and abstract distinctions should give way to plainer interests and to more obvious and simple rules of conduct."[10]

Just what Hamilton relied upon in place of scientific reasoning is difficult to state precisely. Although he sometimes spoke of a science of finance or political economy, he seems to have in mind something different from Smith, something closer to the "great art of political economy" as it was conceived by Steuart. Two points may be made. First, Hamilton does not deny that it is possible to reason usefully about such matters. Reasoning must, however, take into account the unpredictable nature of human affairs. Second, Hamilton places great stress on experience, especially the practice of statesmen and nations. One sign of this is that, when Hamilton began to think about economic issues, he thought as if he were a finance minister or a treasury secretary. Partly this reflects Hamilton's ambition to play a role in national affairs, but, more important for our purposes, is that Hamilton's political starting point also reflects something about his general approach to economic affairs. It is generally "enlightened statesmen," not "theorists of political economy," to whom he turns. Where there was a conflict among theories and opinions, Hamilton usually deferred to the general policy of nations. As he would later put the matter in his opinion on the constitutionality of a national bank, in "all questions of this nature the practice of mankind ought to have great weight against the theories of individuals."[11]

Hamilton's argument is extremely significant in view of the economic methodology that Smith devised and helped popularize. Smith, we recall, attempted to look for the underlying continuities and forces shaping economic life. He moved from the surface phenomenon to the purportedly more real but unseen phenomenon—for example, from money price to real price. Hamilton, in contrast, stayed closer to the surface of things.

The Speculative Paradox of Free Trade

Hamilton's first reaction to the theory of free trade illustrates the general points made above. These remarks also help in establishing the continuity of Hamilton's views over time on the issue of free trade. Hamilton's "The Continentalist, No. V" (published in April of 1782) explicitly took up the notion of free trade or, as he put it, the "cant phrase" that "trade must regulate itself." The general purpose of his discussion was to advocate adding "REGULATING TRADE" to the powers of the national government. In this essay and consistently throughout his career, Hamilton understood the power to regulate trade as a very broad power on the part of government to influence commerce, through law and policy, for the public good. In his "Continentalist" essay he included under the power to regulate trade the "right of granting bounties and premiums by way of encouragement, of imposing duties of every kind, as well for revenue as regulation, of appointing all officers of the customs, and of laying embargoes in extraordinary emergencies." This broad understanding of the meaning of the terms, which goes well beyond simply establishing a legal framework for commerce, was common at the time and seems to have been imported into the Constitution of 1787 in the power to "regulate commerce with foreign nations, and among the several states, and with the Indian tribes."[12] Of course, stating the potential scope of the power leaves open just how and to what extent it should be exercised.

Hamilton began by observing that certain past failures on the part of government to regulate prices had called into question the value of all such regulations of trade. Presumably, he had in mind the numerous attempts during the war by the national government and, especially, by the states to control the prices of important commodities in various ways. Hamilton does not make clear who originated this doctrine or who in America had embraced it. Drew McCoy has shown that, at the time of the revolution, there were many enthusiasts for free trade in the United States.[13] He traces the origins of this view to a combination of Physiocracy and a homespun free-trade doctrine elaborated by Pelatiah Webster and Benjamin Franklin. Webster was active in the political journalism of the time, and it is likely that Hamilton had Webster's "Essays on Free Trade and Finance" in mind. In the third of these essays, published in January 1780, Webster urged that Americans *"take every restraint from our trade"* and remarked that "Trade, if let alone, will ever make its own way best, and, like an irresistible river will ever run farest, do least mischief and most good, when suffered to run without obstruction in its own natural channel." Although Webster's defense of "natural liberty" in the area of trade is remarkably similar to Smith's, there is no indication that he had read Smith.[14] Webster's perhaps homegrown free-trade doctrine was, however, reinforced by the writings of Smith and was embraced substantially by Thomas Jefferson and James Madison, among others. As we will see, Hamilton's response to Webster was so general and far-reaching that it anticipated substantially these later variants on the free-trade doctrine. Indeed, Hamilton's response clearly anticipates his great "Report on Manufactures" of 1791.

Hamilton readily granted that the price regulations in question were ineffectual, but he denied that a general presumption against the regulation of commerce could be drawn from their failure. All that could be inferred was that trade "had its fundamental laws, agreeable to which its general operations must be directed; and that any violent attempts in opposition to these would commonly miscarry." Indeed, he dismissed the idea that trade should regulate itself as "one of those wild speculative paradoxes, which have grown into credit among us, contrary to the uniform practice and sense of the most enlightened nations." Any man acquainted with "commercial history" would reject the argument. Hamilton recounted how the legislators of Europe had promoted commerce by judicious laws and policies. Trade in England first expanded under the auspices of Elizabeth I, and "its rapid progress there is in a great measure to be ascribed to the fostering care of government in that and succeeding reigns." In France, under a different "spirit" of government, Jean-Baptiste Colbert "laid the foundation of the French commerce, and taught the way to his successors to enlarge and improve it." The Dutch, to whom Hamilton granted "pre-eminence in the knowledge of trade," had, by a "judicious and unremitted vigilance of government," been "able to extend their traffic to a degree so much beyond their natural and comparative advantages."[15]

Hamilton's account, though brief, reveals much. As Elkins and McKitrick have pointed out, Hamilton shared Hume's interest in the "sociology of economic development," as distinct from Smith elaboration of general laws of economic behavior.[16] Important as this insight is, it does not go far enough, because it suggests that Smith and Hume (and Hamilton) were simply talking about different things: one about the establishment of a free-market economy; the other about the operations of a free-market economy. Specifically, it does not take into account Smith's belief that his general laws were of universal applicability and thus, as he explicitly says, were applicable to North America. The critical difference really concerns the ways in which each man used history. Like Smith, Hamilton looked to history, but by "commercial history" he had in mind *actual* rather than the conjectural history of the *Wealth of Nations*. Furthermore, the context for commercial history is political history, specifically the history of the administrations of the regimes discussed. More generally, Hamilton saw the spread of commerce and the rise of European civilization not as part of a historical process powered by economic forces but as the result of the deliberate policy and enlightened practices of the times. As I have noted, although Smith used actual history a great deal, his turn to history was ultimately to a conjectural economic history that was independent of politics. Smith's claim was that this conjectural economic history could provide a guide for politics. In contrast, history for Hamilton was, in essence, the accumulated experience of political men. This kind of history showed, among other things, the interdependence of politics and economics. Specifically, this kind of history showed conclusively the beneficial effects of certain regulations of trade.

Hamilton suggested further that the writings of the "very ingenious and sensible" Hume had contributed to the emergence of a doctrine so at odds with experience and common sense. Hume's essay "Of the Jealousy of Trade" was the critical document. This essay, first published in 1758, represented the culmination of Hume's reckoning with the free-trade issue. Hamilton's reading of the essay is, perhaps, open to question, in that it may understate the extent of

Hume's gradual shift to a free-trade position, but this issue is less important than what Hamilton's reading says about his own economic views.[17] His comments deserve extensive quotation and close examination:

> The scope of [Hume's] argument is not, as by some supposed, that trade will hold a certain invariable course independent on the aid, protection, care or concern of government; but that it will, in the main, depend upon the comparative industry moral and physical advantages of nations; and that though, for a while, from extraordinary causes, there may be a wrong balance against one of them, this will work its own cure, and things will ultimately return to their proper level. His object was to combat that excessive jealousy on this head, which has been productive of so many unnecessary wars, and with which the British nation is particularly interested; but it was no part of his design to insinuate that the regulating hand of government was either useless, or hurtful. The nature of government, its spirit, maxims and laws, with respect to trade, are among those constant moral causes, which influence its general results, and when it has by accident taken a wrong direction, assist in bringing it back to its natural course.[18]

The first point to note is that Hamilton believes that Hume's position, at least as he understands it, is the correct position. Nations need not always or even usually fear the prosperity of other nations. Furthermore, trade between states is not necessarily a zero-sum game. Given this opinion, we should not be surprised that later in his career Hamilton favored a trading system that was substantially free, both at home and abroad. In the 1779 letter mentioned earlier, Hamilton affirmed that the "prosperity of commerce" depends on the "spirit of enterprise and competition."[19] His approach is certainly not the puzzle that some contemporary scholars have suggested it is.

It must be added, however, that Hamilton's position is that only an "excessive jealousy" is foolish. A prudent jealousy requires a certain amount of government action to ensure that the nation's interest is being followed. In addition, it is important to highlight Hamilton's notion of the natural course of trade: trade does not take an "invariable" course independent of the active encouragement of government. What Hamilton calls the natural course of things is, to a large extent, the product of the "moral causes" that act on the nation and over which the government, through its laws and institutions, has an important influence. Government and society remain interdependent; thus, to a significant degree, the "comparative advantages" of a nation are created rather than natural, strictly speaking. For Hamilton, the natural course of trade was not, as it was for Smith (and Webster), the necessary result of the workings of the desire to better our condition. Thus, he concludes, the maxim "trade must regulate itself" is reasonable if it is extended only to the idea that violent attempts in opposition to the natural course of trade are likely to miscarry.[20] The implication is important. The natural-versus-artificial distinction, so critical to the argument of the *Wealth of Nations,* is transformed. Hamilton equates artificial with violent intervention, rather than with government intervention as such. Put otherwise, government intervention is natural and in keeping with the "fundamental laws" of trade if it takes the form of wise and moderate measures. For Smith, the reader will recall, once a legal framework for commerce is established, government intervention is always unnatural and for the most part unreasonable. Furthermore, Hamilton's reference to the spirit of each of the leading nations of Europe is important. Like Steuart, he thought that commercial policy must be tailored to the particular character, or spirit, of each nation.

One might object that Hamilton's early writings here are made less important because he was, in all likelihood, not yet aware of Smith. The same might be said about the Physiocrats, for, although Hamilton took a strong interest in French affairs and may have been indirectly aware of the Physiocrats through his reading of Hume, his statement that the benefit of regulation "is everywhere admitted by all writers on the subject; nor is there anyone who has asserted a contrary doctrine" immediately after his discussion of Hume strongly suggests that he had read neither the Physiocrats nor Smith at this stage. Indeed, it has been argued that Hamilton underwent a change of heart on the question of free trade after reading Smith and that this change is reflected in the differences between his early pamphlets, including "The Continentalist," and his later reports.[21] I do not see any such recantation. For a prima facie confirmation of this view, I simply quote from Hamilton's essay on Jefferson's administration. To the "adepts of the new-school" who argued that "[i]ndustry will succeed and prosper in proportion as it is left to the exertions of individual enterprise," Hamilton responded that

> [t]his favorite dogma, when taken as a general rule, is true; but as an exclusive one, it is false, and leads to error in the administration of public affairs. In matters of industry, human enterprize ought, doubtless, to be left free in the main, not fettered by too much regulation; but practical politicians know that it may be beneficially stimulated by prudent aids and encouragement on the parts of Government. This is proved by numerous examples too tedious to be cited; examples which will be neglected only by indolent and temporizing rulers who love to loll in the lap of epicurean ease, and seem to imagine that to govern well, is to amuse the wondering multitude with sagacious aphorisms and oracular sayings.[22]

There is, to be sure, a degree of sarcasm and exaggeration in this attack, but after making allowances for this element, there is no reason to doubt that Hamilton did not mean what he said: the dogma of free trade is true as a general rule but not as an exclusive one. Although the language is similar, Hamilton had in mind something different from Smith's idea of free trade as a general rule subject to limited exceptions. To repeat, the source of the difference is a different notion of what constitutes the natural course of things. Smith thought it was shaped by the desire to better one's condition. For Hamilton, the distinction between nature and artifice is not so sharp. Government can exert a positive influence, whereas for Smith all government interference is unnatural and usually harmful. This is not to say that Hamilton's views did not change on some points.[23] It is clear that he moderated the crude mercantilism of his earliest pamphlets. I believe that the mature Hamilton arrived in about 1779, with the first of a series of financial letters. After this time, he changed his mind on specific questions, but his basic approach, including his opinion of the doctrine of free trade, remained the same.

The Passions, the Interests, and Social Science

To conclude this section, it is useful to speculate more broadly on the significance of Hamilton's reservations about the role of theory in political life in light of the development of social science. This will help to establish the broadest context for the consideration of Hamilton's term as treasury secretary that follows. Although Hamilton identified the trend toward speculatism early in his career, he, like Edmund Burke, believed it was the French Revolution that was the most extreme manifestation of the inappropriate injection of theory into political life. Writing to the Marquis de Lafayette, in the very early stages of the French Revolution, Hamilton wished the French well in their bid for liberty but gave three reasons for caution: the vehemence of the French people, the arrogance of their aristocrats, and the "reveries" of France's "philosophic politicians."[24] Hamilton's criticism of the French Revolution increasingly came to center on this last point, the role of philosophical speculation in politics. Hamilton was not, however, as thoroughgoing as Burke in his critique of the role of theory in politics. It was, after all, to *enlightened* statesmen that Hamilton looked for guidance. Hamilton's position is clear from the remarks he made about the unfolding of the French Revolution:

> Wise and good men took a lead in delineating the odious character of Despotism; in exhibiting the advantages of a moderate and well balanced government, in inviting nations to contend for the enjoyment of rational liberty. Fanatics in political science have since exaggerated and perverted their doctrines. Theories of Government unsuited to the nature of man, miscalculating the force of his passions, disregarding the lessons of experimental wisdom, have been projected and recommended. These have everywhere attracted sectaries and everywhere the fabric of Government has been in different degrees undermined.[25]

It is not, then, theory per se that is the problem but particular theories unsuited to the nature of man. In *The Federalist* no. 9, for example, Hamilton readily granted that improvements in the "science of politics" had made the success of republican government more likely.[26]

Hamilton's remarks on the French Revolution also contained his clearest statements about the forces maintaining the cohesiveness of society, in particular the moral influence of religion. These remarks show that society is only to a limited degree held together by enlightened self-interest or reason. Hamilton ridiculed, for example, the liberalization of the French divorce laws as well as the practice of allowing children to testify against their parents. Such innovations threatened "the dissolution of those ties, which are the chief links of domestic and ultimately of social attachment." The greatest and most reckless of the revolution's projects was, he thought, its assault on biblical religion. "Irreligion," he observed, had left "the closets of concealed sophists" and "the haunts of wealthy riot" and had begun to show "its hideous front among all classes." He cautioned that the "politician, who loves liberty . . . knows that morality overthrown (and morality *must* fall with religion) the terrors of despotism can alone curb the impetuous passions of man, and confine him within the bounds of social duty."[27] The "new school" of political economy was clearly not so fearsome as the French Revolution, but it too was guilty of disdaining the lessons of experimental wisdom. Hamilton believed that Smith and his followers had greatly exaggerated the scope for theorizing about economic affairs. The irony here is that Smith's theorizing, along with that of Hume and Montesquieu, was, in part, motivated by a desire to moderate the doctrinairism he saw connected with Whig political theory.

The common thread through all of these expressions of concern is Hamilton's assessment of the strength and influence of the passions. What implications did he draw from his opinion of their strength? Let me suggest two. First, Hamilton saw a greater amount of indeterminacy in human affairs because he thought that the passions played a greater role than did Smith and his followers. It is fundamentally misleading to base one's political speculations on subtle and extended calculations of interest. Interest, though powerful, is less powerful than speculative men either realize or care to admit. Passion will defy predictions based on calculations of interest. Acknowledging indeterminacy does not put political and economic life beyond human control. It leads only to a greater sobriety about the possibility and usefulness of theories of political and economic life.

A second and closely related consideration underlying Hamilton's departures from Smith is that Hamilton's starting point for reasoning about economic affairs is an independent nation, rather than simply society or even the great society of humankind. Hamilton was aware of and approved of the cosmopolitan commercial trends of the times, but nevertheless his perspective begins and, to a large extent, ends with the nation. That said, Hamilton was not a nationalist in our contemporary sense of that term. A dedication to universal principles of liberty and justice is the feature of Hamilton's thought that transcends the priority of national interest. The nation state is, however, the chief means of realizing these principles in practice. As I noted earlier, when Hamilton began to write on economic affairs he immediately put himself in the position of a finance minister; that is to say, he began from a political perspective. He did not adopt a stance of studied scientific objectivity, as do today's economists and social scientists. With these points in mind, in the next section I outline the political framework Hamilton used in contemplating the economic problems he faced as treasury secretary.

THE POLITICAL ECONOMY OF A LARGE REPUBLIC

Modernization or the Rule of Law?

In some ways, Hamilton's reputation as a modernizer is deserved. Symbolic of his efforts in the cause of modernization was his involvement in the ill-fated Society for the Encouragement of Useful Manufactures. The society attempted to establish in New Jersey a manufacturing enterprise greatly beyond the scope of anything yet ventured in the United States. The enterprise was to produce paper, metal, and, especially, cotton goods, among other things. It was to take advantage of the new financial arrangements being put into place in the United States and to make a special effort to use new technology and skilled immigrant labor. Hamilton's high hopes were dashed because of financial and general mismanagement of the enterprise. The experiment was, however, very suggestive of the lines along which he was thinking.[28]

Yet, in another sense, Hamilton is miscast when he is portrayed as a modernizer. As we will see, Jefferson and Madison were devoted to capitalist economic development in the United States, though of a particular kind that made liberal use of the new political economy of Adam Smith. Their agrarian republicanism was far removed from that of Aristotle, Xenophon, Harrington, or even the English Country faction. But it must be remembered that modernization implies much more than a modern economy; it implies "modern thinking."[29] Jefferson's characterization of the Federalists as "anti-philosophers" provides the clue to the true nature of the conflict. Madison and, especially, Jefferson were much more devoted to modern thinking than Hamilton was: a shift toward secularization, a revision of traditional property and familial relationships, and a revolution in the forms and principles of government. Our earlier discussion should have made it clear that Hamilton balked at the modern thinking of many of his contemporaries. Rather than modernization, it is better to say that his program was aimed at establishing constitutional government, or simply the rule of law in the new United States. His program was informed by the comparatively conservative political science of Hume, Montesquieu, and Blackstone. It was inspired by a love of fame that Hamilton felt deeply and that he thought was the "ruling passion of the noblest minds."[30]

What were the terms of the debate over forms of government that engaged Hamilton? Few, if any, Americans embraced completely the ancient republic as it was described by Montesquieu. Their preferences for commerce and liberty pointed them in the direction of large societies governed by representative bodies. Moreover, a modern republic devoted to liberty was clearly incompatible with the general and rigorous superintendence of morals necessary to support the kind of virtue that would always lead a citizen to prefer the common good to his own good. That said, many parts or elements of the ancient republics were attractive to some of the advocates of modern liberty: a similarity and closeness between rulers and ruled; a jealousy of power, especially when it is vested in few hands; and popular participation in government. Transferred to the modern context, these elements suggested a preference for states' rights, opposition to economic policies that increase inequality, reliance on a militia, and efforts to reign in the least democratic parts of government. This line of thinking was greatly reinforced, perhaps transformed, by the liberal republican thinking of Jefferson, Madison, and Thomas Paine and by the new political economy of Smith. The new liberal-republican thinking and political economy promised to solve what Montesquieu identified as a fatal defect of large republics. Montesquieu taught that the common good is more easily felt, known, and within reach of citizens in small republics, whereas in large republics "the common good is sacrificed to a thousand considerations."[31]

Hamilton made the case for a more high-toned government: a strong executive; a liberal construction of the Constitution; and an active use of the powers granted by the Constitution. In his famous June 18 speech at the Constitutional Convention of 1787, Hamilton asserted that the great issue dividing the convention was that "[g]entlemen differ in their opinion concerning the necessary checks, from the different estimates they form of the human passions."[32] Given Hamilton's assessment of the strength of the human passions, the institutions and policies preferred by the new liberal republicanism were simply inadequate to the task of governing a country the size of the United States. The size of the American republic raised in the starkest form the problem of the common good identified by Montesquieu. How can it be identified and pursued in a large and diverse republic? One element of a solution, accepted by both Hamilton and his rivals, was to make the end of government liberty, rather than a demanding conception of virtue. Yet this was not enough. I turn next to Hamilton's analysis of the problem of the common good in the new United States and then to Hamilton's solution to this problem: constitutional government. Hamilton argued that only a strong Union would be able to follow the common good. In surveying Hamilton's argument for Union, one begins to see the origins of his political and economic program, as well as of the great controversies those programs would provoke.

The Large Republic and the Common Good

Hamilton's thoughts on the problem of the common good in the United States are evident in his contributions to *The Federalist*. In arguing the case for a strong Union, Hamilton had to banish certain "airy phantoms" that flitted before the "distempered imaginations" of some of his countrymen. These phantoms were conjured on the basis of certain unwarranted assumptions about the nature of relationships between independent states, including republics. From Montesquieu, Smith, and Hume, among others, many republicans had learned a dangerously misleading lesson.

> The genius of republics (say they) is pacific; the spirit of commerce has a tendency to soften the manners of men, and to extinguish those inflammable humors which have so often kindled into war. Commercial republics, like ours, will never be disposed to waste themselves in ruinous contentions with each other. They will be governed by mutual interest, and will cultivate a spirit of mutual amity and concord.[33]

This statement may be restated in the form of three propositions: the spirit of republics (as opposed to that of monarchies) is pacific; commerce softens mores; commercial republics will be bound together by mutual interest.

To adopt these propositions, Hamilton replied, would be to "forget that men are ambitious, vindictive, and rapacious, . . . to disregard the uniform course of human events, and to set at defiance the accumulated experience of the ages." It is the strength of the human passions, those "inflammable humors," that makes perpetual peace between independent states a paradoxical and visionary project. Hamilton went on to say that the causes of "hostility" among nations are "innumerable." The love of power and dominion frequently caused war, as did their opposites: jealousy of power and desire for equality and safety. Sometimes the purely private passions of the leading individuals of a society, or the favorite of a king or a people, are causes of war.[34] Let us look more closely at each of the three propositions in question.

A more perfect Union would, Hamilton argued, allow the United States to imitate the situation of Great Britain, whose isolation had protected it from the constant threat of invasion, thereby preserving its liberty. The division of the American continent into a number of partial confederacies or, even worse, into an infinity of small, jealous republics, would, he believed, set in motion a course of events that would end in the extinction of liberty in the New World. The collapse of the Union would, sooner or later, unleash those "engines of despotism" that had been the "scourge of the old world." On the Continent of Europe, the constant threat of war had necessitated the maintenance of large standing armies that, Hamilton stated, "bear a malignant aspect towards liberty and economy." Furthermore, it is, he argued, in "the nature of war to increase the executive at the expense of the legislative authority." Standing armies might not be introduced immediately, because of the American people's jealousy of military establishments. But the people would, he argued, eventually accommodate themselves to the "standard" of the "natural course of things" and relinquish their "jealousy of military establishments" in the face of evident necessity. To republicans, he delivered a sobering message: "Safety from external danger is the most powerful director of national conduct. Even the ardent love of liberty will after a time give way to its dictates. . . . To be more safe, they at length become willing to run the risk of being less free."[35] This principle was likely to be forgotten when the danger seemed remote. It was especially likely to be forgotten by a commercial and formerly colonial people who had not yet learned to think like an independent nation.

Hamilton drew particular attention to the causes of war that might arise from commercial competition. "Has commerce hitherto done anything more than change the objects of war?" he asked.[36] This is not to say that the spread of commerce does not result in significant changes in the way of life of a people. Hamilton acknowledged that there was a sharp contrast between the "industrious habits of the people of the present day, absorbed in the pursuits of gain, and devoted to the improvements of agriculture and commerce" and that of "the condition of a nation of soldiers, which was the true condition of [the ancient] republics." Furthermore, commerce had brought about a revolution in the science of war. It had made professional armies essential, because it is necessary for a large part of the population to devote itself to creating the wealth required by modern warfare. In addition, improvements in the science of finance, especially public borrowing, opened up vast stores of wealth to be used in war. This development made public credit one of the highest political priorities. Hamilton denied the common charge that modern finance increased the chances of war by making it easier. Wars were, he granted, probably longer, but they were no more frequent. Moreover, because of the greater importance of wealth and the greater respect for property rights, modern war was less likely to result in the complete devastation of civilian society that had so often been the case in earlier times.[37]

Still, if habits of justice, industry, and frugality prevail in the majority and if the majority is the moving force in a republic, will not war be less likely? Hamilton said no. Consider, he urged, the case of Great Britain, where commerce was the "predominant pursuit" for "ages" but where there "have been . . . almost as many popular as royal wars. The cries of the nation and the importunities of their representatives have, upon various occasions dragged their monarchs into war, or continued them in it, contrary to their inclinations, and sometimes contrary to the real interests of the state." Hamilton illustrated the point with the most recent Anglo-Spanish war. British merchants had violated Spanish trade laws. The Spanish response exceeded the bounds of "just retaliation" and was chargeable with "inhumanity and cruelty." In the aftermath, "by the usual progress of a spirit of resentment, the innocent were after a while confounded with the guilty in indiscriminate punishment. The complaints of the merchants kindled a violent flame throughout the nation." Hamilton concluded that a war ensued that "overthrew all the alliances that but twenty years before had been formed with sanguine expectations of the most beneficial fruits."[38]

In *The Federalist* no. 7, Hamilton pointed to a number of specifically economic areas where conflict was likely in the United States.[39] First, different systems of commercial policy result in "distinctions, preferences, and exclusions, which would beget discontent."[40] This discontent was likely to be great because of significant regional differences, especially between the commercial northern states and the agricultural southern states. If the Union were fractured, a system of policy designed for a society characterized by an unbridled spirit of enterprise would be pitted against one designed to preserve an agricultural economy based on slavery.[41] Second, taxation would be a fertile source of conflict, because states would be tempted to use geographic and other advantages to shift tax burdens to their neighbors. Third, the public debt would be a major source of conflict. There were, first, the grave difficulty of establishing a rule for apportioning the war debt among the states and, furthermore, "dissimilar views among the states as to the general principle of discharging the debt." Some states exhibited "an indifference, if not a repugnance, to the payment of the domestic debt at any rate."[42] Finally, he pointed to the frequency with which the states had hitherto passed laws violating private contracts. If continued, these laws would be considered acts of aggression by states whose citizens were affected. Hamilton's identification of these various points of actual or potential conflict foreshadow with great accuracy the bitter controversies his economic program would later provoke.

The Constitution and the Economy

Hamilton appealed not to an invisible hand to reconcile the various interests that made up the United States but, rather, to good government and national character. Furthermore, Hamilton thought Madison's plan, printed in *The Federalist* no. 10, for a "republican remedy for the diseases most incident of republican government" was inadequate. It was easier for majority factions to form than Madison imagined. What was needed, in addition to representative institutions, was a vigorous use of the executive power, both to resist popular passions and to shape public policy. A national government would be charged with the task of formulating a *national* system of commercial policy, one that would reconcile the various competing interests and thus placate—or, at least, control—those competitions that otherwise would end in war. Only a "unity of government" could bring about "a unity of commercial . . . interests."[43] Hamilton realized that this would be no easy task. At the end of "The Continentalist, No. V," he remarked on what he regarded as an unfortunate element of the "national temper"; namely, that it was "too much characteristic of our national temper to be ingenious in finding out and magnifying the minutest disadvantages, and to reject measures of evident utility even of necessity to avoid trivial and sometimes imaginary evils." He continued:

> We seem not to reflect, that in human society, there is scarce any plan, however salutary to the whole and to every part, by the share, each has in the common prosperity, but in one way, or another, and under particular circumstances, will operate more to the benefit of some parts, than of others. Unless we can overcome this narrow disposition and learn to estimate measures, by their general tendency, we shall never be a great or a happy people, if we remain a people at all.[44]

To take one crucial example, Hamilton observes in *The Federalist* no. 12 that enlightened statesman acknowledge that the interests of commerce and the interests of agriculture are "intimately blended and interwoven." Yet this simple truth about the common good was often obscured by a "spirit of ill-informed jealousy, or of too great abstraction and refinement."[45] As Hamilton explained later in his "Report on Manufactures," it was necessary to state publicly the interdependence of the two parts of society and to undertake measures that contributed to the "*substantial* and *permanent order* in the affairs" of the country.[46] Only an energetic national government could formulate and implement such measures, for even "the regular and gentle influence of general laws" by which Hamilton hoped to effect an assimilation of interests was gentle only when compared with the alternative of reconciling clashing interests by the sword.[47]

Hamilton saw his responsibility as being more than to formulate an economic plan; his plan was to be an integral step in establishing the authority of the new government. Thus the Constitution was both a means and a goal in Hamilton's thinking. His advocacy of a liberal construction of the national government's powers has led to a false impression of his assessment of the importance of a written constitution. The importance of the Constitution, indeed, seemed to rise in Hamilton's estimation as the character of American political life became more and more clear to him. Although he considered the Constitution of 1787 deficient in certain respects, what concerned him most was what he thought to be the abandonment of its spirit and, to some extent, its letter.[48] Hamilton viewed the Constitution as the instrument for converting a multiplicity of interests into the public interest. Only constitutional government promised to blend popular will and sufficient space for statesmanship to secure a wise administration. The spirit of the Constitution was evident in its purposes. Hamilton considered its language broad and general, because "[c]onstitutions of civil government are not to be framed upon a calculation of existing exigencies, but upon a combination of these with the probable exigencies of ages, according to the natural and tried course of human affairs." Hamilton's assessment of the "probable exigencies of the ages" stressed two considerations: first, the impossibility of predicting the type and scope of national emergencies, and, second, the necessity that all governments undertake "liberal or enlarged plans of public good."[49] The "nature and objects of government itself" recommend that constitutional powers, especially those which concern the "general administration," be liberally construed, because the "means by which national exigencies are to be provided for, national inconveniences obviated, national prosperity promoted, are of such infinite variety, extent and complexity that there must, of necessity be great latitude of discretion in the selection and application of those means."[50]

Hamilton's interpretation of the financial and commercial powers granted by the Constitution followed in the spirit of these remarks. He argued the case for the constitutionality of a national bank on the grounds that it bore a "natural & direct" relationship to several of the enumerated powers of the national government and, therefore, came within the ambit of the necessary and proper clause. Furthermore, Hamilton saw in the Constitution a design "to vest in congress all the powers requisite to the effectual administration of the finances of the United States." "As far as concerns this object," he continued, "there appears to be no parsimony of power." As I observed, Hamilton understood the power to regulate commerce among the states and foreign commerce in a similarly broad way. Under "commerce," he included all forms of trade, manufacturing, and agriculture; and by "regulation," he envisaged much more than what Smith termed "an exact administration of justice." Legitimate regulations of trade may involve the active encouragement of commerce. Hamilton thought it natural that the laws of the United States "give encouragement to the enterprise of our own merchants and to advance our navigation and manufactures." Thus a national bank established for the purpose of providing "facilities to circulation and a convenient medium of exchange and alienation . . . is to be regarded as a regulation of trade." Hamilton granted that such regulation would, of necessity, have an impact on state and local commerce, but he believed that a meaningful distinction could be drawn between interstate and state commerce. He observed that regulations which relate to the "details" of buying and selling fall "more aptly within the province of the local jurisdiction than within that of the general government, whose care must be presumed to have been intended to be directed to those general political arrangements concerning trade on which its aggregate interests depend." It is also clear from various remarks that Hamilton thought the Constitution manifested a design to involve the national government deeply in the protection of property rights. This was, above all, evident to him from the prohibitions on the state governments from interfering in the rights of property.[51]

Hamilton emphasized the text of the Constitution itself in its ordinary meaning as the chief guide to interpreting the document. He did not, however, believe that this method would remove all grounds for controversy. In the first place, controversy over the actual meaning of the Constitution would remain. In such cases, "a reasonable latitude of judgement must be allowed." Second, the Constitution leaves open the possibility of laws that are constitutional but imprudent. The nature of the objects of federal power required that the powers granted to the national government be construed liberally. Against Madison's claim that liberal construction was more appropriate when applied to the state constitutions, Hamilton responded that the national government's powers concern "the variety and extent of public exigencies, a far greater proportion of which and of a far more critical kind are the objects of National than of State administration." He continued that the "greater danger of error, as far as is supposable, may be a prudential reason for caution in practice, but it cannot be a rule of restrictive interpretation." The "expediency of exercising a particular power, at a particular time, must indeed depend on circumstances; but the constitutional right of exercising it must be uniform and invariable—the same today as tomorrow." To illustrate the point, Hamilton brought up the example of whether the Constitution gave the national government the power to establish companies with exclusive privileges or monopolies. He observed that, although grave doubts about the utility of such companies were justified, he could not find any reason to question the constitutional authority of the United States to establish them.[52]

A broader point must be made here. The Constitution embodied many of the presuppositions of what is now known as classical liberalism. Hamilton, Smith, and the Constitution seem to agree that individuals are responsible for making their own way in the world. One need only look at the rights mentioned in the Constitution and the Bill of Rights to see that there is no suggestion that the national government is responsible for the material welfare of individuals. In other words, there is no opening for an "entitlement" state. Beyond this, however, it must be stressed that the Constitution did not embody a particular economic theory—mercantilist or Smithian—that might specify the means or policies that the government ought to pursue. In keeping with this, there was, in Hamilton's understanding of the Constitution, no substitute for a "wise administration."

FINANCE

Public Credit

In this section and the next I consider the two chief elements of Hamilton's economic plan: the restoration of public credit, and the encouragement of manufactures. Hamilton's thinking on these two issues amounts to a comprehensive view of the government's role in the economy.[53] I try to bring out the economic and political assumptions behind his program in such a way as to make the contrast with Smith. The first element of Hamilton's plan, and the element to which he accorded first priority, was the restoration of public credit. The contrast with Smith on manufactures is clear, but the contrast regarding financial matters is just as great and at least as important. Hamilton took up his position as treasury secretary in September 1789. His "First Report on Public Credit," tendered to Congress on January 9, 1790, called for a total revision of the nation's financial system, one that would have far-reaching political implications. Unlike his "Report on Manufactures," the plan for restoring public credit was, for the most part, implemented. This success though came only after a bitter battle. Hamilton's rivals saw the plan as an attempt to change the direction of the nation—and they were right.

As McDonald has observed, Hamilton closely followed Necker's advice when it came to his duties as treasury secretary. Necker urged finance ministers to act decisively and to explain their policies clearly and confidently to the public.[54] The "First Report on Public Credit" adopted a very high tone: nothing short of the character and reputation of the nation was at stake in this seemingly limited question of public finance. The gravity of the debt situation was the clearest reason for such a tone. By the time Hamilton took office, payment of the interest on much of the domestic debt and on portions of the foreign debt had been suspended. Prior to the ratification of the Constitution, there seemed little chance that payments would be resumed. Default was a real possibility.[55] The economic consequences of a default would have been enormous, but Hamilton feared something in addition to economic disaster. He repeatedly stressed that the modern system of war made sound public credit essential to national defense. Easy access to loans, especially foreign loans, allowed nations to sustain and pay for wars without devastating their national wealth.[56] A further reason for the high tone of the report was his belief that the actions of the "infant government" on this matter would set the tone for future activities of the government, because the plan would establish habits for the people and the government. Hamilton told Washington that even though the report's proposals might appear to be tainted by an unnecessary rigor, the times demanded a "peculiar strictness and circumspection."[57]

I will consider Hamilton's plan by discussing the five major issues dealt with in his financial reports: discrimination; assumption; revenues; funding; and the national bank. Each of these issues corresponds to an element in Hamilton's overall vision of a remodeled U.S. economic and political system. Each also contains a lesson about the founding of a commercial republic. In addition to his official reports, I will make substantial use of his "Defense of the Funding System," written in about July 1795, soon after he left the treasury, but not completed or published by him. "Defense of the Funding System" provides key insights into Hamilton's deepest thoughts on the issue of public credit.

Discrimination: Justice

The first great issue to arise in the debate over Hamilton's plan was that of discrimination. Hamilton's plan made no distinction between the current and the original holders of the public debt. This was criticized by many, James Madison included, on the grounds that it involved an injustice to those original holders of the debt who had parted with their securities at prices far below par.[58] Without measures to compensate these original holders, there would be at least an impression that the original holders had been sacrificed for the benefit of speculators in the debt. Hamilton replied that honoring the precise terms of the contracts was dictated by reasons of justice, constitutional obligation, the obligation of contracts, and good policy. He granted that there might be cases of hardship or inequity, but perhaps not as many as the advocates of discrimination contended. He noted that the original holders might have sold their holdings for good reasons or bad and that a similar uncertainty applied to the buyers. Moreover, to discriminate would be to penalize those who had shown faith in the government's ability to meet its commitments. Hamilton further argued that the Constitution prohibited discrimination by stating that "all debts contracted and engagements entered into before the adoption of the Constitution shall be as valid against the United States under it, as under the confederation."[59]

Hamilton's chief argument against discrimination centered on the obligation of the government to meet the precise terms of the contract. The public debt was issued on the basis of a contract between the government and the original owners of the debt, or their assignees. In making such an agreement, he would explain in his last official report, the government "exchanges the Character of Legislator for that of a moral Agent, with the same rights and obligations as an individual. Its promises may be Justly considered as excepted out of its power to legislate, unless in aid of them." This "great principle" governed the case and prevented interference with the obligation of contracts in any way, whether by discrimination or, as Congress later contemplated, by taxing stock transfers. Where there were reasons to believe that the original contracts were invalid, this was a judicial matter, not the proper object of legislation. Any violation of this principle was "in the nature of a resort to first principles."[60] By "first principles" Hamilton appears to have meant the principles applicable in the state of nature. Such measures would, he thought, alarm an important class of citizens who had hoped for relief under the Constitution.[61] The rejection of discrimination, on the other hand, would be an important signal to the monied interest that the national government could now be regarded as the chief guardian of an important species of property.

Hamilton's use of first principles to understand the nature of contracts is of peculiar significance. It bears out Marshall's remark in *Ogden* v. *Saunders* (1827) that "we must suppose that the framers of our constitution were intimately acquainted with the writings of those wise and learned men whose treatises on the

laws of nature and nations have guided public opinion on the subject of obligation and contract."[62] Hamilton's wide interpretation of the nature of contract
foreshadowed Marshall's great judicial decisions that insulated a large section of
economic life from state interference.[63] McDonald has speculated that it was
Hamilton who was responsible for placing the contracts clause in the Constitution.[64] Whether true or not, there is certainly every reason to believe that Hamilton heartily endorsed the provision and thought it wise for the national government to follow its spirit. With respect to the constitutional prohibition on
interference with the obligation of contracts by the states, Hamilton observed
that the "example of the national government in a matter of this kind may be expect'd to have a far more powerful influence, [than] the precepts of its constitution."[65] Thus, as we will observe again and again, Hamilton's strategy was to
give meaning to words through action.

Assumption: Nationalism

Assumption of the state debts was the most far-reaching of Hamilton's proposals. Assumption refers to the transfer of responsibility for the states' war debts
to the national government. With a single stroke, the entire financial system of
the United States was transformed. As I noted earlier, Hamilton believed that
the Constitution manifested a design to place the management of the public finances in the national government. Assumption appeared to him to be a constitutional measure that would replace fourteen separate financial systems with one
unified system under the supervision of the national government

As with discrimination, assumption recommended itself to Hamilton for reasons of justice *and* policy. In this case too, complete and exact justice was impossible. The settlement of the intergovernmental debts arising from transfers between the national and state governments during the war posed a particular
problem for establishing the precise amount of the debts to be assumed.[66] But,
on balance, Hamilton believed assumption to be the best of the possible alterna-
tives. The war debt was, in his high phrase, "the price of liberty." It was only just
that the nation as a whole should pay for debts incurred in a national struggle.
Justice was further served in that assumption significantly increased the
prospects for meeting the needs of the state creditors. If matters were left to the
discretion of the individual states, creditors would be unlikely to receive equal
treatment. Moreover, in view of past indiscretions by the states, there were reasons to believe that the state creditors would fare much worse than would the
creditors of the national government.[67]

Five strong reasons of policy also favored assumption. First, assumption
would facilitate management of the debt by allowing the burden of taxes to be
spread across the nation. Without assumption, it would be impossible to establish an efficient taxation policy throughout the country, because states would
compete with the national government for resources and because competition
among the states would be intensified. Second, a unified financial system would
unite the public creditors, thereby removing potential sources of conflict

between the creditors of different states and between state and national creditors in the same state. This was particularly important from the point of view of gaining support for the government and for facilitating management of the debt.[68] Third, by removing the issue from the reach of the states, assumption was likely to better secure the interests of the public creditors. Hamilton did not regard the mere parchment provisions of the Constitution against interference with contracts as a sure guarantee that they would be observed, especially if a state found itself in difficulty as a result of the heavy debt burden. It was wise, he argued, to second the spirit of those provisions "by removing as far as it could be constitutionally done out of the way of the States whatever would oblige or tempt to further tampering with faith credit & property."[69]

Hamilton's fourth reason is of critical importance. As we saw in the previous section, the size of the United States was a major political concern for Hamilton, in that he had questioned the ability of any government to govern a nation of so great an extent. Economic factors had to be managed in such a way that they did not exacerbate this inherent problem. Without assumption, disruptive population movements were likely. In the first place, states with heavy debt burdens would be depopulated. Furthermore, heavy taxes in the original thirteen states might provoke a westward movement that would "retard the progress in general improvement and . . . impair for a greater length of time the vigor of the Nation by scattering too widely and too sparsely the elements of resource and strength. It [would] weaken government by enlarging too rapidly the sphere of its action and . . . by stretching out the links of connection between the different parts." Moreover, to give such an impulse would be to lay "artificial disadvantages" on the settled parts of the country.[70]

Finally, Hamilton argued that assumption would help increase the popularity of "our infant Government by increasing the number of ligaments between the Government and the interests of Individuals." Hamilton, as we have noted, believed the most dangerous challenges facing the Union to be those of "controlling the eccentricities of state ambition and the explosions of factious passions." Assumption presented itself as a constitutional measure that extended the national government's reach into the "internal concerns" of the states. It would win new friends for and manifest the powers of the national government. In "Defense of the Funding System" Hamilton claimed, however, that "it was the consideration upon which I relied least of all." This remark is significant because of the emphasis placed on this motive by generations of historians, beginning with Charles Beard, and by the Republicans at the time.[71] Before dismissing Hamilton's claim as a defensive afterthought, his reasons ought to be considered, along with the general context of his actions. The influence of the debt, Hamilton observed, was temporary and limited, because it would ultimately be extinguished and, moreover, because it would gradually be accumulated in fewer and fewer hands. Furthermore, he noted, assumption necessitated the imposition of new and unpopular taxes that would hurt the government's popularity among the public as a whole.[72]

The more general context must also be considered. Hamilton's initial appeal to the commercial classes who held the debt was, in several respects, a necessity. The restoration of public credit was the first priority for economic reasons and for reasons more strictly political. Public credit was intimately related to private credit. With the system of public credit in tatters, it was impossible to believe in a return to prosperity. For the public credit to be reestablished, it was essential that the confidence of the public creditors be boosted; otherwise, they would not be bullish enough to bring about the desired appreciation in the price of government securities.[73] Moreover, some sort of war with Great Britain was a real possibility. Without credit, resistance to the British would be doomed. Hamilton had to make his policies appeal to the nation's creditors. Finally, in the short run, there was simply no one else to whom they could turn. Any appeal to the people would be problematic until the benefits of the new administration were brought home in more tangible ways. Even then, there was no guarantee that the system of public credit would gain support. "The effect of energy and system," he remarked, "is to vulgar and feeble minds a kind of magic which they do not comprehend and thus they make false interpretations of the most obvious facts."[74] The commercial classes could, in contrast, understand what was in their own best interests. Hamilton many times refers to the commercial and financial classes as "reasonable" or "enlightened," by which he seems to mean that they are more farseeing than are the other classes.[75]

Hamilton's belief that liberty and an unequal distribution of wealth went hand in hand did not mean that he believed in government solely for the interests of the wealthy. Joyce Appleby, who has repeated the Jeffersonian criticism of Hamilton, claims that it was the Republicans who held out a vision of hope for the common man.[76] The economic aspects of Appleby's general view have been developed further by John Nelson, who argues that Hamilton's whole "stabilization policy" turned on the appeasement of the monied interest.[77] This is an exaggeration. Hamilton's preferences for the wealthy are those that are necessarily associated with the liberal understanding of property. But this is not to say that Hamilton's program did not envisage substantial benefits for the ordinary man.[78] The difference between Hamilton and Jefferson concerned the means of providing the benefits.

Taxes: The Rule of Law

The issue of taxes was many-sided, involving concerns of economics, administration, politics, and even the meaning of liberty itself. In order to meet the new government's financial needs, Hamilton's "First Report on Public Credit" recommended an increase in various existing import duties and the introduction of an excise duty on distilled spirits made in the United States. A version of his excise-tax recommendations was finally passed into law on March 3, 1791. Hamilton's "Defense of the Funding System" reveals another, fuller, dimension of his thinking on the assumption question. There he remarked that it would have been easiest for the national government to forego assumption. This policy would have allowed the government to avoid raising taxes and put it in a better position to court popularity. Two reasons, however, argued against this approach. In the first place, such an unwillingness to risk "reputation & quiet" would have shown "pusyllanimity & weakness" in the responsible individual. It would, moreover, be shortsighted because, in the long run, a "weak and embarrassed government never fails to be unpopular." Tackling difficult problems is the only way to establish respect. Hamilton saw a second reason for assuming the burden at that particular time. It was an opportunity to "leave the field of revenue more open to the US & thus secure to [the] government for the general exigencies of the Union including defense & safety a more full & complete command of the resources of the Nation."[79]

Hamilton remarked in *The Federalist* no. 30 that the resources of a nation are seldom more than equal to its needs. No legal limit, then, should be set on the resources available to the national government once it has been charged with potentially unlimited ends.[80] Hamilton believed that the Constitution conferred such power but that political obstacles remained. As Publius, he had noted that resistance to taxation, especially excises, was characteristic of Americans.[81] He was no doubt also aware of the fate of Horace Walpole's administration in Great Britain, which collapsed partly as a result of attempting to introduce an excise.[82] Hamilton, however, reasoned that a delay in exercising these powers would be construed as a disapproval of this form of taxation. On the other hand, circumstances were propitious for implementing an excise immediately, because of the popularity of both Washington and the government after ratification.[83] The object of assumption presented itself as a chance to "occupy the ground" in new areas of taxation by way of a seemingly unobjectionable excise tax on distilled spirits. One might conclude that if assumption was a pretext for anything, it was for the introduction of new forms of taxation. Hamilton's excise scheme, it should be added, was also important in light of his objective of increasing the prominence of the national government. The imposition of an excise tax, however confined, extended the reach of the national government into those internal concerns that Hamilton saw as central to obtaining the allegiances of the people as a whole.

As it turned out, in order to execute the excise law, the national government literally had to "take command" and "occupy the ground" of western Pennsylvania during the Whiskey Rebellion of 1794.[84] Hamilton's handling of this problem is highly illuminating, because it is an indication of his views on how to establish the authority of a new government. He was quite aware that there would be difficulties in implementing this new form of taxation. Although he showed a willingness to try to improve the provisions of the excise law, he nevertheless quickly signaled his desire to see it strictly upheld. Writing to Washington, he called for vigorous measures against offenders, noting

> that it is indispensable, if competent evidence can be obtained, to exert the full force of the Law against the Offenders, with every circumstance that can manifest the determination of the Government to enforce its execution; and if the processes of the Courts be resisted, as is rather to be expected, to employ those means, which in the last resort are put in the power of the Executive.[85]

Writing as "Tully" during the height of the disturbances in 1794, Hamilton made clear the reason for his concern:

> What is the most sacred duty and the greatest source of security in a Republic? . . . An inviolable respect for the Constitution and the Laws—the first growing out of the last. Respect for law is the great security against enterprises by the rich and powerful and demagogues who would climb on the shoulders of faction to the tempting seats of usurpation and tyranny.[86]

Hamilton's contention that respect for law maintains the greatest security of republican government is striking. Just as striking are his views on how the suppression of the rebellion might enhance respect for the law. The rebellion presented an opportunity to manifest the *full* powers of the national government while avoiding actual bloodshed by deploying an overwhelming number of troops.[87] Historian Jacob Cooke remarks that the rebellion showed "Hamilton at his most imperious."[88] Hamilton might respond that, at times, governments must be imperious and be seen to be imperious. It is not so much that there is a balance to be struck between liberty and force but, rather, that the two are sides of the same coin—free or republican government that is equal to the task of governance.

Hamilton's thinking in this regard highlights the critical lacuna in Smith's account of the development of society. Smith's evolutionary account of justice neglected the question of how an exact administration of justice is established. This neglect is evident as well in later political theories influenced by Smith that emphasize spontaneous order or civil society. The omission is twofold in nature. It omits the way in which government is a check on "uncivil" associations; and it omits the way in which government gives shape to "civil" associations. This second role for government goes beyond establishing a mere legal framework to actually placing a stamp on the character of civil associations through its actions and example.

Funding: Confidence

Funding referred to the practice of providing for the payment of interest on public debt by earmarking specific revenues for that purpose on a permanent basis.[89] Funding may or may not be accompanied by provision for the retirement of the principal of the debt. The question of funding takes us to the heart of some of the most important issues that separate Hamilton and Smith. It also serves to illustrate, perhaps, the most important element of Hamilton's thinking on the issue of public finance. For public and private credit to flourish, the government must create a climate of confidence. In this respect, Hamilton's goal of boosting the confidence of the public creditors was as much an economic strategy as it was a political one. In an early letter, Hamilton had described the essence of successful financial policy as a union of "public authority and private influence."[90] Smith disapproved of funding, observing that "it has gradually enfeebled every state which has adopted it" (*WN* V.iii.57).[91] His reasons are traceable to his view of money as both a representative of real value and a medium of exchange that was important for instrumental reasons only. Hamilton did not endorse unlimited government borrowing. He noted, however, that there were "respectable individuals, who from a just aversion to an accumulation of Public debt, are unwilling to concede to it any kind of public utility, who can discern no good to alleviate the ill with which they suppose it pregnant." Although he could not agree with those individuals, he granted that there would come a time when the accumulation of debt ceased to be useful. "Where this critical point is," he continued, "cannot be pronounced; but it is impossible to believe, that there is not such a point."[92]

A number of commentators have noticed that Hamilton's "First Report on Public Credit" established only an appearance or illusion that the debt would be paid off.[93] Again, for the purpose of policy it was the appearance that counted as much as the reality of the situation. The "sinking fund" Hamilton proposed at that time was more an instrument for economic management than a means of extinguishing the debt. It was really a means of supporting the price of public securities during difficult times by "open-market operations." This was, he believed, all that could be done at the time. Hamilton's "Report on a Plan for the Further Support of Public Credit," the so-called "Valedictory Report," recommended the creation of a larger sinking fund, one that planned for the retirement of the debt over a period of thirty years. The original sinking fund was expanded and given legislative protection against political interference. The report recommended that, as a "rule of administration," any new debt be accompanied with the means for its extinguishment in a specified time. Hamilton was serious about this provision, and it remains one of the most orthodox aspects of his financial program. Hamilton, it must be added, envisaged a leisurely extinguishment of the existing debt. Moreover, his sinking fund was more flexible than the British precedents upon which he drew. He reasoned that although the debt would take longer to pay off, a less-demanding sinking fund was less likely to be violated by the legislature. In this way, a reputation for sound financial management could be preserved even during difficult times.[94]

Funding appealed to Hamilton for a number of reasons. First, a more rapid extinguishment of the debt was simply impossible, given the resources of the nation. Second, a system that earmarks funds for the provision of public debts on a permanent basis is superior to any that relies on annual provisions. With funding, creditors have a greater assurance of the permanent value of their holdings. Moreover, such a guarantee would be the surest way of raising the price of the depreciated securities to their par value, after which they would become "an object of ordinary and temperate speculation." Hamilton made a clear distinction between speculative purchases of the debt and investments that would be to the long-term benefit of the nation. But, he remarked, "virtuous and sensible men lamenting the partial ills of all over-driven speculation know at the same time that they are inseparable from the spirit & freedom of Commerce & that the cure must result from the disease."[95] Speculation in the debt led to two "bubbles." On both occasions, Hamilton's treasury acted to bring matters to a head and, through the sinking fund, to support the price of government securities.[96]

Third, once securities were at or near par, foreign purchases would cease to be a drain on the nation's wealth. The inflow of capital could then be used for productive purposes. Hamilton did not fear foreign investment in the debt, because he saw it as absolutely necessary for a nation in the condition of the United States. Only with a continual inflow of hard money from abroad would it be possible to develop the nation's resources in an effective way. Finally, once prices stabilized, the securities could act as money in a capital-starved United States.[97]

These last two arguments were crucial to Hamilton's scheme. Both were connected with his opinion that the United States faced a critical shortage of capital. Hamilton's first priority was the restoration of public credit, but he saw this goal as both a direct and an indirect means of stimulating trade and industry in the United States. He believed that the monetization of the public debt was a powerful means of increasing the amount of capital available for economic development, because it was *"an artificial increase of capital"* that would pave the way for *"an absolute increase in capital or an accession of real wealth."* Thus the increase in "artificial wealth" was "an engine of business, or an instrument of industry and commerce," the positive effects of which had been demonstrated by the European nations, especially Great Britain. Hamilton's reasoning on this issue deserves close attention, because it represented a significant departure from Smith.[98]

Hamilton dealt with Smith's argument in his "First Report on Public Credit," and he returned to it several times in his later reports. His response to certain "Theoretical Writers on Political Economy" takes the allegedly superficial view of money seriously. Hamilton begins by denying that the raising of funds by issuing securities involves the destruction of capital. "'Tis evident," he said, it is "not annihilated, they only pass from the individual who lent to the individual or individuals to whom the Government has disbursed them. They continue in the hands of their new masters to perform their usual functions, as capital."[99] Hamilton took seriously the appearance—"'Tis evident"—that the purchasing power lives on, in the sense that it is simply transferred from one group of citizens to another via the government. (Implicitly, Hamilton denies Smith's distinction between productive and unproductive labor.) According to Hamilton, not only is purchasing power or capital not destroyed, it is increased:

> [T]he lender has the bonds of the Government for the sum lent. These from their negotiable and easily vendible nature can at any moment be applied by him to any useful or profitable undertaking which occurs; and thus the Credit of the Government produces a new & additional capital.[100]

Hamilton's "Report on Manufactures" attributes the "negotiable and easily vendible nature" of the bonds to the "estimation in which they are usually held by Monied men" and suggests that, "in a sound and settled state of public funds, a man possessed of a sum in them can embrace any scheme of business, which offers, with as much confidence as if he were possessed of an equal sum of Coin."[101] He explains, in "Defense of the Funding System," that the public debts are a form of "property": "All property is capital, that which can quickly and at all times be converted into money is active capital."[102] Thus Hamilton defined capital not in terms of prior transformations of matter by labor but in terms of the "estimation" in which various objects were held by the business community. Hamilton pointed to the experience of Great Britain as confirmation, as well as to the "prevailing opinion of the men of business, and of the generality of the most sagacious theorists of that country."[103] Again Hamilton relied on common experience and the views of enlightened statesmen rather than on theories, however persuasive, elegant, or systematic.

Just as Hamilton made a clear distinction between enterprise and speculation, so did he make one between money and wealth:

> But though the funded debt is not in the first instance, an absolute increase in Capital, or an augmentation of real wealth; yet by serving as a New power in the operations of industry, it has within certain bounds a tendency to increase the real wealth of the Community, in like manner as money borrowed by a thrifty farmer, to be laid out in the improvement of his farm may, in the end, add to his Stock of real riches.

In essence, Hamilton's plan relied on future prosperity to pay off current indebtedness. It is clear that Hamilton did not see this as an exceptional way to stimulate economic activity. The funded debt operated in much the same way as "bank credit and in an inferior degree every species of private credit."[104]

The decision to honor the precise terms of the contracts and provide revenues for a funding system was, however, subject to one great and rather embarrassing difficulty: the resources of the nation were insufficient to meet the obligations of those contracts. Hamilton's handling of this problem is instructive. He had to find a way that modified the immediate demands placed on the resources of the national government without losing the confidence of the public creditors. Such a modification would have to take place on "fair and equitable" principles. On this basis, every proposal put to the public creditors "ought to be in the shape of an appeal to their reason and to their interest; and not to their necessities." Although Congress did not adopt Hamilton's plan as a whole, it deserves our consideration.[105]

The compromise Hamilton hit upon involved raising new loans, to which creditors could subscribe in the public debt. The new loans were to be raised by issuing securities that yielded an annual average rate of interest of 4 percent but that were redeemable only at specified times. Hamilton believed that this last feature presented an attractive prospect for investors because of the greater certainty involved. The old debt paid 6 percent but was redeemable at the pleasure of the government. These securities would be particularly attractive if, as expected, interest rates were to fall. Hamilton also recommended that these securities be issued in a variety of forms (six in all), reasoning that in "nothing are the appearances of greater moment, than in whatever regards credit. Opinion is the soul of it, and this is affected by appearances, as well as realities. By offering an option to the creditors, between a number of plans, the change mediated will be more likely to be accomplished. Different tempers will be governed by different views of the subject."[106] The variety of forms would cater to different expectations held by public creditors. The plan as a whole would improve the public credit by creating the appearance of an improvement. The more quickly the government could rearrange its finances so that it could meet its interest commitments, the more quickly its credit would be restored, because then the embarrassment of heaping up arrears of interest would be removed. Because this effect would be achieved by a reduction in the payment of interest, not by an improvement in the financial situation of the country, it would exist more in the mind than in the realities of the situation. But, as Hamilton stressed, appearances were as important as realities in such matters.

National Bank: Stability and Growth

Hamilton saw a national bank as essential for the completion of his economic program. Hamilton's bank drew on English precedents, but his plan was deliberate and far-reaching in a way that exceeded the ad hoc development of the Bank of England. In addition to facilitating public finance, Hamilton's bank was intended to be a powerful instrument for the promotion of national prosperity over the long run.[107]

Hamilton began the "Report on a National Bank," which he presented to Congress on December 13, 1790, by observing that the question of banking was one in which the policies of "the principal and most enlightened nations" and the views of both "Theorists and men of business" were in agreement. Adam Smith was among those who had described the benefits of banking. He even approved of the Bank of England, which he described as a "great engine of state" (*WN* II.ii.85). There are, however, subtle but important differences between the two men on the question of banks. Hamilton agreed with Smith that banks had the power to increase the active capital of the nation by allowing merchants to place their idle balances in deposits and to rely on credits for the conduct of their day-to-day business. Without this access to credit, they would have to keep cash on hand for ordinary operations and emergencies. This advantage of bank money permitted the nation a saving on the expense of its circulating capital in the form of hard money, which, as Smith pointed out, has to be purchased with goods produced in the country. Any surplus quantity of precious metals could then be exported and materials for productive activities purchased. In the North American colonies, Smith attributed the persistent shortage of precious metals to the excessive enterprise of Americans, which made them unwilling to see part of their capital tied up in the form of species. Smith believed there is a determinate amount of bank money that can be issued profitably and that the amount is equal to the value of the amount of coin otherwise needed for everyday business. If this amount is exceeded, then the paper will be returned to the bank to be exchanged for species.[108]

Hamilton goes beyond Smith in one critical respect. Hamilton saw the expansion of the supply of paper money as, in itself, a stimulus to economic activity. Smith would not have acknowledged the extra stimulus given to industry by the expansion of paper credit, because he believed that the level of economic activity was determined by other factors. For him, the paper circulated is simply a replacement for precious metals otherwise necessary. This in mind, Hamilton's seeming agreement with Smith that the circulation of bank money is self-limiting takes on a different light. Both argue that emissions in excess of demand will be returned to the bank. The issue, however, is, what determines the level of demand?

Hamilton's emphasis on bank money and his prediction that the monetization of the debt would act as a stimulus to economic activity may be placed in the context of his broader thinking on economic issues. Hamilton, unlike Smith, did not see money as an epiphenomenon, or even simply as a means of lowering the transaction costs, to use a contemporary term that refers to the difficulties which attend the conduct of exchanges without money. For Hamilton, money "is the very hinge on which commerce turns. And this does not mean merely gold & silver; many other things have served the purpose with different degrees of utility."[109] A constant theme of his reports is the necessity of providing an adequate medium of circulation for the purpose of avoiding stagnation.[110]

The different understanding of the role of money is evident in several places. To begin with, even though Hamilton approved of the use of paper money, he was concerned with increasing the stock of precious metals within the nation. The "Report on a National Bank" took up the question of whether banks in general tend to banish the precious metals. Hamilton thought this to be the most serious objection to banks. He noted the "most common" (and essentially Smithian) answer to this objection: "the thing supposed is of little or no consequence . . . and that the intrinsic wealth of the nation is to be measured, not by the abundance of the precious metals, contained in it, but by the quantity of the productions of its labor and industry." Hamilton granted that this answer was "not destitute of solidity," but he objected that the "positive and permanent increase or decrease of the precious metals . . . can hardly ever be a matter of indifference" because "as the money of the world, *it is of great concern to the state, that it possesses a sufficiency of it to face any demands, which the protection of its external interests may create.*"[111] The precious metals, Hamilton stressed, are important for the protection of the nation's external economic and military interests. Species is the international currency and is, therefore, necessary for international trade and for the purchase of foreign supplies in wartime. Smith had granted that this was to an extent true, but he relegated it to the position of an exceptional concern, thus minimizing the importance of a favorable balance of trade as a source of species. Hamilton's different assessment of national needs may be traced in part to a different assessment of the demands of foreign affairs. The position of a new nation made these national-security demands especially acute.[112]

Furthermore, because money in the form of the precious metals "is the commodity taken in lieu of every other, it is a species of the most *effective* form of wealth." Hamilton vividly captured the psychological attractions of money in

The Federalist no. 12. The prosperity of commerce, he observed, was desirable because by

> multiplying the means of gratification, by promoting the introduction and circulation of the precious metals, *those darling objects of avarice and human enterprise,* it serves to vivify and invigorate the channels of national industry, and to make them flow with greater activity and copiousness. . . . [A]ll orders of men look *forward* with eager *expectation* and with growing alacrity to this pleasing reward to their toils.[113]

By contrast, stagnation is the consequence of "an inadequate circulating medium."[114] Precisely how this abundance of money provides an incentive needs to be explained. The abundance of purchasing power provides an incentive to industry, because buyers can be found and lenders are willing to part with their money on easy terms.[115] An adequate circulation creates a climate of confidence, which then feeds on itself. To a large degree, it is the incentive which money, particularly precious metals, provides that elicits human endeavor. Hamilton's argument surely reminds us of Locke's claim that money, in the form of gold or silver, is the universal commodity, one which is accepted everywhere and which, because of its steady value, is desirable without bounds. Hamilton also shared with Locke a concern for the role of species money as a pledge for future value, the characteristic that makes it so desirable. Hamilton had, however, a much more flexible idea of what might constitute money, in that he attributed a role to opinion which is not evident in Locke's account.

As I have noted, Hamilton was convinced that an increased supply of paper money was essential to the economic development of the United States. The immediate reason was that the Revolutionary War and the instability which followed had created a scarcity of all forms of money. Smith denied that there could be such a thing as a scarcity of money in normal times. Such complaints, he thought, were always the product of prospective borrowers without adequate credit. Hamilton agreed that scarcity is a complaint of all times, one in which "the imagination must ever have too much scope." Yet, he argued, there were telltale signs of real scarcity of money, chiefly a greater prevalence of direct barter in the interior of the country and a general difficulty in selling improved real estate. A return to financial stability promised some improvement on this front. An even deeper problem was inherent in the situation of the United States economy, one that went beyond any temporary instability. On this score, Smith and Hamilton differed significantly. Hamilton realized that, for many years to come, the labor of the United States would be devoted primarily to developing the natural resources of the nation, especially its agriculture. The improvement of the frontier required the diversion of resources into activities that would pay off only after a significant period of time. This meant that, in the interim, there would be a continual shortage of funds for investment in other areas, such as manufacturing. This, in turn, threatened to exacerbate the problem of foreign trade. Without industries that could produce exportable good or provide substitutes for imports, the trade imbalance would result in a continual drain of precious metals from the country.[116]

Smith explicitly warned against the establishment of banks for "public spirited purposes." Yet Hamilton's national bank was deliberately intended to
achieve such a purpose. "Public utility," he argued, "is more truly the object of
public Banks than private profit. And it is the business of Government to constitute them on such principles, that while the latter will be the result, in a sufficient degree, to afford competent motives to engage in them, the former be not
made subservient to it."[117] Hamilton's bank would provide an important source
of capital for the development of the country. To a degree, it is true that Hamilton intended to do this on the basis of largely fictitious wealth, but, as McDonald has observed, he was counting on the future to make good the returns.
McDonald describes that bank as an instrument for the "institutionalization of
future expectations," which, by so doing, could provide the wherewithal for development.[118] It was a daring plan. In this regard, we might note Hamilton's
opinion of the notorious John Law, gambler, duelist, banker to France, and architect of the infamous Mississippi Scheme. Of John Law, Hamilton remarked
that he "had more penetration than integrity." But of Law's plan for French finances, Hamilton remarked that the "foundation was good but the superstruc-
ture was too vast." He concluded that it "will be our wisdom to select what is
good in this plan, and in others that have gone before us, avoiding their defects
and excesses."[119]

Hamilton's bank had many similarities to a modern central bank. Its position
as the government's exclusive banker gave it a disproportionate influence on the
economy. One must also remember that, at the time, only three other banks existed in the entire United States. Given this, some comment is required on
Hamilton's decision to place the bank substantially under private control.
Hamilton considered the possibility of establishing a wholly national bank that
would allow the government to reap the profits of its activities. Such an idea was,
however, open to "insuperable objections." Full confidence in the institution required that it be under private direction, to free it from the suspicion that it
would become an arm of government and "in certain emergencies, under a feeble
or too sanguine administration would, really be liable to being too much influenced by *public necessity*." Although it would clearly be in the government's interest not to abuse its influence, Hamilton argued that, given human nature, it almost certainly would. "The keen, steady, and, as it were, magnetic sense, of their
own interest, as proprietors, in the Directors of a Bank, pointing invariably to its
true pole, the prosperity of the institution is the only security, that can always be
relied upon, for a careful and prudent administration."[120] This is not to say that
the state was to have no control over the bank. In addition to being a minority
shareholder and possessing an unqualified right to be appraised of all the bank's
workings, the charter of the bank was for a limited time only. If its performance
was unsatisfactory, the charter could be allowed to lapse. Hamilton also seems to
have assumed that there would be a certain harmony of understanding among
practical men as to what was beneficial for the economy as a whole and therefore,
eventually, for each part. Thus, it was unlikely that the bank's directors would
pursue policies too much at odds with enlightened opinion.

Conclusion

Hamilton was aware of the risks that went along with his scheme of incentives. As he argued with respect to the other passions, the passion for gain ought to be governed by reason or reasonable habits, which in this case are those of industry and enterprise. He spelled out the dangers in his discussion of the prudent limits on the accumulation of public debts. If these are exceeded, "the greatest part of it may cease to be useful as a Capital, serving only to pamper the dissipation of idle and dissolute individuals." Likewise, if productive uses were not found for the inflow of foreign capital, it would be "quickly exported to defray the expense of an extraordinary consumption of foreign luxuries." Late in December 1791, soon after the first speculative bubble, he warned that "[t]here is at the present juncture, a certain fermentation of the mind, a certain activity of speculation and enterprise which if properly directed may be made subservient to useful purposes; but which if left entirely to itself, may be attended with pernicious effects."[121] One means of making this spirit "subservient to useful purposes" was skillful management of the nation's finances. But Hamilton believed that more was necessary. It is in light of this problem especially that the significance of his program to encourage manufactures is visible.

TRADE AND INDUSTRY

The Encouragement of Manufactures

In many respects, the "Report on Manufactures" is a theoretical document. Although it foreshadows significant changes, it lacks any specific recommendation comparable in scope with, for example, the assumption of the states' war debts. But there is no reason to suggest, as Nelson has, that Hamilton was either not serious or hopelessly in error in his efforts to encourage manufactures.[122] Nelson sees the report as a function of Hamilton's stabilization policy that emphasized the monied interest more than the interests of merchants and small manufacturers. A better explanation would begin by considering what Hamilton said his intentions were, the character of the report, and the circumstances in which it was presented. Hamilton pondered long before issuing the "Report on Manufactures," nearly two years after his "First Report on Public Credit." The situation, he thought, required him to "investigate principles, to consider objections, and to endeavour to establish the utility of the thing proposed to be encouraged."[123]

Though there were disagreements about the appropriate means, the end of restoring public credit was not controversial. This was not the case with manufacturing, especially large-scale manufactures. Many people not only questioned the economic value of manufactures but saw them as, in some way or another, a threat to republican government. In this context, Hamilton wished to set the record straight on certain issues relating to manufacturing, which, once accomplished, could be the basis for a more detailed and far-reaching plan. He also wished to consider the obstacles that stood in the way of the development of such a plan, including the constitutional limitations.

Hamilton's report opened with a summary of the position against the encouragement of manufactures. His statement of the opposing position is a virtual paraphrase of Smith's assessment of the condition of North America in the *Wealth of Nations:*

> In every country . . . [a]griculture is the most beneficial and productive object of human industry. This position, generally, if not universally true, applies with peculiar emphasis in the United States. . . . To endeavour, by the extraordinary patronage of Government, to accelerate the growth of manufactures, is, in fact, to endeavour, by force and art, to transfer the natural current of industry from a more, to a less beneficial channel.[124]

This is the opinion to be evaluated. Hamilton granted that the argument had "respectable pretensions," but he denied that it was applicable to the United States. "Most general theories," he continued, "admit of numerous exceptions, and there are few, if any, of the political kind, which do not blend a considerable portion of error, with the truths they inculcate."[125] In the sequel, Hamilton gives what is in effect a running commentary on many of the key contentions of the *Wealth of Nations.*[126]

Agriculture and Manufacturing

Hamilton begins with a discussion of the comparative economic merits of manufacturing versus agriculture. He takes up, first, not Smith but the Physiocratic claim that agriculture is the sole productive activity. Physiocracy had its sympathizers in the United States: Thomas Jefferson and John Taylor, to name two. Given the growing respectability of Smith's views, Hamilton made a clever rhetorical move by using his main antagonist, Smith, against the Physiocrats.[127] Hamilton followed Smith in arguing that the Physiocratic position was not only contrary to common sense but also contained logical errors. Even if the labor of artificers and merchants produces no equivalent to the rent on land, it does produce sufficient to maintain those laborers during the year and, therefore, represents an increase in the national produce for the year over what there would have been without their labor. Hamilton's rejoinder to Smith's assertion of the superior productivity of agriculture is more interesting. Recall that Smith had argued for the superior productivity of agriculture over manufacturing on the ground that manufacturing yields nothing that is the equivalent of the rent on land and, therefore, where profits are equal among competing uses, agriculture is capable of putting into motion an additional quantity of labor.

Hamilton began with Smith's claim that, in agriculture, nature labors along with man. This argument, he remarked, "may be pronounced both quaint and superficial." Labor by a single man on a complex object, he explained, may be productive of more value than the labor of man plus nature directed toward a simple object. Even more important, he says, is the fact that, in manufacturing, labor could be aided by mechanical powers; a circumstance that removed "even the appearance of plausibility" from Smith's argument. Labor in manufacturing is, in addition, more constant and regular than labor in agriculture and is more open to improvements by human ingenuity. In spite of the implausibility of Smith's claim, Hamilton did not lay much weight on his own theoretical rebuttal, remarking that "[c]ircumstances so vague and general, as well as so abstract, can afford little instruction in a matter of this kind."[128]

Hamilton considered the principal argument in favor of agriculture to be that manufacturing yields nothing which is the equivalent of rent. He dismissed this argument as "rather verbal than substantial." "It is easily discernible," he argued,

> that what in the first instance is divided into two parts under the denominations of the ordinary profit of the Stock of the farmer and the rent to the landlord, is in the second instance united under the general appellation of the ordinary profit on the Stock of the Undertaker; and that this formal or verbal distribution constitutes the whole difference in the two cases.

Put otherwise, Smith had not treated land as capital and the rent on land as a return on that capital. The real question is whether capital or stock laid out on the purchase and improvement of land yields a return greater than an equal sum employed in the prosecution of a manufactory. This is an empirical question, which can be settled only by inquiry. Hamilton, indeed, attempted such an inquiry. He commissioned a national survey on the extent of manufacturing activity in the United States. The results were not conclusive, but he believed that they "served to throw doubt upon, [rather] than to confirm the Hypothesis, under examination."[129] Although he did not argue for giving preeminence in every case to manufacturing, he concluded that there was no persuasive reason to believe that the encouragement of manufactures would result in a diversion of resources from more productive pursuits to less productive ones. The question of the merits of agriculture and manufacturing would have to be decided on the basis of other arguments.

In this regard, Hamilton proceeded to list seven factors connected with manufacturing which, he contended, influence "the total mass of industrious effort in a community" and together "add to it a degree of energy and effect, which are not easily conceived":[130] (1) the division of labor; (2) an extension of the use of machinery; (3) additional employment for the classes of the community not ordinarily engaged in business; (4) the promoting of emigration from foreign countries; (5) furnishing greater scope for the diversity of talents and dispositions that discriminate men from each other; (6) the affording of a more ample and various field for enterprise; and (7) the creating, in some instances, of new demand and the securing, in all instances, of more certain and steady demand for the surplus produce of the soil. Several of these factors warrant closer consideration.

Both Hamilton and Smith thought that the division of labor was capable of far greater extension in manufacturing than in agriculture. Hamilton's discussion of the benefits of the division of labor is more or less a paraphrase of Smith. But Hamilton stresses the benefits of the division of labor within an independent nation, not the division of labor in the abstract. Furthermore, Hamilton's emphasis on natural talents and the importance of different types of labor is striking, in that Smith denied the relevance of natural differences and chose, instead, to analyze economic growth in terms of the accumulation of quantities of homogeneous labor. Hamilton concludes that substantial improvements in productivity would flow from having a manufacturing sector within the United States. Hamilton went on to single out machinery as a factor of "great importance" in favor of manufacturing, noting the "prodigious effect" of the cotton mill on English manufacturing. This is a significant difference. Smith had attempted to subsume technological change under the rubric of the extension of the division of labor or, more generally, of the natural progress of opulence. Hamilton, as Caton argues, shows an awareness of the dramatic change in economic affairs that the full-scale application of modern science to industry would bring about. In Caton's words, Hamilton's political economy "pierced the barrier of the commercial phase of modernity, summarized in the *Wealth of Nations,* and opened a political perspective on the high technology manufacture that was to dominate the next century. [It] was a growth economics animated by insight into the distinctly modern sources of growth."[131] The point is not so much that Smith should have known about these effects; it is that Smith thought he had hit upon an all-encompassing framework that could take future changes in technology into account.

Hamilton comments extensively on the effects of manufacturing on the people. His remarks are, perhaps, directed to American critics who saw manufacturing as antirepublican, but they also respond to Smith's famous criticisms of the effects of manufacturing on the workforce in book 5 of the *Wealth of Nations.* Hamilton's argument points to the addition to the labor and industry of the nation resulting from a release of new talents and energies. But he also points to certain moral benefits that accompany manufacturing. Manufacturing would immediately provide employment for idle or underutilized labor (including women and children). Of much more importance, he thought, from the point of view of "the general scale of national exertion" would be, first, the greater potential for making use of the diverse talents to which human nature gives rise and, second, the expansion of the objects open to the "spirit of enterprise." With respect to the first, Hamilton wrote that "minds of the strongest and most active powers" will atrophy if they do not find a proper outlet. But when "all the different kinds of industry obtain in a community, each individual can find his proper element, and can call into activity the whole vigour of his nature."[132] With respect to the spirit of enterprise, he remarked that "every new scene, which is opened to the busy nature of man to rouse and exert itself, is the addition of a new energy to the general stock of effort." Indeed, even "things in themselves not positively advantageous, sometimes become so, by their tendency to provoke exertion."[133] Thus the immediate result of diversifying the objects of human endeavor would be an increase in the nation's stock of industry and talent. The political and social consequences would be to change the character of society. Although Hamilton did not dwell on this point, he was acknowledging something that the opponents of manufacturing had charged. The difference was that Hamilton saw benefits in such a change.

Hamilton's remarks on the benefits of manufacturing grow in significance when they are placed alongside his treatment of American agriculture. His reservations about American agriculture were long-standing. He wrote to Robert Morris on April 30, 1781, that Americans "labour less now than any civilized nation of Europe."[134] In the South, he said elsewhere, there prevailed a "voluptuous indolence" that made the people oblivious to their true interests, even at times of profound crisis. That "commerce which presided over the birth and education of these states" suited them for "the chain"; and, he lamented, "the only condition they sincerely desire is that it may be a golden one."[135] As he noted in *The Federalist,* significant elements of American life did not fit this pattern, especially in the area of navigation, but the general rule was otherwise.[136] In 1796 Washington wrote to Hamilton complaining that

> to every man who considers the Agriculture of this country, (even in the best improved parts of it) and compares the produce of our lands with those of other countries, no ways superior to them in *national fertility,* how miserably defective we are in the management of them; and that if we do not fall on a better mode of treating them, how ruinous it will prove to the landed interest.[137]

Washington went on to note that exploitative farming methods would accelerate westward expansion, along with all its attendant economic and political difficulties. He directed Hamilton to incorporate these thoughts and a proposal for the establishment of an agricultural society for the furthering of this "great national object" into a draft of his last annual message to Congress. There is no reason to doubt that Hamilton shared Washington's scathing assessment of the agricultural practices of his countrymen.

This inference is confirmed by a close examination of Hamilton's "Report on Manufactures." Hamilton treads lightly over the issues, but his concern is clear. The report leaves a reader with a first impression that Hamilton accepted the conventional wisdom that, as Jefferson had said, those who work the land are "the chosen people of God, if ever He had a chosen people."[138] He identifies the many attractions of the agricultural life and predicts that it will be the primary activity of Americans for many years to come. But, on a second glance, both of these observations turn out to be indications of a great problem along the lines identified by Washington. What if nothing were done to improve agricultural practices? Cities would be depopulated and the land exhausted, leaving large segments of the people addicted to an easy, thoughtless frontier existence. Over the course of the report, Hamilton qualified his initial favorable comments on agriculture. Agricultural work is "in a great measure periodical and occasional . . . while that occupied in many manufactures is constant and regular." Labor is used more effectively in manufacturing, and examples of "remissness" are probably fewer. The natural fertility of the soil encourages "carelessness" in the mode of cultivation. Manufacturing, in contrast, "opens a wider field to the exertions of human ingenuity" than does agriculture. Furthermore, the "exertions of the husbandman will be steady or fluctuating, vigorous or feeble, in proportion to the steadiness or fluctuation, adequateness or inadequateness, of the markets on which he must depend."[139]

This last factor was of great importance, because American farmers, as Hamilton pointed out, depended on demand from Europe and the West Indies, which was subject to all the political and economic vicissitudes of international relations. It was, observed Hamilton, "a primary object of the policy of nations, to be able to supply themselves with subsistence from their own soils; and manufacturing nations, as far as circumstances permit, endeavour to procure, from the same source, the raw materials necessary for their own fabrics." As a result of this policy, "the foreign demand for the products of Agricultural Countries is, in a great degree, rather casual and occasional, than certain or constant." In addition, "natural causes" make foreign demand for agricultural products precarious. The vagaries of the seasons, in particular, make gluts a regular possibility. The only way to secure a steady demand for agricultural products is to create an extensive domestic market by promoting a sizable manufacturing sector. Not only does manufacturing increase the demand for raw materials, it also increases the variety of materials required. Moreover, whatever labor is diverted from expanding the extent of agriculture into manufacturing is more than likely compensated by the "tendency to promote a more steady and vigorous cultivation" of existing farmlands. Hamilton rejected the notion that there was a conflict between agricultural and commercial states. An economic strategy that sought to create a balanced economy would, in the long term, bind agricultural and commercial interests more closely and, in particular, the interests of the North and the South.[140] Hamilton was particularly sensitive to this last concern, as we will see when we discuss his specific proposals.

Hamilton's desire to commercialize agriculture points to a significant difference with Smith (and the Republicans). Smith noted that country gentlemen are seldom industrious but that merchants turned country gentlemen are the best improvers. Hamilton would have agreed. Smith and Hamilton differed, however, as to whether the yeoman farmer is naturally industrious and intelligent.[141] Smith believed that industry and independence go together, and he attributed the rapid progress of North America to the diligence of its small farmers. Hamilton was not so sure. To a large extent, Hamilton's doubts were the result of the prevalence of slavery in a significant part of the nation. Slavery is not a sufficient explanation, however. Hamilton doubted whether what Smith termed the desire to better one's condition was a spontaneous and independent force. Hamilton's comparable phrase was the "spirit of improvement." As we will see, he thought that such a spirit was unlikely to spread without the "incitement and patronage" of government.

Free Trade

After presenting general reasons for expecting manufactures to increase the total mass of industry and labor in the community, Hamilton took up a series of arguments against the encouragement of manufactures relating to the particular circumstances of the United States. The gist of the essentially Smithian argument Hamilton addressed is as follows: it is in the interest of a nation with vast tracts of uncultivated land, and which is not closed to foreign commerce, to specialize in agriculture and thereby to benefit from the advantages of the international division of labor.

Hamilton explicitly addressed Smith's idea of a "system of perfect liberty."[142] If such a system prevailed among nations, he granted that the "arguments which dissuade a country, in the predicament of the United States, from the zealous pursuit of manufactures, would doubtless have great force." The system of perfect liberty was not, however, a material consideration, because the prevailing system of nations "has been operated by an opposite spirit." The United States, in particular, was an unequal partner in several of its most significant trading relationships, which could "not but expose them to a state of impoverishment, compared with the opulence to which their political and natural advantages authorize them to aspire." Yet Hamilton adds that "[r]emarks of this kind are not made in the spirit of complaint. 'Tis for the nations, whose regulations are alluded to, to judge for themselves, whether, by aiming at too much, they do not lose more than they gain." The task for the United States was "to consider by what means they can render themselves least dependent on the combinations, right or wrong of foreign policy."[143] Hamilton's attitude toward the international trading system was the result of a recognition that, on one hand, benefits were to be had from a substantially free trade but, on the other hand, nations legitimately and sensibly engage in the promotion of their own industries.

McCoy has shown that Smith's analysis of these issues greatly influenced the foreign policies of Jefferson and Madison. Smith had urged retaliatory measures where there was a prospect of forcing the opponent to remove discriminatory practices. Jefferson and Madison began from a perception, which might easily have been derived from a study of the *Wealth of Nations,* that Great Britain was peculiarly vulnerable to such pressures. McCoy has also shown how these views were behind their policy of commercial warfare against Great Britain. It was the eventual failure of these policies that forced Jefferson and Madison into a position of supporting the encouragement of manufactures as a central element of national policy.[144] In contrast, the Revolutionary War had dispelled any illusions Hamilton may have harbored about the relative power of the United States and Great Britain.[145] As a result, he saw no value in a retaliatory policy that could not be backed up immediately with force. To him, the aggressive Republican stance toward Great Britain was foolhardy bluster that showed little appreciation of the true position of the United States. Hamilton's constant advice to Washington was to negotiate *and* to prepare for war.[146]

That said, it is true that Hamilton preferred a "British connection." At least three factors seem to have influenced Hamilton on this matter. First, he was more concerned with gaining control of the mouth of the Mississippi, which was controlled by Spain, than with the Western Territories or Canada, which were controlled by Britain. Second, Hamilton envisaged the extension of an already

broad and mutually beneficial trading relationship between Great Britain and
the United States. Madison and Jefferson thought that the United States' extensive and predominant trading relationship with Britain was "artificial" because it
had developed under the mercantile system. They believed that the more "natural" commercial relationship was with the rest of Europe, especially France.
There were political reasons for their French preference, but the idea that the
Great Britain–United States trading relationship was fundamentally unnatural
could have been—and probably was—taken straight from the *Wealth of
Nations*.[147] Finally, Hamilton preferred a connection with Britain because he believed that, despite the revolution, the nations were much closer, with regard to
principles of government and manners, than were the United States and revolutionary France.

Hamilton turned next to the central tenet of Smith's political economy;
namely, the proposition "that Industry, if left to itself, will naturally find its way
to the most useful and profitable employment." This maxim implies that "manufactures without the aid of government will grow up as soon and as fast, as the
natural state of things and the interest of the community may require." Against
the solidity of Smith's "hypothesis," Hamilton believed "very cogent reasons
may be offered." He mentions four factors that operate against the hypothesis:
(1) "the strong influence of habit and the spirit of imitation"; (2) "the fear of
want of success in untried enterprises"; (3) "the intrinsic difficulties incident to
first essays towards a competition with those who have previously attained to
perfection in the business to be attempted"; and (4) "the artificial encouragements with which foreign nations second the exertions of their own Citizens."
Hamilton ranked the last mentioned as the "greatest obstacle."[148]

Hamilton's remarks on the force of habit and on the effects of the fear of failure deserve comment because of their contrast with Smith. Smith had described
economic progress as the accumulation of many individual efforts. Hamilton lays
greater stress on the activities of a few adventurers who, by breaking into new areas, pave the way for the majority to follow. "Experience teaches," he observed,

> that men are often so much governed by what they are accustomed to see and
> practise, that the simplest and most obvious improvements, in the most ordinary
> occupations, are adopted with hesitation, reluctance, and by slow gradations. The
> spontaneous transition to new pursuits, in a community long habituated to differ-
> ent ones, may be expected to be attended with proportionably greater difficulty.

A "general spirit of improvement" is, then, not necessarily a spontaneous growth
even in a free society. It sometimes requires the "incitement and patronage of
government." Government, Hamilton thought, could raise the confidence of
"cautious and sagacious capitalists."[149] This would involve giving them some
protection from the most significant obstacles that might threaten new undertakings, especially the activities of foreign governments.

Hamilton granted that such encouragements could be seen as having a tendency "to enrich particular classes, at the expence of the Community."[150] This

objection had been central to Smith's critique of mercantilism. It was particularly pertinent in the United States because of the marked regional differences. Hamilton first noted that although this was, perhaps, true in theory, there were reasons to believe that prices would not necessarily increase as an immediate result of the protection of domestic manufactures. More important, he thought, is the principle that, once a manufacture has been brought to perfection, it necessarily falls in price. He concluded that "it is in the interest of a community, with a view to eventual and permanent economy, to encourage the growth of manufactures. In a national view, a temporary enhancement of price must always be well compensated by a permanent reduction of it."[151]

The general character of Hamilton's disagreement with Smith over free trade is, however, much more readily discernible than are the ultimate grounds of the disagreement. Why in the long run is a global "common market" not a possibility? The arguments concerning the Union from *The Federalist* addressed earlier in this chapter suggest three distinct but interrelated grounds. First, where the common good is not evident—that is, when the permanent and aggregate interests of the community are not clear—there is considerable room for the passions, which are felt immediately and sharply, to disturb a sober and rational calculation of interest. A "unity of government" is necessary for there to be a "unity of commercial interests." Where there is no government to adjust competing claims, passion will always intervene. Second, Hamilton states in *The Federalist* no. 11 that the "world may politically, as well as geographically, be divided into four parts"—America, Europe, Asia, and Africa—"each having a distinct set of interests."[152] These political differences are paramount, in that they shape each nation's and each region's perception of its commercial interest. Trade between regions is not, for this reason, to be discouraged, but it must be recognized that such trade is always subject to political interference. Lastly, one can discern in both Hamilton's political thought and his statesmanship as a whole the belief that the victory of interest over the passions was an impossibility. For better or worse, the passions would continue to play a decisive role in human affairs.

Policies for Encouragement

Hamilton provided a detailed commentary on the merits of various means of encouraging manufactures and made a number of specific recommendations. In addition, he raised various constitutional questions with respect to deficiencies of the Constitution for providing assistance to manufactures. Of Hamilton's specific recommendations, only those for relatively modest increases in import duties were implemented.[153] Nevertheless, Hamilton's discussion here is particularly interesting in light of later views of him as a statist political economist. As he foreshadowed in his "Continentalist" essays, he favored a substantially free trade that made use of the forces of enterprise and competition.

Hamilton first took up the value of import duties as a means of encouraging manufactures and as an important source of revenue. Hamilton considered the propriety of this species of encouragement so uncontroversial that it "need not be dwelt upon."[154] His discussion leaves open the important question of how the competing priorities of revenue versus encouragement should be weighed. This trade-off was particularly acute in the early republic because import duties were the only significant source of revenue. Smith had argued that revenue concerns were the only rational concern. Although he did not accept Smith's reasoning, Hamilton, too, seems to have accorded revenue concerns first—though not exclusive—priority. Hamilton's emphasis on revenue has led some contemporary scholars to the remarkable conclusion that he was not very interested in promoting manufactures. As I mentioned earlier, Nelson has argued that Hamilton's economic program emphasized the restoration of credit to the exclusion of all other concerns. Nelson wonders why Hamilton did not favor a real protective tariff. He concludes that Hamilton lost the support of manufacturers and mechanics for this reason and that the conventional view of Republicans as partisans of agrarianism needs to be reevaluated in light of the actual support the Republicans received from the manufacturing interest.[155]

Yet it is easy to divine a number of reasons for Hamilton's attitude toward import duties more in keeping with what he said his intentions were. First was the issue of timing. Hamilton thought that the first priority of the national government should be to restore the public credit. Increases in duties beyond a certain point would cut into revenues, thus impairing the capacity of the national government to restore the public credit. Second, Hamilton regarded import duties as a blunt instrument that helped the industrious and the lazy alike. Where possible, he preferred more precise and selective means of encouragement. Third, tariffs would pit manufacturing against agricultural interests. He thought there were better ways. Fourth, he was deeply concerned by the prospect of war with Great Britain. As we have noted, this made the restoration of public credit the first necessity. Finally, he feared that the commercial-warfare policies of the Republicans would lead to war. It is possible that, in part, his approach in the report was designed in part to avoid throwing fuel on their fires.

With regard to complete prohibitions on the import of certain articles, Hamilton expressed severe reservations. These could only be beneficial where domestic competition was sufficient to ensure an adequate supply at a reasonable price. There were, he thought, perhaps only a few cases in which such a policy was justified. Conversely, prohibitions on the export of the raw materials for manufactures "ought to be adopted with the greatest circumspection, and only in very plain Cases." He noted that such prohibitions would fall most heavily on agriculture.[156]

Hamilton was much more favorably disposed to bounties (that is, subsidies) as a means of encouraging manufactures, even though they were "less favoured by public opinion."[157] Bounties are, Hamilton argued, "more positive and direct" and have "a more immediate tendency to stimulate and uphold new enterprises." Bounties also have less of a tendency to increase prices or to produce a scarcity of the particular good than do most other forms of assistance. Hamilton drew attention to the way in which bounties might reconcile agricultural and manufacturing interests by using the revenues from duties on foreign manufactures that use raw materials which are also available domestically to subsidize local industry that either produces those raw materials or that uses domestic raw materials in production. In each case, the effect is to stimulate local production. There was, Hamilton admitted, a degree of prejudice against bounties because of the perception of giving away public money and enriching "particular classes, at the expense of the Community." He responded that "the acquisition of a new and useful branch of industry," though it might result in a "temporary expence," was more than offset by "an increase of industry and Wealth, by an augmentation of resources and independence, & by the circumstance of eventual cheapness." Bounties were appropriate for new industries, but, Hamilton added, the continuance of bounties on manufactures long established is almost always a questionable policy. "Because a presumption would arise, in every such case, that there were natural and inherent impediments to success."[158]

Hamilton believed that bounties could be provided under the authority of the "general welfare" clause, to which he gave a characteristically broad interpretation: "there seems to be no room for doubt that whatever concerns the general Interests of *learning* of *Agriculture* of *Manufactures* and of *Commerce* are within the sphere of the national Councils, *as far as regards an application of money*." The only qualification he admitted was that the objects of the appropriation be general, not local, in purpose. It is of note that Hamilton did not try to make the case for the constitutionality of bounties under the commerce clause. Instead, he chose to make the more difficult and radical case for an open-ended interpretation of the general-welfare clause. His reasons are not difficult to guess. He was probably paving the way for gaining constitutional support for other forms of government support for commerce, such as internal improvements. Hamilton quoted Smith in support of public patronage for improvements in transportation. Again, however, he was forced to note that "it were to be wished that there was no doubt of the power of the national Government to lend its direct aid on a comprehensive plan."[159]

Hamilton, like Smith, endorsed the granting of premiums "to reward some particular excellence or superiority, some extraordinary exertion or skill." Such rewards touched the chords of emulation and of interest, making them "a very economical means of exciting the enterprise of the whole community." In what could be seen as a complementary measure, he recommended the establishment of regulations for the inspection of manufactured commodities "to preserve the quality and character of the national manufactures."[160] He agreed with Smith in advocating patent and copyright laws and, in addition, argued for direct pecuniary awards to inventors. Hamilton also recommended the extension of this benefit to the introducers of new technologies from abroad, as well as to domestic authors and inventors. Here he noted that there was again a question as to whether the appropriate constitutional authority existed.

Hamilton's discussion of the particular kinds of manufactures to be encouraged contains few surprises, in view of his measured discussion of the appropriate means. His most extensive recommendations concern manufactures connected with national security. Here he is quite emphatic that national self-sufficiency is the goal: "Every nation, with a view to those great objects, ought to endeavour to possess within itself all the essentials of national supply. These comprise the means of *Subsistence habitation clothing* and *defence*." It was, he added, "the next great work to be accomplished."[161] Hamilton remarked that until the United States acquired a powerful navy to protect its foreign commerce, it would be all the more essential to ensure an adequate domestic demand by encouraging manufactures. It is clear, however, from Hamilton's many remarks in support of an "active commerce,"[162] that he desired both a navy and the encouragement of manufactures. There is little equivocation in his remarks. As Caton observes, "Hamilton was a mercantilist and expected war."[163] Thus, for Hamilton, talk of trade-offs between defense and opulence was somewhat beside the point.

Conclusion

In the conclusion of his "Report on Mnaufactures," Hamilton recommended the creation of a "Board" for the promotion of "Arts, Agriculture, Manufactures and Commerce." Under its auspices, funds would be dispensed to encourage immigration, to introduce useful discoveries, and for premiums and other support such as Congress might authorize. Throughout his report, Hamilton stressed the need for selective measures that promoted or utilized competitive forces and that emphasized innovation and excellence, rather than the simple protection of existing industries. The recommendations followed the maxim stated in the second draft of the "Report on Manufactures": that measures should be "gradual systematic and progressive efforts rather than forced into maturity by violent and disproportioned exertions."[164] His only marked departures from this general principle were in the area of national security.

HAMILTON'S COMMERCIAL REPUBLICANISM

A number of features of Hamilton's commercial republicanism distinguished it from that of his rivals. As I have suggested, Hamilton's approach to commercial republicanism was largely shaped by Montesquieu's analysis of the problem of the common good in large republics. The nub of that problem is that as the society becomes larger and more diverse, it becomes more and more difficult to identify and pursue the common good. Hamilton did not accept that an invisible hand would reconcile the clashing interests and passions of a large society. Nor did he think that representation was a sufficient solution to the problem. In addition, and more so than Montesquieu, Hamilton considered war a permanent possibility in human affairs. Hamilton's response to these problems was to point to the role of the "more permanent branches" of the government established by the Constitution, especially the executive, in identifying and pursuing the common good. Hamilton always assumed that the underlying political culture was and would remain republican. The problem was that, although it "is a just observation that the people commonly *intend* the PUBLIC GOOD . . . their good sense would despise the adulator who should pretend that they always *reason right* about the *means* of promoting it."[165]

Hamilton's views on the executive have been the subject of extensive scholarly commentary.[166] Furthermore, in the preceding sections we have seen many examples of what Hamilton thought to be the proper use of executive power. For present purposes, perhaps the most important issue is what Hamilton thought would be the effects of his economic program on the underlying republican culture of the nation. The issue is important because he was accused at the time of favoring measures that would subvert a republican system of government. Concern about the effects of commerce on society came from many quarters. Smith went some distance in this direction with his criticism of the effects of manufacturing on the character of ordinary laborers. More importantly, Jefferson and Madison saw Hamilton's plan as a conspiracy to subvert the republican system. In his "Anas," Jefferson wrote that Hamilton's whole fiscal scheme had but two objects: first, "as a puzzle, to exclude popular understanding and inquiry"; and second, "as a machine for the corruption of the legislature." Each step of the plan threw "pabulum to the stock jobbing herd," thereby adding new recruits to the "phalanx of the Treasury." The national bank was, Jefferson believed, the means of perpetuating a system that would eventually result in an English-style monarchy.[167] He and Madison saw banks and high finance as unrepublican, because they gave rise to a taste for luxury and provided a fund for the corruption of the government. For similar reasons, they opposed any significant encouragement of manufacturing. Hamilton's program, they thought, threatened to corrupt republican government by creating a class of government pensioners and subjecting a large section of society to a degrading form of labor.

On the issues of public credit and manufactures, Madison and Jefferson maintained complex and, perhaps, not entirely consistent positions. Perhaps the deepest difficulty was that, although they were opposed to Hamilton's program, they were not opposed to economic liberty. As a result, they appear to have been willing to accept the long-run consequences of economic development. As McCoy has noted, both Madison and Jefferson seem to have accepted something like Smith's idea of a natural progress of opulence. One might say that Jefferson and Madison attempted to find a republican niche within Smith's account of the natural progress of opulence by prolonging as long as possible the agrarian phase of economic and social development. Whereas Jefferson had an unshakable faith in American exceptionalism, McCoy observes that Madison anticipated a problem— a "crisis," in fact—arising from the long-term implications of economic development for republican government.[168] What would happen when the United States reached the final stages of economic development? There is certainly something to this argument, but it may understate the degree to which Madison (and Jefferson) thought these problems could be reduced by establishing the correct institutions and by spreading the doctrine of the rights of man. Whatever the case, Hamilton's account of the benefits of economic development is of great interest today, because the United States has forever passed beyond agrarian democracy.

Hamilton was acquainted with the so-called luxury debate. His position was strikingly similar to Hume's. Hume thought that it was impossible for a legislator to remove every vice and replace it with a virtue. When faced with a choice, he would be wise to choose luxury over indolence, because luxury is accompanied by many goods and indolence by none. As he remarked elsewhere: "No advantages in this world are pure and unmixed."[169] Furthermore, Hume pointed to the benefits in terms of culture, politics, and morality that follow along with economic progress. Economically advanced societies display greater politeness, a more refined sense of honor, greater humanity, and, of course, more extensive learning than do those that are less advanced. Hume's economic essays argued that the "infallible and universal" "method" for rousing men from their lethargy is to excite other forms of industry that afford the agricultural laborers a ready market for their surplus produce.[170] Steuart reasoned similarly, distinguishing between "luxury," which he saw as a stimulus to industry, and "excess," which he saw as a threat to both government and society.[171]

In his "Valedictory Report" on public credit, Hamilton briefly mentioned the objections that some "speculative men urge against national and individual opulence" and remarked that "perhaps upon careful analysis of facts they would be found to have much less support in them than is imagined, inasmuch as they attribute to those systems effects which are ascribed more truly to the passions of men and perhaps to the genius of particular governments."[172] His clearest statement on the problem of luxury occurs in "Defense of the Funding System." Hamilton followed Hume and Montesquieu in believing that the military discipline of the ancient republics was unnatural. A modern republic will rely on a more realistic assessment of man's capacity for virtue. The "true politician," he remarked, will not attempt "to travel out of human nature and introduce institutions and projects for which man is not fitted."[173] Like Hume, Hamilton viewed progress as something of a two-edged sword. Science, opulence, national strength, public credit, even liberty itself give rise to certain abuses. Opulence, for example, may promote "luxury extravagance dissipation and effeminacy." Hamilton responded that

> Tis the portion of man assigned to him by the eternal allotment of Providence that every good he enjoys, shall be alloyed with ills, that every source of his bliss shall be a source of his affliction—except Virtue alone, the only unmixed good which is permitted to his temporal Condition.[174]

The "true politician," he concluded,

> will favour those institutions and plans which tend to make men happy according to their natural bent, which multiply the sources of individual enjoyment and national resource and strength—taking care to infuse in each case all the ingredients which can be devised as preventives and correctives of the evil which is the eternal concomitant of temporal blessing.[175]

Hamilton's thinking provides a rule of prudence for the liberal statesman dealing with the question of progress. Hamilton emphasized again and again that, in public affairs, there are few courses of action which do not entail some disadvantages.[176] With respect to Hamilton's republicanism, his advocacy of moderation and energetic government were two sides of the same coin. The zeal for liberty must be moderated, in order to permit the energy that all governments require. Here his moderation points to a prudent regard to the mixed character of public life.[177]

Despite his similarities to Hume, Hamilton did not view progress with what Ralph Lerner has termed Hume's "breezy equanimity."[178] He stressed that even beneficial progress must be managed and its unwholesome side effects mitigated; and, to this extent, it might be said that Hamilton was concerned with corruption. As we have seen, his political economy consciously strove to confine acquisitiveness to useful ends and to cultivate certain virtues such as industry, probity, and law-abidingness. Of particular note is Hamilton's belief that strict adherence to honesty, justice, and law are the distinguishing features of a republican citizenry. In this belief Hamilton departed from classical republicanism's stress on devotion to the public good. But his views are highly consonant with the foundations of modern liberal republicanism, especially the version of it that stresses constitutional government. As I suggested earlier, Hamilton increasingly came to see fidelity to the Constitution as the key to the American republican experiment.

Several other features of his attitude toward economic progress deserve mention. He departed from Hume on the implications of opulence for national security. Hume had argued that resources, including human resources, can be shifted easily from civilian to military uses when emergencies arise.[179] Hamilton, in contrast, insisted on the utility of standing armies. A favorite project of Hamilton's (and Washington's) was a military college for the purposes of keeping alive "military *spirit* and military knowledge."[180] In addition, I suspect that Hamilton balked at Hume's notorious freethinking. He certainly did at Jefferson's. Particularly after the French Revolution, Hamilton showed a considerable eagerness to bolster religious views among the people. In his draft of Washington's "Farewell Address," a speech Hamilton hoped to render "*importantly* and *lastingly* useful," he wrote that morality needs the aid of "generally received and divinely authoritative Religion."[181] However devoted to modernization Hamilton might have been, he did expect that it would undermine the religious element of the foundation of society. The question of Hamilton's own beliefs is impossible for us to answer, but it is sufficient here to note that he was more than convinced of the political utility of revealed religion.

The coherence of Hamilton's political program to establish an effective republic, to use Flaumanhaft's term, and his economic program is visible from another perspective.[182] His political program demanded that the tone of the government be set as high as possible, within the limits of the Constitution. The great offices of state were to be filled by men of quality and weight who sought to win a name for themselves. His economic program aimed to create a diverse, vigorous, and modern society, in which property and law were respected. While recognizing the primacy of agriculture in the United States in the foreseeable future, Hamilton's plan proposed to give a weight to the cities that they would not otherwise have received. Caton observes that the growth of cities necessarily increases the number of professionals, the class which Hamilton saw as playing the crucial political role of impartial judges of the various interests that make up the nation.[183] Such a nation would be a far cry from the homogeneous, agrarian republic Jefferson sometimes said he desired. If I am correct in seeing Hume's influence on Hamilton's understanding of the progress of society, then there is every reason to believe that Hamilton expected the refined sensibilities which he himself possessed to continue in a commercial society, and perhaps even prosper. One might conclude that he saw his economic program and republican government as not merely compatible but essential to the perfection of republican government.

POLITICAL
ECONOMY *and*
STATESMANSHIP

SMITH AND HAMILTON

THE FIRST PURPOSE OF OUR STUDYING Smith and Hamilton was to begin to clarify the role of the liberal statesman with respect to the economy. The second purpose was to contribute to the debate over the construction of a new political economy. Now is the time to consider what have we learned. Smith and Smithians would argue that economic developments in the United States would have proceeded much as they did even if Hamilton's economic program had never existed. This was essentially the argument Smith made against the mercantile system. The surface appearance that the mercantile system was the cause of Europe's economic revival hid the deeper truth: the mercantile system was really a drag on progress.

From Hamilton's perspective, the matter would appear quite differently. In the first place, the establishment of an exact administration of justice, an objective of which Smith approved, was hardly a simple administrative matter. Indeed, from the point of view of political practice, there is a critical lacuna in Smith's thought on this point. Smith wrote about the evolution of our sense of justice, rather than the establishment of a system of justice. That Hamilton had to confront this task in the circumstances of a republican government made it all the more difficult. It required all the skill of the statesman to cajole and, at times, prod the American people to accept the rule of law. Second, it is indisputable that Hamilton's financial system was vitally important in breathing life and energy into the new nation.

Third, aspects of Hamilton's economic program became integral to both American economic policy and American economic thinking for more than a century. After lapsing for a period during Madison's presidency, Hamilton's financial system was revived until the time of Jackson, when it was dismantled—with disastrous results. Furthermore, even though Hamilton's "Report on Manufactures" was not implemented, manufacturing was eventually encouraged by government, although in fits and starts and chiefly by war, embargo, and, eventually, by a protective tariff. Perhaps just as importantly, many of Hamilton's arguments were republicanized by men such as Henry Clay, who successfully promoted an "American system," including a protective tariff that became a cornerstone of American economic policy.[1] Even Jefferson and Madison were forced by circumstances to make substantial concessions to the Hamiltonian view on manufacturing. It was, however, in the Marshall Court that Hamilton's legacy was most faithfully upheld. Hamilton's understanding of the Constitution and of the proper role of the national government was perpetuated more or less intact by the Marshall Court. It is true that American economic development took a course different from that which Hamilton had envisaged. The pace of westward expansion far exceeded anything Hamilton thought either wise or even manageable. Although this pattern of development had certain economic benefits, including a stimulus to American manufacturing, it placed an extraordinary political stress on the nation. And one must wonder whether Hamilton was not proved correct by the terrible consequences of the struggle over slavery in the territories.

Perhaps Hamilton would take another route in his own defense. When faced with a conflict between theories, he looked to enlightened statesmen and to the general policy of nations as guides for political practice. Has the general policy of nations changed much since Hamilton's time? It seems not. At times, a more liberal world order has prevailed, but this has had more to do with the political situation of the day than with economic considerations. Furthermore, there are successful mercantilist states in Europe and Asia. In these respects, mercantilism cannot be said to have been simply refuted.[2] Indeed, it is remarkable that economic science has been unable to settle certain fundamental debates that have characterized it from the beginning. The Smith–Hamilton debate is just one example; others include: wage reductions versus job-creation solutions for unemployment; easy money versus tight money as means to growth; and demand-side versus supply-side approaches to economic management. What is just as remarkable is that mainstream economics, now represented by neoclassical economics, has maintained essentially the same basic theory for one hundred or perhaps, as I have suggested, for two hundred years. This is not to say that economists have been inactive. With the aid of mathematics, they have focused on refining certain basic insights. But as Alexander Rosenberg has observed, such stability is unheard of in the natural sciences.[3] It is possible that politicians are invincibly stupid and will always be tempted to stray from orthodoxy, but the curious combination of theoretical refinement within a given research program and practical stalemate is suggestive of a deeper problem within economic theory. Indeed, the practice of economic policy would seem to confirm Hamilton's suspicion about the limits of theory.

. . .

By way of conclusion, I make three proposals that grow out of the study of Hamilton's economic statesmanship. Taken together, these proposals suggest that the relationship between the science of political economy and statesmanship needs to be rethought. The problem is not that the kind of scientific inquiry in which Smith engaged is worthless but that it has been greatly overrated. In the final section, I address a possibly grave objection to looking to Hamilton for assistance.

An Enterprise Economy

Many of the issues that separate Smith from Hamilton have an antiquarian flavor. Smith's argument for the superior productivity of agriculture, for example, could today only be pronounced "quaint and superficial," just as Hamilton said. The same might now be said of Hamilton's concern about precious metals. My purpose, however, was to consider these arguments for the light they shed on the way in which Smith and Hamilton approached economic affairs. This is important, because Smith established an enormously influential school of thought that maintained his basic approach even though it rejected some of his specific opinions.[4]

Smith's political economy was an economics of exchange. Because economic outcomes depend on a vast multitude of similar causes, the economy resembles a mechanism, and because economic progress is smooth and predictable, it is a suitable subject for scientific analysis. Not only is the economy a mechanism, it is a benevolent one. This view of the economy has its analog in Keynesian and socialist economics, which also regard the economy as a mechanism, though, to varying degrees, a malevolent one. Such an approach is open to the objection that the economy does not move in a smooth and predictable manner. Neither the uncertainty associated with economic affairs, especially in a money economy, nor the efforts of individual entrepreneurs or inventors figured prominently in Smith's analysis. Smith explained away this volatility by pointing to two factors. First, sometimes governments create volatility by distorting the natural course of things. The second and less contingent factor is that the economy is not as volatile as we first might think, in that the surface economy described in ordinary speech is not the real economy. By escaping from the ambiguities of common speech, which reflects the apparent complexity of human affairs, to a more solid and precise realm suitable for scientific analysis, Smith hoped to reveal the smooth and predictable character of economic progress behind the world of appearances.

What would an alternative conception of the economy look like? Hamilton did not view economic growth in terms of incremental change based on frugality and industry. It was not that he rejected these virtues or discounted their importance for economic growth. Rather, he saw economic growth as a more complex and volatile process that depended, to an important extent, on the extraordinary efforts of some, rather than on the ordinary efforts of many. This difference from Smith is evident in several areas. Most clearly, Hamilton favored the protection of infant industries. Furthermore, as Caton has observed, Hamilton displayed a keen insight into the technological elements of economic growth.[5] Caton tends, however, to neglect the financial or, what he terms "commercial," aspect of Hamilton's program. Hamilton sought to provide incentives sufficient to elicit the vast amount of energy and activity necessary for the exploitation of the human and material resources of the nation. He saw two conditions as essential: a climate of confidence among consumers and entrepreneurs; and the provision of a medium of exchange sufficient to incite industry and enterprise. Caton's preoccupation with Hamilton's industrialism obscures the fact that Hamilton's liberal political economy differs significantly from the European statist tradition. Hamilton relied most on financial incentives to move the enterprising. The result is a kind of capitalism more volatile than its European or Asian counterparts. The enormous energy created in its private sector compensates for this volatility. Hamilton's conception of the economy contains elements that may be found in Keynes, Schumpeter, and even the Austrian School. And, no doubt, these later thinkers present more-sophisticated accounts of certain aspects of the economy. What makes Hamilton's account particularly useful is that it is integrated into a comprehensive political framework.

Constitutionalize Political Economy

Despite Smith's fame as a proponent of spontaneous order, his solution to the problem of economic progress was, in a fundamental sense, technocratic.[6] His continual references to history and his advocacy of incremental change disguise this aspect of his thought. Smith attempted to establish universal laws of justice and policy that showed the way to reconciling natural liberty with the protection of private rights and the public good. He relied on the unanticipated consequences—both short term and long term—of human actions to bring about this reconciliation. The presupposition of his entire project is that there are independent and spontaneous economic forces that can be understood by science. Smith makes statesmanship subordinate to political economy, practice to theory. Our consideration of Hamilton has pointed to two problems with this view: theory is severely limited in its capacity to grasp reality; and theorists disagree. The significance of this second problem was just becoming apparent in Hamilton's time. Theories attract zealous adherents; and, furthermore, theory can be used for political purposes, because the authority of science is a powerful rhetorical tool.

I want to suggest replacing Smith's pairing of the science of political economy and statesmanship with Hamilton's pairing of constitutional government and statesmanship. The advantages of this substitution are twofold. First, the Constitution displays a fruitful ambiguity toward statesmanship, in that it both limits statesmanship and provides it with opportunities. Second, the Constitution provides a normative anchor for statesmanship. By appealing to the spirit of system, Smith obscured his own moral anchor. Contemporary economics goes farther and confines such concerns to the netherworld of "values." The practical implication of a pairing of constitutional government and statesmanship is that the statesman's primary or ordinary task is the fostering of a political and economic culture that preserves constitutional government. The secondary or extraordinary task of statesmanship is to deal with those situations that threaten to escape the boundaries of limited government, such as wars (including cold wars and trade wars) and Great Depressions.

What I am proposing amounts to a reversal of the powerful current trend of extending the economic approach to political matters. Constitutionalizing political economy requires the subordination of the economy to the priority of preserving constitutional government. As understood by Hamilton, constitutional government meant limited government. Ironically, then, the thorough politicization of economics in this way might arrive at many of the same practical conclusions as today's Smithian-inspired economic constitutionalists, such as James Buchanan and Gordon Tullock.

Recognize a Place for Statesmanship

Finally, the hierarchy Smith established, placing a statesman guided by knowledge of the general course of things above the crafty and opportunistic politician, must be rethought. In the wake of Smith, economics became a professional pursuit with a wide influence in both the academy and in the polity. Smith, perhaps, anticipated such an empire over men's minds. The system of natural liberty contains all the elements that Smith thought essential for a successful theory. It is elegant, simple, comprehensive, and founded on the familiar principle of self-interest. Smith sought to move political men through an appeal to their interests and by channeling ambition into the spirit of system. This kind of appeal was made necessary by his belief that, as a class, political men are moved chiefly by ambition. Both his political science and his political economy taught moderation in the interest of effectiveness, thereby reconciling public good, private ambition, and moderate politics. Smith did not anticipate the emergence of social scientists, who stand ambiguously somewhere between philosophers and statesman. Nevertheless, Smith's basic notion—that theory can directly guide practice—is enshrined in contemporary universities and government. Smith's hierarchy is reflected not only in the social sciences' neglect of the perspective of the statesman but also in their proclivity to attribute the lowest of motives to anyone engaged in politics.

The analysis of the spirit of system was Smith's most original contribution. It involved a significant revision of the understanding of statesmanship associated with both Aristotle and Machiavelli.[7] This tradition located the nobility of statesmanship in the difficulty of the task that confronted the statesman. The accomplishment of great tasks constituted the proof of the statesman's virtue. Smith pointed, instead, to the aesthetic appeal of ideal plans of government as the secret motive behind much public-spirited activity. Public service, in this sense, is not so much the proving ground of one's virtue as the vehicle for satisfying one's psychic need for esteem.

In contrast, there were few general principles Hamilton was willing to grant as everywhere valid. Moreover, he made a point of stressing that too great a "spirit of abstraction and refinement" is not suitable for understanding political and economic affairs, noting "how apt the imagination is to be heated" in theoretical inquiries. His caution in this area forbade surrender to any general theories of politics and counseled him to defer to experience. By experience he meant not so much scientific experimentation as the tried practice of nations and statesmen. Hamilton leaves greater room for what we might call judgment or the particular skill or knack that chooses the right means to given ends in particular circumstances.[8] Furthermore, Hamilton's greatest ambitions were bound up in the particular decisions and judgments for the founding of the commercial republic.

What does this mean, practically speaking? First, Hamilton substantially agrees with Smith in holding that the objective of government policy is to provide the conditions that enable individuals to pursue their interest. Smith, however, underestimated the role of government in bringing about these conditions. In particular, he failed to deal fully with the steps that must be taken to bring the commercial republic into being. Second, acknowledging that the economy is not a mechanism would have the effect of moderating our expectations about its quarterly or yearly performance. This approach rules out the kind of fine-tuning associated with Keynesian economics, but it leaves open the possibility of supply-side *and* demand-side interventions in times of real crisis or fundamental change. In ordinary times, the focus of short-term policy ought to be on preserving the political and economic culture of the nation that is the foundation of long-term prosperity.

What role is left for what Smith called "speculative men"? As I noted, abstract reasoning of the kind Smith engaged in is not simply useless. What is necessary is to realize fully its limitations. Hamilton thought that the free-trade position was reasonable as a general rule but not as an exclusive one. The study of economic statesmanship is a fruitful way both to recognize the limits of theory and to consider the application of general rules. Furthermore, it ought to be remembered, Hamilton took his bearings from an idea of a just society outlined by "wise and good men" who delineated "the odious character of despotism." He evaluated policies and institutions in light of this end. The speculative man today can contribute to clarifying the nature of the just society and the activities of statesmen. The great task of bringing into being such a society is, however, left to citizens and statesmen acting in a world of chance and change.

FROM THE EIGHTEENTH CENTURY
TO THE TWENTY-FIRST CENTURY

The foregoing argument is open to a potentially powerful objection. Hamiltonianism, today, is out of place or even dangerous. It gives support and authority to those who wish to expand the scope of government in the economy and society at a time when there seems to be a clear need to bring the scope of government under control.[9] More generally, even if one grants that there are difficulties in Smith's political economy, Hamiltonianism is a standing threat to limited government in a way that Smithian free-market economics is not. By itself, the rhetoric of Smithian political economy—its optimism and its persuasiveness—is a powerful support for the idea of limited government.

In light of this problem, what does Hamilton have to offer? Clearly, something for new and developing nations.[10] From his point of view, the American experience was not as exceptional as many of his contemporaries believed. Hamilton knew that America was to be the decisive testing ground for the republican experiment, but he was certain it would have to deal with the problems that beset all nations. Thus the experience of the first "new nation" and its leading men has much to offer the rest of the world.

But what of the United States today? In the first place, the gap between Hamilton and today's advocates of the free market is narrower than might first appear. There is little doubt that Hamilton would have recoiled at the rise of the entitlement state since the New Deal. As much as Smith or any of today's advocates of the free market, Hamilton valued the habits of industry, frugality, and enterprise for the sake of both polity and economy. Furthermore, Hamilton would be stunned at the range of activities now within the sphere of the national government. In *The Federalist* no. 17, Hamilton wondered why any official of the national government would stoop to consider anything other than the great objects of state: "commerce, finance, negotiation, and war."[11] I suspect that Hamilton would recommend reducing the role of the national government for the sake of more effectively pursuing the tasks it should be doing. Thus, to invert the famous formula of Herbert Croly, he would pursue Hamiltonian ends using Jeffersonian means. Finally, the "general spirit of improvement" that Hamilton sought to establish in the United States is probably as well founded here as in any nation in the world. Thus there is no reason for further extensive government encouragement. It must be remembered, as well, that Hamilton favored a *substantially* free trade.

Notwithstanding the above, there would still be a gap. Hamilton was too attuned to the workings of the human passions to believe in a general theory that promised to inject a "benevolent and philosophic spirit" into political life. Perhaps most of all, Hamilton would regard the intersection of science, military power, and the private sector as a necessary focus of activist government. Hamilton's example has something else to offer. In a word, it is sobriety. From at least the late eighteenth century onward, an element of what Smith called the spirit of system entered into political speculation. The word *enthusiasm,* which Smith reserved for religious zealotry, might also be appropriate. Whether Smith's own speculation was free of this spirit is open to question. What is clear is that Smith sought to channel this spirit in others, especially the politically ambitious, in a useful direction. To be sure, Hamilton was, at times, impetuous, but this side of his character reflected partly an intense desire for true fame and partly a sincere belief that decisive action was a necessary part of effective politics. It is clear that both of these qualities are sorely lacking today. That Hamilton needed a Washington to keep him in check only underscores the point. But in any case, Hamilton's political and economic reasonings remain a model of sobriety. As Hamilton put it in his "Report on Manufactures," "it interests the Public Councils to estimate every object as it truly is; to appreciate how far the good in any measure is compensated by the ill, or the ill by the good. Either of them is seldom unmixed."[12] Enthusiasm, or a spirit of system, destroys the ability to think clearly about means and ends.

In closing, I cite two examples from the realm of economic policy that testify to the need for a clear understanding of the merits of alternative policies when at a critical juncture in history. In each case, a decision was made on the basis of a theory or system of policy that purported to supersede Hamilton's constitutionally limited statesmanship. The first case is that of Thomas Jefferson, who explained his change of mind on the question of the encouragement of manufactures by asking, "[W]ho in 1785 could foresee the rapid depravity which was to render the close of that century the disgrace of the history of man? . . . We have experienced what we did not then believe, that there exists both profligacy and power enough to exclude us from the field of interchange with other nations."[13] Jefferson's remarks reveal a belated recognition of what Hamilton had argued time and again is the natural course of things. Consider also the case of Franklin D. Roosevelt. When Roosevelt announced in his "Commonwealth Club Address" that the "day of enlightened administration has come," he was not speaking in Hamiltonian terms.[14] Roosevelt had in mind both the scientific management of public policy and the transcendence of traditional constitutional politics. Perhaps, if he had had a clearer grasp of administration in the Hamiltonian sense, he would not have seen boisterous American capitalism as incompatible with a truly wise administration.

INTRODUCTION

1. One of the better such comparisons is Robert Gilpin, *The Political Economy of International Relations* (Princeton, N.J.: Princeton University Press, 1987), pp. 33–34, 172–73, 180–81.

2. Prominent contemporary examples are James Fallows, *Looking at the Sun: The Rise of a New East Asian Political System* (New York: Pantheon, 1994); Robert Kuttner, *The End of Laissez-Faire: National Purpose and the Global Economy after the Cold War* (New York: Alfred A. Knopf, 1994); and Robert Reich, *The Work of Nations: Preparing Ourselves for 21st Century Capitalism* (New York: Alfred A. Knopf, 1991). For a classic statement of this view, see John K. Galbraith, *Economics and the Public Purpose* (Boston: Houghton Mifflin, 1973).

3. See James Buchanan and Gordon Tullock's seminal *The Calculus of Consent* (Ann Arbor: University of Michigan Press, 1962), as well as Dennis Mueller's survey, *Public Choice II* (Cambridge, England: Cambridge University Press, 1989). A clear, thorough, and recent account that stresses the policy implications of the public-choice perspective is William C. Mitchell and Randy T. Simmons, *Beyond Politics: Markets, Welfare, and the Failure of Bureaucracy* (Boulder, Colo.: Westview Press, 1994).

4. For criticism of public choice, see James Ceaser, *Liberal Democracy and Political Science* (Baltimore, Md.: Johns Hopkins University Press, 1990), pp. 78–87; and Harvey C. Mansfield Jr., "Social Science and the Constitution," in *Confronting the Constitution,* ed. Allan Bloom (Washington, D.C.: AEI Press, 1990), pp. 431–35. Donald P. Green and Ian Shapiro, *Pathologies of Rational Choice Theory* (New Haven, Conn.: Yale University Press, 1994), assess public-choice theory from the perspective of conventional social science and find it wanting.

5. Colin Wright, "Competing Conceptions of Political Economy," in *From Political Economy to Economic—and Back?* ed. James Nicholls and Colin Wright (San Francisco: ICS Press, 1990), pp. 74–76.

6. For reflections on the study of statesmanship and social science, see Leo Strauss's essay "An Epilogue," in *Essays in the Scientific Study of Politics,* ed. Herbert J. Storing (New York: Holt, Rinehart, and Winston, 1962), pp. 305–27. On the problems of the fact–value distinction, see Leo Strauss, *Natural Right and History* (Chicago: University of Chicago Press, 1953), pp. 35–80.

7. Donald McCloskey, *The Rhetoric of Economics* (Madison: University of Wisconsin Press, 1985), pp. 97–98.

8. As Robert Skidelsky has remarked (*The Road from Serfdom* [New York: Penguin, 1995], p. 190), the most important name missing from contemporary debates in political economy is that of John Maynard Keynes. Skildelsky understates, however, the problems inherent in Keynes's policy prescriptions. The best account of Keynes's project

is Athol Fitzgibbons, *Keynes's Vision: A New Political Economy* (Oxford: Oxford University Press, 1988).

9. See, especially, Jean Baptiste Say, *Treatise on Political Economy* (New York: Augustus M. Kelley, 1964), p. xxxviii: "until the epoch of [the] publication [of *Wealth of Nations*], the science of political economy did not exist." See also the judgment of the great neoclassical economist, Alfred Marshall, in *Principles of Economics* (London: Macmillan, 1920; reprint, London: Macmillan, 1974), App. B, Sec. 3, p. 626: "wherever [Smith] differs from his predecessors he is more nearly right than they; while there is scarce any economic truth now known of which he did not get some glimpse. And since he was the first to write a treatise on wealth in all its chief social aspects, he might on this ground alone have a claim to be regarded the founder of modern economics."

10. See Salim Rashid, "Adam Smith's Rise to Fame: A Reexamination of the Evidence," *The Eighteenth Century* 23, no. 1 (1992):64–85; and Salim Rashid, "Adam Smith's Interpretation of the History of Economics and Its Influence in the 18th and 19th Centuries," *Quarterly Review of Economics and Business* 27, no.3 (1987):56–69. Smith's political economy is a kind of revisionist history of the preceding centuries. On Smith's neglect of the "mercantilist program for liberty, enlightenment, and progress," see Hiram Caton, "The Preindustrial Economics of Adam Smith," *Journal of Economic History* 45, No. 4 (1985), p. 842, n. 34.

11. Walter Bagehot, "Adam Smith and Our Modern Economy," in *Economic Studies,* ed. Richard Holt Hutton (Stanford, Calif.: Academic Reprints, 1953), pp. 108–10; Joseph Schumpeter, *History of Economic Analysis* (New York: Oxford University Press, 1954), pp. 184–86. For the record, Schumpeter thought Hamilton's economic reports to be "'applied economics' at its best" (p. 199).

12. Even Rashid implicitly grants this, in "Adam Smith's Rise to Fame," pp. 56–57.

13. Joseph Cropsey, *Political Philosophy and the Issues of Politics* (Chicago: University of Chicago Press, 1977), p. 54. See also Joseph Cropsey, *Polity and Economy: An Interpretation of the Principles of Adam Smith* (The Hague: Martinus Nijhoff, 1957). Peter Minowitz's *Profits, Priests, and Princes: Adam Smith's Emancipation of Economics from Politics and Religion* (Stanford, Calif.: Stanford University Press, 1993) is the first serious effort to revise Cropsey's deflection thesis in light of recent Smith scholarship. Minowitz's Smith is, perhaps, more Socratic than the Smith presented here, in that his Smith is more concerned with understanding than with action. Minowitz is not unaware of the tensions within Smith's thought on this matter (*Profits, Priests, and Princes,* pp. 156–57). In *Adam Smith's Discourse: Canonicity, Commerce, and Conscience* (New York: Routledge, 1994), Vivienne Brown reaches conclusions similar to Minowitz's, but by a very different route. Her postmodernist reading of Smith makes him a retiring philosopher with an almost fatalistic resignation concerning the world's imperfections, including those brought about by the deflection of philosophy and society toward political economy.

14. See especially Donald Winch, *Adam Smith's Politics: An Essay in Historiographic Revision* (Cambridge, England: Cambridge University Press, 1978); Knud Haakonssen, *The Science of a Legislator: The Natural Jurisprudence of David Hume and Adam Smith* (Cambridge, England: Cambridge University Press, 1981); and Richard Teichgraeber, *Free Trade and Moral Philosophy: Rethinking the Sources of the Wealth of Nations* (Durham, N.C.: Duke University Press, 1986). Winch seems to have coined the term "liberal-capitalist perspective" (*Adam Smith's Politics,* p. 23). The revisionist literature is reviewed by Edward S. Cohen, "Justice and Political Economy in Commercial Society: Adam Smith's Science of a Legislator," *Journal of Politics* 51, no. 1 (1989):50–72.

Jerry Z. Muller synthesized much of this new scholarship in *Adam Smith in His Time and Ours: Designing the Decent Society* (New York: Free Press, 1993).

15. John Marshall, *The Life of George Washington* (New York: Wm. H. Wise, 1925), vol. 5, p. 202. In "Anas" (in *The Life and Selected Writings of Thomas Jefferson*, ed. Adrienne Koch and William Peden [New York: Modern Library, 1944], p. 127), Thomas Jefferson remarked on Hamilton's "singular" character.

16. Consider the following opinions. Talleyrand ranked Hamilton above Napoleon and Fox, whom he regarded as the other two great men of his day. See Allan McLaine Hamilton, *The Intimate Life of Alexander Hamilton* (New York: Charles Scribner's Sons, 1911), p. 255. See also Walter Bagehot, "The American Constitution at the Present Crisis," in *Bagehot's Historical Essays* (Garden City, N.Y.: Anchor, 1965), pp. 352–56; Lord Charnwood, *Abraham Lincoln* (New York: Henry Holt, 1917); and James Bryce, *The American Commonwealth* (New York: Macmillan, 1933), vol. 2, pp. 6–8. Cf. the judgment of Woodrow Wilson in *The New Freedom* (Englewood Cliffs, N.J.: Prentice Hall, 1961), p. 47: "A great man, but, in my judgement, not a great American."

17. For Hamilton as Walpole, see Lance Banning, *The Jeffersonian Persuasion: Evolution of a Party Ideology* (Ithaca, N.Y.: Cornell University Press, 1979); Drew McCoy, *The Elusive Republic: Political Economy and Jeffersonian America* (Chapel Hill: University of North Carolina Press, 1980); and, in a more qualified way, Forrest McDonald, *Alexander Hamilton: A Biography* (New York: W. W. Norton, 1979). For Hamilton as a classical republican and mercantilist, see Joyce Appleby, *Capitalism and a New Social Order: The Republican Vision of the 1790s* (New York: New York University Press, 1984); and John R. Nelson Jr., *Liberty and Property: Political Economy and Policy Making in the New nation, 1789–1812* (Baltimore, Md.: Johns Hopkins University Press, 1987). It is of interest to observe that, with the exception of McDonald's work, all of these scholars have Jefferson as their primary focus. Hamilton appears as a foil.

18. March 4, 1805, in Jefferson, *Writings,* p. 342 (emphasis added). Hamilton, of course, was dead by this date, but his thinking lived on in what remained of the Federalist Party.

19. Shannon C. Stimson, "Reflections on the Economic Interpretation of the Constitution," in *Writing a National Identity: Political, Economic, and Cultural Perspectives on the Written Constitution,* ed. Vivien Hart and Shannon C. Stimson (Manchester, England: Manchester University Press, 1993), p. 157.

20. Hiram Caton, *The Politics of Progress: Origins and Development of the Commercial Republic, 1600–1835* (Gainesville: University of Florida Press, 1988), pp. 473–76, 529; Caton, "Preindustrial Economics of Adam Smith," pp. 846–49; McDonald, *Alexander Hamilton,* pp. 160–61, 233–36.

21. Stanley Elkins and Eric McKitrick, *The Age of Federalism: The Early American Republic, 1788–1800* (New York: Oxford University Press, 1993), pp. 107–14.

22. Gerald Stourzh, *Alexander Hamilton and the Idea of Republican Government* (Stanford, Calif.: Stanford University Press, 1970), p. 177.

23. For other early reactions to Smith's systematizing, see Samuel Hollander, *The Economics of David Ricardo* (Toronto: University of Toronto Press, 1979), pp. 33–40.

24. On Pitt's eulogy for Smith, see Rashid, "Adam Smith's Rise to Fame," pp. 82–83.

25. John Maynard Keynes, *The General Theory of Employment, Interest and Money* (London: Macmillan, 1973), p. 32. The remarks in Rashid, "Adam Smith's Interpretation"; Rashid, "Adam Smith's Rise to Fame," and Caton, "Preindustrial Economics of Adam Smith" are relevant here.

CHAPTER 1: SMITH'S POLITICS RECONSIDERED

1. See Ronald Hamowy, *The Scottish Enlightenment and the Theory of Spontaneous Order* (Carbondale: University of Southern Illinois Press, 1987). The puzzle I am pointing to resembles Chandran Kukathas's account of the difficulties encountered by a more recent advocate of the theory of spontaneous order, F. A. Hayek. See Chandran Kukathas, *Hayek and Modern Liberalism* (Oxford: Clarendon Press, 1989), esp. chap. 6.

2. For both the old and the new debate over classifying Smith's politics, see Shannon C. Stimson, "Republicanism and the Recovery of the Political in Adam Smith," in *Critical Issues in Social Thought,* ed. Murray Milgate and Cheryl B. Welch (New York: Academic Press, 1989), pp. 91–112.

3. Emma Rothschild notes that Stewart, along with all liberal progressives, was on the defensive at this time because of the excesses of the French Revolution. More important, she draws attention to the radical or "French" Smith, who admired Voltaire and Quesnai. She argues that Smith's renowned Scottish caution was something of a disguise: "The public Smith was hiding his real sentiments from conservative public opinion" (Emma Rothschild, "Adam Smith and Conservative Economics," *Economic History Review* 45, no. 1 (1992):89).

4. Baron de Montesquieu, *The Spirit of the Laws,* trans. Anne M. Cohler, Basia Carolyn Miller, and Harold Samuel Stone (New York: Cambridge University Press, 1989), XXI.20.

5. Walter Bagehot, "Adam Smith as a Person," in *Bagehot's Historical Essays* (Garden City, N.Y.: Anchor Books, 1965), p. 165.

6. Albert O. Hirschman, *The Passions and the Interests: Political Arguments for Capitalism before Its Triumph* (Princeton, N.J.: Princeton University Press, 1977), pp. 100–14.

7. Alexander Hamilton, James Madison, and John Jay, *The Federalist* (New York: Mentor, 1961), no. 6, pp. 56, 59.

8. Winch, *Adam Smith's Politics,* p. 5.

9. Minowitz, *Profits, Priests, and Princes,* p. 11.

10. For Smith's views on the dangers of letter writing, see his letter to William Strahan, December 2, 1776, in Adam Smith, *Correspondence of Adam Smith,* ed. E. C. Mossner and T. S. Ross, Glasgow ed. (Oxford: Oxford University Press, 1977; Indianapolis, Ind.: Liberty Classics, 1987; hereafter cited as *Correspondence*), no. 18.

11. Minowitz provides a helpful discussion of this general issue in *Profits, Priests, and Princes,* pp. 6–9.

12. Ibid., chaps. 7–10.

13. Rothschild, "Adam Smith and Conservative Economics," p. 94.

14. Other examples are *system, political economy, natural liberty,* and *sympathy.*

15. Smith uses the terms *philosophy* and *science* interchangeably. See W. P. D. Wightman's "Introduction" to *Astronomy,* 11–13. Smith claimed to be in the process of writing a "sort of philosophical history of all the different branches of Literature, of Philosophy, Poetry and Eloquence" (Letter to Rochefocauld, November 1, 1785, *Correspondence,* no. 248).

16. On these points, see Andrew Skinner, "Adam Smith: Philosophy and Science," *Scottish Journal of Political Economy* 19 (1972):307–19.

17. Smith recommends that even common people be exposed to "geometry and mechanics," the necessary introductions "to the most sublime as well as to the most useful sciences" (*WN* V.i.f.55).

18. Deborah Redman, "Adam Smith and Isaac Newton," *Scottish Journal of Political Economy* 40, no. 2 (1993):210–30. Redman makes the important point that Smith may himself have drawn on Voltaire's popularized version of Newton's philosophy. According to Redman, it was Voltaire who created the impression that Newton's philosophy was rigidly mechanistic. This, however, does not imply that Smith was not trying to imitate the form and substance of what he understood to be Newton's philosophy.

19. The broad outlines of this dichotomy in Smith have been noticed before. See Minowitz, *Profits, Priests, and Princes,* pp. 233–34; Paul A. Rahe, *Republics: Ancient and Modern: Classical Republicanism and the American Revolution* (Chapel Hill: University of North Carolina Press, 1992), pp. 318–20.

20. Nathan Rosenberg deals with this question from the perspectives of economics ("Adam Smith on the Division of Labor: Two Views or One?" *Economica* 32 (May 1965):127–39) and of law ("Another Advantage of the Division of Labor," *Journal of Political Economy* 84, no. 6, pt. 1 (August 1976):861–68. I deal with it from the perspective of political philosophy.

21. Nevertheless, Smith believes philosophy to be a "masculine" characteristic (*TMS* I.iii.3.6).

22. The inclusion of moral and political philosophy is implied in the discussion of education in *WN* V. It is explicit in the "Early Draft" (20, 30–31) of the *Wealth of Nations* (which is to be found in the Glasgow edition of Smith, *Lectures on Jurisprudence,* pp. 570, 574).

23. Cf. Niccolò Machiavelli, *The Prince,* trans. Harvey C. Mansfield Jr. (Chicago: University of Chicago Press, 1985), chaps. 3, 6, 18. Minowitz, *Profits, Priests and Princes,* explores the contrast between Smith and Machiavelli at a number of levels (see esp. pp. 82, 97–98, 137–38, 225–26).

24. David McNally, *Political Economy and the Rise of Capitalism* (Berkeley: University of California Press, 1988), pp. 189–92, makes a similar point but develops it in a very different way.

25. On Smith's use of mankind as a standard, see Cropsey, *Polity and Economy,* pp. 57–58.

26. When making this observation, Smith perhaps had Colbert in mind. Cf. *WN* IV.ix.3.

27. In the *Theory of Moral Sentiments,* Smith does seem to hold out the hope that some rare human beings might acquire the superior prudence he so admires. Marcus Aurelius, for example, whom Smith mentions favorably twice, does seem to conform to that high standard (VI. ii. 3. 5–6; VII. ii. 1. 35). Yet there are reasons to discount the significance of his example. In modern times, the division of labor is carried to a far greater extent than it was in ancient times. As a result, individuals are less likely to have the multifaceted characters possessed by members of less-civilized societies. As it is, Smith's language is somewhat qualified on the issue of whether Aurelius successfully combined all the virtues. Perhaps a more important reason is that the rarity of such men itself suggests that they will have a limited influence on the course of human affairs. Smith's analysis of the course of history in both the *Wealth of Nations* and the *Lectures on Jurisprudence* stresses the overwhelming influence of classes and groups rather than individuals on social outcomes.

28. In *Science of a Legislator,* pp. 132–33, Haakonssen draws attention to Smith's claim that sovereign power must be placed somewhere, even if it is divided, as it is in Great Britain. One wonders, however, whether Smith, in saying this, was laying down a normative principle or simply making a statement of fact. Where power is equally

divided, a struggle for supremacy will ensue; at some point the struggle will come to an end, with one party victorious. Where power is unequal, the strongest party is by definition subject to no higher power.

29. Consider in this regard Smith's analysis of the problems for the English constitution caused by its colonial empire (*WN* IV.ii.43–45). His chief recommendation is not to add to those problems but rather to gradually solve the existing problems.

30. This distinction bears some resemblance to that which Walter Bagehot made between the "dignified" and the "efficient" parts of the English constitution. See his *The English Constitution* (1867) (Ithaca, N.Y.: Cornell University Press, 1963), p. 61.

31. See David Hume, "Of Original Contract," in *Essays: Moral, Political and Literary,* ed. Eugene Miller (Indianapolis, Ind.: Liberty Classics, 1985), pp. 465–87.

32. The two accounts are, I think, identical. That of the *Theory of Moral Sentiments,* however, employs more consistently Smithian rather than Humean terminology.

33. There appears to be a transcription error in this passage. In the manuscript the last word is *utility,* when clearly it should be *authority.*

34. See Smith's discussion of infanticide in *TMS* V.2.15–16.

35. See, in particular, Thomas Hobbes, *Leviathan* (Harmondsworth, England: Penguin Books, 1968), chaps. 16–17; and John Locke, *Two Treatises of Government,* ed. Peter Laslett (New York: New American Library, 1963), II, chap. 8.

36. Smith begins his *Lectures on Jurisprudence* by observing that "To acquire proper notions of government it is necessary to consider the first form of it, and how the other forms arose out of it" (*LJB* 19).

37. On the first point, see *WN* V.ii.k.74. On the second, consider the discussion of how the "high-spirited" men in the American colonies could be "managed" at *WN* IV.vii.c.78 and context.

38. In *LRBL* II.126–27 Smith noted the importance attached to the place of items in a list. The central place naturally belongs to the most important item, because this position is the most effective for influencing the reader.

39. As the editors of *Theory of Moral Sentiments* point out, there is a certain kinship between Smith's analysis of the spirit of system and Jean D'Alembert's critique of the spirit of system in his introduction to the *Preliminary Discourse to the Encyclopedia of Diderot,* trans. Richard N. Schwab (Indianapolis, Ind.: Bobbs-Merrill, 1963). D'Alembert's criticism is, however, narrowly focused on the problem of theory cut loose from empirical confirmation rather than on politics. Moreover, D'Alembert thought that the spirit of system had outlived its usefulness, whereas Smith finds room to praise it (*Preliminary Discourse,* pp. 94–95. The critical difference is that whereas Smith thought his own theorizing was free of the spirit of system, he saw the usefulness of that same spirit in moving others.

40. It is difficult to know what to make of the change in terminology from "public spirit" to "public virtue." Perhaps it is an indication of the moral neutrality of "public spirit" when separated from the other virtues, especially humanity.

41. Donald Winch, "Science and the Legislator: Adam Smith and After," *Economic Journal* 93 (September 1983):503; also Edward Harpham, "Liberalism, Civic Humanism, and the Case of Adam Smith," *American Political Science Review,* 78 (September 1984):772–73.

42. These passages were added to the sixth edition of the *Theory of Moral Sentiments,* perhaps in response to the French Revolution (editorial note 6, by D. D. Raphael and A. L. Macfie, *TMS* VI.ii.2.12).

43. Minowitz, *Profits, Priests, and Princes,* p. 207.

44. The philosopher, the interpreter of the natural course of things, stands in the background, unseen, but perhaps as much or more a leader and director as any statesman in that he is the author of the "system." It is of interest that in the discussion of the spirit of system in *TMS* IV.i there is no parallel in the political realm to the role of the invisible hand in the economic realm (cf. Minowitz, *Profits, Priests, and Princes,* pp. 137–38).

45. Letter to William Cullen, September 20, 1774, *Correspondence,* no. 143.

46. He seems to have in mind here a distinction between those students of noble birth and those of common but at least moderately wealthy families. See *WN* V.1.f.35, where he refers to "all gentleman and men of fortune." Perhaps he has in mind the distinction between the politically useful class, the natural aristocracy, and the upper class proper, which does not usually serve a political purpose.

47. "Advertisement" for the sixth edition of *Theory of Moral Sentiments* (reprinted in Glasgow edition, p. 3).

48. In the case of the education of the poorer sort of people, he was more inclined toward state intervention (*WN* V.1.f.52).

49. Cf. Hobbes, *Leviathan,* pp. 717–29. Cropsey, *Polity and Economy,* p. 84, n. 6, comments on Smith's descent from Hobbes.

50. Cf. George Stigler, "Smith's Travels on the Ship of State," in *Essays on Adam Smith,* ed. Andrew Skinner and Thomas Wilson (Oxford: Clarendon Press, 1975), pp. 237–46.

51. Brown, *Adam Smith's Discourse,* pp. 116–20.

52. Ibid., pp. 120–40.

53. It does not, however, have a part in Smith's thought comparable to that played by justice in Plato's *Republic,* the necessary and sufficient condition of the best life for an individual and a city. Nor does it have the expansive meaning it had for Aristotle when he wrote, in the *Nicomachean Ethics,* of justice as complete virtue. See Plato, *Republic,* trans. Allan Bloom (New York: Basic Books, 1968), book II; and Aristotle, *Nicomachean Ethics,* trans. Martin Ostwald (Indianapolis, Ind.: Bobbs-Merrill, 1962), book V, chap. 3.

54. Smith presents indignation as partaking of the irrational—for example, when we imagine the sufferings of someone who has died even though they feel nothing. With irrationality comes the strong possibility of excess. This realization leads him to recommend that the desire to punish be held in check and that individuals and societies observe a "count-to-ten rule." Indignation, however, serves a purpose. "The want of proper indignation is a most essential defect in the manly character, and, upon many occasions, renders a man incapable of protecting either himself or his friends from insult and injustice" (*TMS* VI.iii.16).

55. On the English and American antimonopoly tradition, see Michael Connant, *The Constitution and the Economy* (Norman: University of Oklahoma Press, 1991), pp. 213–19.

56. Rights acquired by contract or promise are "personal rights." They are distinguished from "real rights," which pertain to possessions. The two make up property rights as a whole.

57. The factors behind this development are: the increasing volume and variety of commerce; the increasing political means of supporting property rights; the increasing sensitivity of people to injury; and the increasing sophistication of language (which is necessary to deal with complex transactions).

58. Smith describes five ways in which property might be acquired: occupation; accession; prescription; testamentary succession; and voluntary transfer.

59. See Haakonsen, *Science of a Legislator,* pp. 104–7, for a helpful discussion.

60. One is tempted to say that *natural* justice is equivalent to *social* justice where the society referred to is "the great society of mankind" and that political justice is confined to actual societies. But this goes too far, because it seems that even the great society of mankind would at times have to sacrifice the interests of the individual to those of society.

61. In a discussion of smuggling, Smith gives an illuminating twist to the issues addressed here:

> The hope of evading . . . taxes by smuggling gives frequent occasion to forfeitures and other penalties, which entirely ruin the smuggler; a person who, though no doubt highly blameable, for violating the laws of his country, is frequently incapable of violating those of natural justice, and would have been in every respect, an excellent citizen, had not the laws of his country made that a crime which nature never meant to be so. (*WN* V.ii.k.64)

62. The distinction is well brought out by Haakonsen, *Science of a Legislator*, pp. 95ff.

63. The necessity of such laws is, perhaps, the deepest reason that led Smith to observe that in

> no country do the decisions of positive law coincide exactly, in every case, with the rules which the *natural sense of justice* would dictate. Systems of positive law, therefore, though they deserve the greatest authority, as records of the sentiments of mankind in different ages and nations, yet can never be regarded as accurate systems of the rules of justice. (*TMS* VII.iv.36, emphasis added)

64. The remark is revealing because of the light it throws on the transition from the particularism of Montesquieu to the universalism of Hume and Smith. This is a point of considerable significance, because it provides compelling evidence that Smith's assessment of the obstacles to the emergence of liberal societies was much more optimistic than Montesquieu's. On Smith's universalism, see P. E. Chamley, "The Conflict between Montesquieu and Hume: A Study in the Origins of Adam Smith's Universalism," in *Essays on Adam Smith*, pp. 274–305.

65. Winch, *Adam Smith's Politics*, p. 64.

66. Cf. "In all the courts of Europe the power of the nobility declined from the *common causes*, the improvement of the arts and commerce" (*LJB* 59, emphasis added). Winch, *Adam Smith's Politics*, p. 64, speaks of Smith's search for "constant causes."

67. Minowitz sees Smith's emphasis on history as a concomitant to his depreciation of politics (*Profits, Priests, and Princes*, pp. 28–34). Brown sees it as reflecting a kind of fatalistic resignation about progress (*Adam Smith's Discourse*, pp. 120–40). Both agree that the emphasis on history reduces the role for a legislator. Ronald Meek, *Social Science and the Ignoble Savage* (Cambridge, England: Cambridge University Press, 1975), and Andrew Skinner, "Adam Smith: An Economic Interpretation of History," *Essays on Adam Smith*, pp. 154–78, emphasize the deterministic side of Smith's history. They also discuss the large body of commentary on the general issue.

68. Cropsey, *Polity and Economy*, pp. 94, 95.

69. Duncan Forbes, "Sceptical Whiggism, Commerce and Liberty," in *Essays on Adam Smith*, pp. 201, 199. In this essay Forbes refined the position he took in an earlier essay, "Scientific Whiggism: Adam Smith and John Millar," *Cambridge Journal* no. 7 (August 1954), pp. 643–70. There he provided a very helpful formulation of Smith's

contribution to the study of history. He spoke of Smith's two laws of history: the law of progress, and the law of the heterogeneity of ends. The former refers to Smith's notion of "the natural course of things," or economic progress, and the latter refers to the secondary, but to an extent predictable, consequences of this natural course, the "unintended consequences." Forbes's more recent argument represents a denial that the law of progress gives rise to the unintended consequences, civilization and freedom.

70. Haakonssen, *Science of a Legislator*, pp. 182–83, 188.

71. See Cropsey, *Political Philosophy*, p. 75, n. 37.

72. Pierre Manent claims that Smith wrote under the "authority of history" (*La Cité de l'homme* [Paris: Fayard, 1994], p. 125). Manent is certainly correct in saying that Smith took for granted that history conforms to a pattern.

73. The example of England under Cromwell also illustrates the point (*LJA* IV.97).

74. Haakonssen provides a very thorough account of this issue in *Science of a Legislator*, pp. 165–71.

75. Rosenberg, "Another Advantage."

76. John Danford emphasizes the greater humanity of commercial society in "Adam Smith, Equality, and the Wealth of Sympathy," *American Journal of Political Science* 24, no. 4 (1980):674–95.

77. Montesquieu, *Spirit of the Laws* XXI.5; see also XX.1–2, XX.23, and XXI.20.

78. Forbes, "Sceptical Whiggism," p. 200.

79. Montesquieu, *Spirit of the Laws* XIV–XVII; for comment, see Thomas L. Pangle, *Montesquieu's Philosophy of Liberalism: A Commentary on The Spirit of the Laws* (Chicago: University of Chicago Press, 1973), pp. 161–77.

80. *WN* II.v.22; *WN* V.ia.44; *WN* V.ii.c.6. On these issues, see Haakonssen, *Science of a Legislator*, pp. 175, 179; and Minowitz, *Profits, Priests, and Princes*, pp. 109–13.

81. But Smith is either self-contradictory or tantalizingly ambiguous on this issue. The difficulty is evident in his discussion of the poor boy who leaves his country home, where he is watched by everyone, for the city, where he is "sunk in obscurity and darkness" and is in danger of losing his character. He is saved by becoming part of a small religious sect. "His brother sectaries are, *for the credit of the sect*, interested to observe his conduct" and to punish him if he departs from its moral code (*WN* V.i.g.12, emphasis added). What is puzzling about this statement is that it suggests that the desire to better our condition is not spontaneous and independent, because it needs to be supplemented by religion.

82. See Cropsey, *Polity and Economy*, chap. 3; Danford, "Adam Smith"; Muller, *Adam Smith*, chap. 10.

83. Max Weber, *The Protestant Ethic and the Spirit of Capitalism* (New York: Charles Scribner's Sons, 1958), p. 181.

84. David Hume, "Of Civil Liberty," in *Essays*, pp. 88–89. The two maritime powers were England and Holland.

85. See Minowitz, *Profits, Priests, and Princes*, p. 207.

CHAPTER 2: THE POLITICAL ECONOMY OF PROGRESS

1. Brown, *Adam Smith's Discourse*, p. 126.

2. An exception is *WN* IV.iii.c.8, where he distinguishes between the ways of a "great trader" and the "sneaking arts of underling tradesmen."

3. James Steuart, *An Inquiry into the Principles of Political Economy*, ed. Andrew Skinner (Chicago: University of Chicago Press), pp. 16–17, 122.

4. Brown's audacious reading of the *Wealth of Nations* on this point cannot be sustained (*Adam Smith's Discourse,* pp. 154–61; cf. *WN* I.x.c.25; *WN* IV.vii.54). Her contention is that the *Wealth of Nations* is not a book about "political economy" because it is critical of the various systems of "police" (policy) that preceded it. It is really a philosophical work. She all but robs the book of its practical significance, somehow overlooking the vast practical implications of the book in the areas of trade, taxation, regulation, finance, and even religious policy. Of course it is a practical book, but it is a practical book that grows out of the science of political economy, not out of the "clamour and sophistry" of merchants, as Smith thought the mercantile system did.

5. It might be better to say theoretical and applied economics, on the one hand, and public policy, on the other. See *Palgrave's Dictionary of Political Economy* (London: Macmillan 1899), s.v. "Political Economy," by Henry Sidgwick, vol. 3, pp. 129–33, for an illuminating discussion of the development of the term from signifying an aspect of the "art of government" to signifying an independent science. Sidgwick stresses Smith's ability to mix theory and policy as a factor in his enormous success. See also Wright, "Competing Conceptions of Political Economy."

6. Cf. Locke, *Two Treatises,* II, sect. 61.

7. The question of the extent to which Smith was aware of the profound changes that the Industrial Revolution would bring is difficult to answer. Smith's emphasis on the division of labor has been interpreted as revealing a stunning lack of appreciation of the role technological change would play in future economic progress. For a recent statement of this view, see Caton, "Preindustrial Economics of Adam Smith." Smith indicates that he is aware of the way in which technology utilizes the powers of nature. See *WN* I.i.9; "Early Draft" 2, 11; and *LJA* VI.42–43. The last stage of the division of labor seems to be that in which invention itself becomes a trade. Smith concludes that under conditions of free trade there will be the greatest incentives for the adoption of all measures that increase the productive powers of labor, including the adoption of new technologies. According to Smith, no scheme of government encouragement could provide equal incentives. For a generous account of the extent of Smith's awareness of the technological revolution, see Samuel Hollander, *The Economics of Adam Smith* (Toronto: University of Toronto Press, 1973), pp. 208–41, esp. pp. 23–41. Vincent Bladen, *From Adam Smith to Maynard Keynes* (Toronto: University of Toronto Press, 1973), pp. 14–15, places Smith's case for the division of labor in the proper perspective:

> The subject of the book is wealth not equilibrium; discussion of the growth in productivity takes precedence over operations of exchange in the market. I believe that the whole tone of the book makes it clear that Adam Smith would agree with enthusiasm if one said to him: is not freedom to innovate and to reap the rewards of successful innovation the basis of your expectation of increasing wealth?

8. See Hollander's understatement in his *Economics of Adam Smith,* p. 239: "Change is not, on the whole, generated in Smith's system by a minority of creative 'entrepreneurs.' This is not perhaps too surprising, given Smith's characteristic eighteenth century downplaying of innate differences from person to person." It must be added that although Smith believed that men acquire new talents and characters in different ages, he still believed that the underlying human propensities remained the same. See Cropsey, "'Capitalist' Liberalism," in *Political Philosophy,* p. 74.

9. For an insightful discussion of this question, see Minowitz, *Profits, Priests, and Princes,* pp. 71–73.

10. Schumpeter, *History of Economic Analysis,* p. 309.

11. Murray Rothbard, *Economic Thought before Adam Smith: An Austrian Perspective on the History of Economic Thought* (Hants, England: Edward Elgar, 1995), p. 448. For more charitable classical views on Smith, see David Ricardo, *The Principles of Political Economy and Taxation* (London: Everyman's Library, 1984), chap. l, sec. 1, pp. 5–13; and especially Karl Marx, "Grundisse," in *The Marx-Engels Reader,* ed. Robert C. Tucker (New York: W. W. Norton, 1978), p. 240, who described Smith's shift to labor in its "abstract universality" as "an immense step forward."

12. For the arguments of this paragraph, see *WN* I.iv.1–10; *WN* I.v.18–21,23–41; and also *WN* I.xi.21–31; *WN* IV.i.18; *WN* IV.vi.27.

13. Thomas Mun, *England's Treasure by Foreign Trade,* published in London in 1664, but written around 1630, reprinted in *Masterworks of Economics,* ed. Leonard D. Talbott (New York: McGraw Hill, 1973), vol. 1, pp. 6–27. The idea of a mercantile naval empire was proposed by Francis Bacon. See especially "Essays or Councils: Civil and Moral," essay no. 29, and "New Atlantis," both in *Francis Bacon: A Selection of His Works,* ed. Sidney Warhaft (Indianapolis, Ind.: Odyssey Press, 1981), pp. 120–29, 417–59. Bacon was among the first to use the term *balance of trade.* See Jacob Viner, *Studies in the Theory of International Trade* (Clifton, N.J.: Augustus M. Kelley, 1965), p. 8. Bacon's thought is crucial to understanding the emergence of the modern technological and commercial outlook. See Caton, *Politics of Progress,* pp. 32–41, 321–406. Mc-Nally has many interesting observations on Bacon's economics, but in his effort to highlight its agrarianism he fails to see the way in which Bacon anticipates the political and technological revolutions of later centuries (*Political Economy,* pp. 36–40).

14. For the arguments of this paragraph, see Locke, *Two Treatises,* II, chap. 5; and John Locke, "Some Considerations of the Consequences of the Lowering of Interest, and Raising the Value of Money," in *Locke on Money* (Oxford: Clarendon Press, 1991), pp. 233–35, 253–67.

15. Locke, "Some Considerations," p. 292. See the reference to the poverty of Spain in Locke, *Two Treatises,* II, sect. 36. Spain seems to be as poor as the American wilderness.

16. Roy Campbell and Andrew Skinner note the appearance of the paradox of value in Plato, Grotius, Pufendorf, Mandeville, and Hutcheson (*WN* I.iv.13n.31).

17. Caton correctly renders Smith's understanding of homogeneous labor as the "expenditure of animal energy" ("Preindustrial Economics of Adam Smith," p. 850).

18. See Schumpeter, *History of Economic Analysis,* pp. 309–11, for the dominant view. A more sympathetic view, but one that succeeds only in damning with faint praise, is Hollander, *Economics of Adam Smith,* pp. 116–17.

19. Cf. Mark Blaug, *Economic Theory in Retrospect* (Homewood, Ill.: Richard D. Irwin, 1968), pp. 42–46. Hollander, *Economics of Adam Smith,* p. 114, argues that there is a concept of general equilibrium in the *Wealth of Nations* as a whole.

20. Cf. Ricardo, *Principles,* p. 3. H. W. Arndt observes that after J. S. Mill, in particular, "the economics profession turned to other problems, the theory of value and distribution, welfare economics, monetary and trade cycle theory, all these treated almost entirely on static assumptions" (*The Rise and Fall of Economic Growth* [Chicago: University of Chicago Press, 1984], p. 13).

21. Thomas Sowell, *Classical Economics Reconsidered* (Princeton, N.J.: Princeton University Press, 1974), pp. 38–39, 54–55. See also Hollander, *Economics of Adam Smith,* pp. 188–91, 314–15. For a general discussion of Say's Law, see Schumpeter, *History of Economic Analysis,* pp. 62–65.

22. These statements reveal clearly the residual Physiocracy in Smith. A crucial premise of Smith's argument is that rent is a component of price. His argument was immediately challenged by Hume, and the issue figured prominently in Ricardo's criticisms of Smith. See Hume to Smith, April 1, 1776, *Correspondence*, no. 150; and Ricardo, *Principles*, chap. 2. As Hamilton would also point out, without this assumption, it is not self-evident which activity is socially the most advantageous.

23. See, for example, *WN* I.x.c.24; *WN* III.i.5; *WN* III.iv.19; *WN* IV.ii.21; *WN* V.i.g.12.

24. The terminology is Dugald Stewart's (*Account* II.48). Smith's account might be compared to David Hume, "Of Commerce," in *Essays*, pp. 263–64. Hume's account remains closer to the complexity of actual history.

25. The way in which the natural progress of opulence reconciles liberty and the needs of the state is dealt with in the next section.

26. On the other hand, merchants-turned-country-gentlemen are the best of all improvers, according to Smith (*WN* III.iv.3). On the connection between the public interest and that of landlords, see *WN* I.xi.p.9–11. Smith notes that it was the country gentleman who preserved within commercial society the old virtues of generosity and liberality (*WN* II.iii.42). But he does not voice any alarm at the possibility that these virtues might disappear. Contrast the attitude of Edmund Burke, *Reflections on the Revolution in France* (New York: Library of Liberal Arts, 1955), p. 86, when discussing the end of the age of chivalry and the spirit of the gentleman: "If it should ever be totally extinguished, the loss I fear will be great. It is this which has given its character to modern Europe."

27. Smith's account of China occupies a middle ground between Montesquieu's depiction of China as a despotism (*Spirit of the Laws* VIII.21) and Quesnai's contention that China is a model for Europe.

28. On this question, see Istvan Hont and Michael Ignatieff, "Justice and Needs in the Wealth of Nations," in *Wealth and Virtue: The Shaping of Political Economy in the Scottish Enlightenment,* ed. Istvan Hont and Michael Ignatieff (Cambridge, England: Cambridge University Press, 1983), pp. 1–44, who interpret Smith's treatment of needs and justice in light of the jurisprudential tradition of Grotius and Pufendorf. Smith, they point out, found a way to satisfy both concerns.

29. This claim is central to Smith's refutation of Rousseau's theory that commercial progress undermines nature's purposes (Jean-Jacques Rousseau, *The First and Second Discoures,* ed. Roger D. Masters, trans. Judith R. Masters [New York: St. Martin's Press, 1978], *Second Discourse,* esp. pp. 192–203).

30. Although Friedrich List made very clear the cosmopolitical aspect of Smith's thought, he was not sufficiently attentive to this aspect (*The National System of Political Economy,* trans. Sampson S. Lloyd [New York: Longmans, Green, 1904], pp. 97–107). When discussing the economic condition of the disunited German states, List made the following telling observation on the use of the term *society* in political and economic discourse:

> The true conception and the real character of the national economy could not be recognized because no economically united nation was in existence, and because for the distinct and definite term *'nation'* men had every where substituted the general and vague term *'society,'* an idea which is as applicable to entire humanity, to a small country, or to a single town, as to the nation. (p. 158)

31. This is the general tenor of Brown, *Adam Smith's Discourse;* McNally, *Political Economy;* and Teichgraeber, *Free Trade and Moral Philosophy.*

32. One of the earliest, most balanced, and thorough discussions of Smith's view of the role of the state is Jacob Viner, "Adam Smith and Laissez Faire" (1927), in *The Long View and the Short* (Glencoe, Ill.: Free Press, 1958), pp. 213–45.

33. Teichgraeber, *Free Trade and Moral Philosophy,* pp. 166–69, 174–76. See also Richard Teichgraeber, "Less Abused Than I Had Reason to Expect: The Reception of the *Wealth of Nations* in Great Britain," *The Historical Journal* 30, no. 2 (1987):337–66.

34. McNally, *Political Economy,* pp. 209–57; Brown, *Adam Smith's Discourse,* pp. 196–206.

35. The three duties are defense, the administration of justice, and the maintenance of certain public works and institutions. Stewart (*Account* IV.25) reports Smith as saying: "Little else is requisite to carry a state to the highest degree of opulence, from the lowest barbarism, but peace, easy taxes, and a tolerable administration of justice."

36. Cf. Thomas Robert Malthus, *Principles of Political Economy* (New York: Augustus M. Kelley, 1986), pp. 14–16.

37. *Account* IV.6.

38. Smith did, however, reject their controversial single tax proposal (*WN* V.ii.c.7).

39. This discussion draws heavily on Caton, *Politics of Progress,* pp. 410–21. McNally's account in *Political Economy and the Rise of Capitalism* of the Physiocrats is very useful, but he is too anxious to explain the Physiocrats by their historical circumstances.

40. Caton, *Politics of Progress,* pp. 424, 431.

41. Not only did Quesnai embrace the idea of legal despotism, but in 1767 he published an extraordinary panegyric to *le despotisme de la Chine,* a regime that he thought embodied the laws of nature. Quesnai's work of that title appears in *China: A Model for Europe,* trans. Lewis A. Maverick (San Antonio: Paul Anderson, 1946).

42. Rents in kind should be taxed at a higher rate, as should rents on land where the lease prescribes the mode of cultivation (*WN* V.ii.c.13–14). Both of these proposals aim at preserving the freedom and security of tenant farmers. Landlords who, rather than increase rents, charge a fee for the renewal of their leases should also be penalized, because the capitalization of future rents is an imposition on tenants and an enticement to prodigality for landlords, both of which should be avoided (*WN* V.ii.c.12). Most interesting is Smith's proposal that landlords be given a "moderate abatement" of taxes if they cultivate a certain portion of their own land (*WN* V.ii.c.15). This is one of the few occasions when Smith shows any interest in encouraging "projectors." Smith reasons that a landlord's greater capital would give him an opportunity to conduct "experiments" in cultivation. He warns, however, that landlords should only be encouraged to cultivate a small portion of their land because more would be outside the range of their attention and, therefore, likely to be mismanaged.

43. For a subtle discussion of Smith's remarks on technology and warfare, see Minowitz, *Profits, Priests, and Princes,* pp. 109–13.

44. Varying degrees of support for the following policies may be found in Smith's writings: guarantees of fair trading practices; protections for slaves and workers; preventing the engrossment of land in new colonies; temporarily halting corn exports during a dearth; providing for public health; and permitting copyrights and patents. See Viner, "Adam Smith and Laissez Faire," p. 237.

45. This proposal has always shocked free-market economists. It provoked a

famous attack by Jeremy Bentham. His "letters" of 1787 and 1790 are reprinted in *Correspondence,* pp. 386–404.

46. At one point Smith seems to imply (remarkably) that North Americans engage in "unnecessary and excessive enterprize" and were "too eager to become excessively rich" (*WN* V.iii.87).

47. Caton, "Preindustrial Economics of Adam Smith," p. 837.

48. Smith, in passing, gives his support to patents and copyrights for limited terms (*WN* V.i.e.30).

49. Smith was not the first to speak of the pacifying effect of commerce, but because he provided such a compelling economic argument for free trade he was certainly one of the most important. For Smith's influence on the Manchester School, see Geoffrey Blainey, *The Causes of War* (New York: Free Press, 1973), pp. 19–20.

50. Smith suggests that bounties on gunpowder and sailcloth perhaps might be vindicated under this principle (*WN* IV.v.36). He also notes that fine manufactures might be useful during the conduct of a war because they are valuable and easily transportable goods for exchange (*WN* IV.i.30).

51. Cf *WN* V.ii.k.12.

52. Jacob Viner, "Power versus Plenty as Objectives of Foreign Policy in the Seventeenth and Eighteenth Centuries," (1948), in *The Long View and the Short,* p. 293.

53. Hume, "Of Commerce," pp. 253–55, praised "abstruse thinkers" who can delineate the general principles that ought to guide statesmen. He distinguished between these general principles and "particular deliberations."

54. See Aristotle, *The Politics,* trans. Carnes Lord (Chicago: University of Chicago Press, 1984), book VI, chap. 5, sec. 1: "But instituting is not the greatest or only task of the legislator or of those wanting to constitute some regime of this sort, but rather to see that it is preserved; for it is not difficult to be governed in one fashion or another for one, two or three days."

55. See David Stevens, "Adam Smith and the Colonial Disturbances," in *Essays on Adam Smith,* pp. 202–17.

56. It appears that Smith was the author of a memorandum on American affairs sent to his friend Alexander Wedderburn, North's solicitor general, who was at the center of discussions on American policy ("Smith's Thoughts on the State of the Contest with America, February 1778," *Correspondence,* App. B., pp. 377–85).

57. On the issue of taxation and liberty, see Smith's remarkable claim that "Every tax . . . is to the person who pays it a badge, not of slavery, but of liberty. It denotes that he is subject to government, indeed, but that, as he has some property, he cannot himself be the property of a master" (*WN* V.ii.g.11). Cf. *WN* IV.vii.b.44.

CHAPTER 3: HAMILTON AND THE
FOUNDATION OF THE COMMERCIAL REPUBLIC

1. "The Examination, No. III," December 24, 1801, *Papers,* vol. 25, p. 467.

2. "The Continentalist, No. I," July 12, 1781, ibid., vol. 2, pp. 649–52.

3. H to unknown addressee, December 1779, ibid., vol. 2, p. 250.

4. Ibid., p. 248 (emphasis added).

5. Ibid., p. 242.

6. "The Farmer Refuted," February 23, 1775, ibid., vol. 1, p. 94; "The Continentalist, No. V," ibid., vol. 3, p. 77; Hamilton, Madison, and Jay, *The Federalist,* no. 85, p. 526; "Remarks at the Constitutional Convention," June 22, 1787, *Papers,* vol. 4, p. 217;

"Defense of the Funding System," July 1795, *Papers,* vol. 19, p. 67. Hume praises "abstruse thinkers" in "Of Commerce," pp. 253–55.

7. Jacques Necker, *De l'administration des finances de la France* (Paris, 1784), vol. 3, chap. 30, pp. 376–78. (My translation.) See also Necker's contrast of the "hypothetical reckonings" of a geometrician with the more complex kind of reasonings that must characterize public affairs (vol. 2, chap. 11, p. 358).

8. Steuart, *Inquiry,* pp. 8, 124–25, 339, 356–58, 466, 537, 548–50. To explain what Steuart meant by *systèmes,* Skinner's editorial note (p. 8 n. 9) draws attention to a passage in Melon: "One calls a system an assemblage of several propositions linked together, such that the consequences tend to establish a truth or an opinion" (Jean Melon, "Essai politique sur le commerce," in *Économistes-financiers du XVIII siècle,* ed. Eugène Daire (Paris: Guillamin, 1843), chap. 25, p. 820; my translation).

9. John Rae, *Life of Adam Smith* (New York: Augustus M. Kelley, 1964), p. 206; Smith to William Pulteney, *Correspondence,* no. 132, p. 164. Looking forward, one may note similarities between Hamilton and Keynes, who wrote that the

> object of our analysis is not to provide a machine, or method of blind manipulation, which will furnish an infallible answer, but to provide ourselves with an organized and orderly method of thinking out particular problems; and, after we have reached a provisional conclusion by isolating the complicating factors one by one, we have to go back on ourselves and allow, as best we can, for the probable interaction of the factors amongst themselves. This is the nature of economic thinking. (*General Theory,* pp. 297–98)

See also Malthus, *Principles of Political Economy,* pp. 11–12, on the problem of speaking of general rules that are subject to many exceptions.

10. "The Continentalist, No. V," *Papers,* vol. 3, p. 81.

11. "Opinion on the Constitutionality of an Act to Establish a Bank," February 23, 1791, ibid., vol. 8, p. 132.

12. "The Continentalist, No. IV," ibid., vol. 2, p. 670. See Connant, *Constitution and the Economy,* pp. 88–92; and William Letwin, "The Economic Policy of the Constitution," in *Liberty, Property, and the Foundations of the American Constitution,* ed. Ellen Frankel Paul and Howard Dickman (Albany, N.Y.: State University Press, 1989), pp. 124–25.

13. McCoy, *Elusive Republic,* pp. 79–80, 84–85.

14. In Pelatiah Webster, *Political Essays* (New York: B. Franklin, 1969), pp. 65–66, 24.

15. "The Continentalist, No. V," *Papers,* vol. 3, pp. 76–78.

16. Elkins and McKitrick, *Age of Federalism,* p. 107.

17. On Hume, see Eugene Rotwein, *David Hume: Writings on Economics* (Madison: University of Wisconsin Press, 1970), pp. lxxvi–lxxvii.

18. "The Continentalist, No. V," *Papers,* vol. 3, p. 77.

19. H to unknown addressee, December 1779, ibid., vol. 2, p. 250.

20. "The Continentalist, No. V," ibid., vol. 3, p. 76.

21. Louis M. Hacker argues that Hamilton changed his mind on the subject of free trade (*Alexander Hamilton in the American Tradition* (New York: McGraw-Hill, 1957), p. 166. For a similar view of Hamilton as a Smithian, see W. D. Grampp, "Adam Smith and the American Revolutionists," *History of Political Economy,* 11 (Summer 1979), p. 180.

22. "The Examination, No. III," *Papers,* vol. 25, p. 467.

23. For example, McDonald notes a gradual refinement in Hamilton's views on banking (*Alexander Hamilton,* pp. 39–41).

24. "H to Lafayett," October 6, 1789, *Papers,* vol. 5, pp. 425–27.

25. "Views on the French Revolution," 1794, ibid., vol. 26, p. 739.

26. Hamilton, Madison, and Jay, *The Federalist,* no. 9, p. 72.

27. "The Stand, No. III," April 7, 1798, *Papers,* vol. 21, pp. 404–5; "Views on the French Revolution," 1794, *Papers,* vol. 26, p. 739.

28. See McDonald, *Alexander Hamilton,* pp. 231, 240, 244, 249; and Nelson, *Liberty and Property,* pp. 37, 39, 49–50.

29. On the meaning of modernization, see H. W. Arndt, *Economic Development: The History of an Idea* (Chicago: University of Chicago Press, 1987), pp. 111–12.

30. Hamilton, Madison, and Jay, *The Federalist,* no. 72, p. 437. On Hamilton's political thought, see Harvey Flaumenhaft, *The Effective Republic: Administration and Constitution in the Thought of Alexander Hamilton* (Durham, N.C.: Duke University Press, 1992); Morton Frisch, *Alexander Hamilton and the Political Order* (Lanham, Md.: University Press of America, 1991); and Stourzh, *Alexander Hamilton.*

31. Montesquieu, *Spirit of the Laws* VIII.16 p. 124.

32. "Constitutional Convention Speech on a Plan of Government," *Papers,* vol. 4, p. 193.

33. Hamilton, Madison, and Jay, *The Federalist,* no. 6, p. 56, and no. 8, p. 71.

34. Ibid., no. 6, p. 54.

35. Ibid., no. 8, pp. 66–69.

36. Ibid., no. 6, p. 57.

37. Ibid., no. 8, p. 69. On war and finance, see "Defense of the Funding System," July 1795, *Papers,* vol. 19, pp. 56–57.

38. Hamilton, Madison, and Jay, *The Federalist,* no. 6, pp. 58–59. See also Hamilton's analysis of the war parties during the tensions with Great Britain in 1794 (H to Washington, 1794, *Papers,* vol. 16, p. 267). Some Americans, under the influence of "speculative ideas," had been led to "hector and vapor" against Great Britain but either had not acknowledged or, more likely, had not realized that war would result from their actions.

39. Also Hamilton, Madison, and Jay, *The Federalist,* no. 22, p. 144.

40. Ibid., pp. 62–63.

41. Ibid. Note that Hamilton speaks of the enterprising spirit that characterizes the "commercial part" of the country. In the agricultural parts of the country, this spirit was not as strong. On the character of the South, see letters to John Jay, March 14, 1779, and to John Laurens, September 11, 1779, *Papers,* vol. 2, pp. 17–19, 165–69. See also the discussion of regional differences at the "New York Ratifying Convention, Speech of June 20," 1788, *Papers,* vol. 5, pp. 22–23, and "Constitutional Convention Remarks on Equality of Representation of the States in Congress," June 29, 1787, *Papers,* vol. 4, pp. 220–23.

42. Hamilton, Madison, and Jay, *The Federalist,* no. 7, p. 64.

43. Ibid., no. 11, p. 90.

44. "The Continentalist, No. V," April 18, 1782, *Papers,* vol. 3, p. 82.

45. Hamilton, Madison, and Jay, *The Federalist,* no. 12, pp. 41–92.

46. "Report on Manufactures," December 5, 1791, *Papers,* vol. 10, p. 294.

47. "New York Ratifying Convention, Third Speech of June 21," 1788, ibid., vol. 5, p. 58.

48. Consider, for example, H to James Bayard, April 16–21, 1802, ibid., vol. 25, p. 606; and "The Examination, No. XVII," March 20, ibid., vol. 25, p. 576.

49. Hamilton, Madison, and Jay, *The Federalist*, no. 34, 207; Hamilton, Madison, and Jay, *The Federalist*, no. 30, 191.

50. "Opinion on Constitutionality of an Act to Establish a Bank," February 23, 1791, *Papers*, vol. 8, p. 105.

51. Ibid., pp. 122, 126–27, 132. Hamilton cited the following powers: to raise taxes; to raise loans; to regulate commerce; to provide for the common defense; and to make provisions for the property of the United States.

52. Ibid., pp. 102, 105–7, 131.

53. I neglect Hamilton's efforts in the field of public administration, strictly speaking, in order to concentrate on his political economy. Any complete assessment of Hamilton's accomplishments ought to take into account the remarkable efficiency with which his Treasury Department operated. See Leonard White, *The Federalists: A Study in Administrative History* (New York: Macmillan, 1948), pp. 50–66, 88–96, 116–27.

54. McDonald, *Alexander Hamilton*, pp. 135–36.

55. See the editor's introduction to the "First Report on Public Credit," *Papers*, vol. 6, p. 61.

56. Hamilton's stress on the importance of public credit for national security is confirmed by Paul Kennedy's consideration of war and finance in the eighteenth century, *The Rise and Fall of the Great Powers: Economic Change and Military Conflict from 1500 to 2000* (London: Fontana Press, 1989), pp. 98–111.

57. H to Washington, May 28, 1790, *Papers*, vol. 6, p. 438. On the importance of establishing good habits in a new republic, see "Second Letter from Phocion," April 1784, *Papers*, vol. 3, pp. 553, 556–58. This aspect of Hamilton's program is discussed in Mackubin Thomas Owens, "The Surest Guardian of Liberty: Hamiltonian Statesmanship and the Creation of the American Union" (Ph.D. diss., University of Dallas, 1982), pp. 113–39.

58. The congressional debate is reviewed by McDonald, *Alexander Hamilton*, pp. 171–88. E. A. J. Johnson discusses the broader opposition to Hamilton's plan in *The Foundations of American Economic Freedom: Government and Enterprise in the Age of Washington* (Minneapolis: University of Minnesota Press, 1973), pp. 101–19. See also Elkins and McKitrick, *Age of Federalism*, pp. 133–62, for an account of the opposition with particular reference to Madison.

59. "First Report on Public Credit," *Papers*, vol. 6, pp. 73–76.

60. "Report on a Plan for the Further Support of Public Credit," January 16, 1795, ibid., vol. 18, p. 119; H to Washington, May 28, 1790, ibid., vol. 6, p. 436. It was Madison who dubbed Hamilton's January 16, 1795, "Report on a Plan for the Further Support of Public Credit" his "arrogant valedictory Report" (ibid., vol. 18, p. 47, n. 2).

61. Cf. "Conjectures about the new Constitution," September 17–30, 1787, ibid., vol. 4, p. 175.

62. John Marshall, *John Marshall: Major Opinions and Writings*, ed. John Roche (New York: Bobbs-Merrill, 1967), p. 158.

63. Hamilton would have agreed with Marshall's decision in *Fletcher* v. *Peck* (1810), which held that land grants are charters and with his dissent in *Ogden* v. *Saunders* (1827), where he argued that state bankruptcy laws involved an interference with the obligation of contracts. See, respectively, Alexander Hamilton, *The Law Practice of Alexander Hamilton*, ed. Julius Goelbels and Joseph Smith (New York: Columbia University Press, 1980), vol. 4, pp. 356–435; and H to Stephen Van Rensselaer, January 27,

1799, *Papers*, vol. 22, pp. 442–43. Marshall, however, did not embrace Hamilton's very broad reading of the "general welfare" clause.

64. Forrest McDonald, "The Constitution and Hamiltonian Capitalism," in *How Capitalist Is the Constitution?* ed. Robert A. Goldwin and William S. Schambra (Washington, D.C.: American Enterprise Institute, 1982), pp. 57–64.

65. H to Washington, May 28, 1790, *Papers*, vol. 6, pp. 436–37. Hamilton's belief in the power of the example of the national government is also illustrated in his attitude toward the question of whether the national government should issue paper money—that is, "emit bills of credit"—a power the constitution explicitly denied to the states. Hamilton argues that the national government does in principle have this power but that it would be unwise to use it. Hamilton did not object to paper money issued by banks. See "Second Report on Public Credit," December 13, 1790, *Papers*, vol. 7, pp. 321–22.

66. Settlement of these debts was fraught with difficulty, because of poor record keeping and because there were suspicions that some states had engaged in activities not directly connected with the war effort. Hamilton thought it would have been better had each state renounced its particular claims and proceeded "on the principle that each state in the war had exerted itself to the full extent of its faculties." This "great and liberal measure" was impossible because of conflicts among the states. See "Defense of the Funding System," July 1795, ibid., vol. 19, pp. 44–45.

67. "First Report on Public Credit," ibid., vol. 6, pp. 80–81; and "Defense of the Funding System," July 1795, ibid., vol. 19, p. 30.

68. "Defense of the Funding System," vol. 19, pp. 30–31, 36–37.

69. Ibid., p. 32.

70. Ibid., pp. 39–40.

71. Ibid., p. 41; Charles Beard, *An Economic Interpretation of the Constitution of the United States* (New York: Free Press, 1913), pp. 100–101.

72. "Defense of the Funding System," July 1795, *Papers*, vol. 19, p. 41. Hamilton's remarks are confirmed indirectly in Nelson's anti-Hamilton argument when he points to the narrowness of the Federalists' electoral support in the 1790s (*Liberty and Property*, pp. 110–11, 165).

73. See Johnson, *Foundations*, pp. 148–51.

74. "Defense of the Funding System," July 1795, *Papers*, vol. 19, p. 36.

75. See "First Report on Public Credit," ibid., vol. 6, pp. 68, 70, 80, 88, 90, 97, 105.

76. Appleby, *Capitalism*, pp. 14, 53–54, 88. Caton remarks perceptively on the Jeffersonian bias of most recent historians of the Federalist era (*Politics of Progress*, p. 479, n. 25).

77. Nelson, *Liberty and Property*, p. 165.

78. In his economic reports, Hamilton frequently remarks on the prospective benefits for all classes. See "First Report on Public Credit," *Papers*, vol. 6, pp. 67–68; "Second Report on Public Credit," *Papers*, vol. 7, pp. 312–13, 327–28; and "Report on Manufactures," *Papers*, vol. 10, p. 294. On the shifting nature of wealth in American society, see "Second Letter from Phocion," *Papers*, vol. 3, p. 553.

79. "Defense of the Funding System," ibid., vol. 19, pp. 29–30, 43.

80. Hamilton, Madison, and Jay, *The Federalist*, no. 30, p. 190.

81. Ibid., no. 12, p. 93.

82. After praising excise taxes, Smith gave an account of Walpole's demise (*WN* V.ii.k.40).

83. Hamilton had made this tactic clear to Washington (H to Washington, August 18, 1792, *Papers,* vol. 12, pp. 236–37).

84. Jacob Cooke provides a balanced account of Hamilton's involvement in the Whiskey Rebellion in *Alexander Hamilton* (New York: Charles Scribner's Sons, 1982), pp. 146–57. See also Dall W. Forsythe, *Taxation and Political Change in the Young Nation* (New York: Columbia University Press, 1977), pp. 39–51.

85. H to Washington, September 1, 1792, *Papers,* vol. 12, p. 312. Cf. H to John Dickinson, September 25–30, 1783, *Papers,* vol. 3, pp. 451–52, on the means of establishing the authority of new governments.

86. "Tully, No. III," August 28, 1794, ibid., vol. 17, p. 159.

87. H to Washington, August 2, 1794, ibid., p. 16.

88. Cooke, *Alexander Hamilton,* p. 153.

89. Smith provides a helpful discussion of practice at *WN* V.iii.12.

90. H to unknown addressee, December 1779, *Papers,* vol. 2, p. 249.

91. In addition, he attacked the character of the financial classes on the ground that they were useless: "a creditor of the public, considered merely as such has no interest in the good condition of any particular portion of land, or in the good management of any particular portion of capital stock. . . . [I]ts ruin may in some cases be unknown to him, and cannot directly affect him" (*WN* V.iii.56). Variations on this theme appear in the writings of American opponents of the monied interest. See Johnson, *Foundations,* pp. 101–19.

92. "Report on Manufactures," *Papers,* vol. 10, 282.

93. Smith provides a helpful discussion of the nature of sinking funds at *WN* V.iii.27–28. Funding and the sinking fund are discussed by McDonald in *Alexander Hamilton,* pp. 163–88, 223, 248–50, 304–5. On the importance of appearances with respect to sinking funds, see Owens, "Surest Guardian," pp. 134–39.

94. Hamilton, "Report on a Plan for the Further Support of Public Credit," *Papers,* vol. 18, p. 109; "Defense of the Funding System," *Papers,* vol. 19, p. 8; McDonald, *Alexander Hamilton,* pp. 304–5.

95. "Defense of the Funding System," July 1795, *Papers,* vol. 19, p. 62.

96. See McDonald, *Alexander Hamilton,* pp. 222–23, 243–49.

97. With the debt selling below par, yields would be above current interest rates; that is, the government would be paying more than it needed to and would be served better by new borrowings. See "Defense of the Funding System," July 1795, *Papers,* vol. 19, pp. 62–63.

98. "Report on Manufactures," *Papers,* vol. 10, p. 281. Smith discussed the question of public debts in the concluding chapter of the *Wealth of Nations.* That Smith chose to emphasize the "colonial disturbances" and the debt problem in his last words to his readers is a significant indication of the priority he accorded them. He warned of a coming crisis due to the high levels of indebtedness that characterized most European governments. Smith considered and rejected the argument that the public debts are a species of capital which contributes to trade and industry (*WN* V.iii.47). His argument relied on his distinction between productive labor and unproductive labor. The accumulation of public debt involves the destruction of an already existing capital, because a quantity of purchasing power is spent by the government on an activity that does not give rise to a vendible commodity. Smith believed that the fallacies of the mercantile system were the source of the contrary view. His argument tries to dispel the illusion that the purchasing power remains alive in the form of the security issued by the government—which, he grants, may be exchanged for money. Smith's view may be traced back to his understanding of labor

as the "original purchase money" of all things. A commodity represents the various transformations of raw materials provided by nature that labor has produced. A capital is such a commodity or the representation of an existing commodity in terms of money.

99. "Defense of the Funding System," *Papers*, vol. 19, p. 68.

100. Ibid.

101. "Report on Manufactures," ibid., vol. 10, pp. 277–79.

102. "Defense of the Funding System," ibid., vol. 19, p. 67.

103. "Report on Manufactures," ibid., vol. 10, p. 281. Hume, for example, noted the effect of the public debt as a species of capital, although he attacked public debt in general ("Of Public Credit," in *Essays*, p. 93). Hume was concerned about the long-run consequences of the debt. He took a similar position on the closely related issue of the effects of an expansion of the money supply ("Of Money," in *Essays*, pp. 286–87). Keynes, *General Theory*, p. 343, remarked that Hume "had a foot and a half in the classical world. For Hume began the practice among economists of stressing the importance of the equilibrium position as compared with the ever shifting transition towards it, though he was still enough of a mercantilist not to overlook the fact that it is in the transition that we actually have our being." Smith denied the significance of the transition phase altogether in his treatment of money: cf. *LJB* 253: "[Hume] seems however to have gone a little into the notion that public opulence consists in money." As McDonald observes, Steuart's views appear to be closest to Hamilton's (Forrest McDonald, *Novus Ordo Seclorum* [Lawrence: University Press of Kansas, 1985], pp. 137–42). Steuart, *Inquiry*, pp. 406–7, held that "Symbolical or paper money is but a species of credit: it is no more than the measure by which credit is reckoned." It is a promise to be fulfilled in the *future* and thus does not necessarily represent a commodity that exists *now*.

104. "Report on Manufactures," *Papers*, vol. 10, pp. 281–82.

105. "First Report on Public Credit," ibid., vol. 6, pp. 87–88. Congress adopted a less-sophisticated but more politically acceptable plan based on a clumsy formula. The compromise forced Hamilton to change his plan to monetize the debt in certain ways. See McDonald, *Alexander Hamilton*, pp. 185–88, 192–93.

106. "First Report on Public Credit," *Papers*, vol. 6, p. 97.

107. Bray Hammond has argued that Hamilton was one of the first great theorists of central banking; and he draws attention to Hamilton's origination of fractional-reserve requirements (*Banks and Politics in America* [Princeton, N.J.: Princeton University Press, 1957], pp. 142–43). On Hamilton's intentions and use of precedents, see McDonald, *Alexander Hamilton*, pp. 194–95.

108. Hamilton was aware of Smith's argument. See H to Washington, August 18, 1792, *Papers*, vol. 12, p. 244. For Smith's discussion of paper money in North America, see *WN* V.iii.78–87. "Bank money" refers to bank-issued credits, promissory notes, and so forth that serve the purposes of money. The confidence that this paper can be converted into money at any time is what keeps it in circulation.

109. "Opinion on Constitutionality of an Act to Establish a Bank," *Papers*, vol. 8, p. 126.

110. "Second Report on Public Credit," ibid., vol. 7, pp. 310, 318; "Report on Manufactures," ibid., vol. 10, pp. 288–89.

111. "Second Report on Public Credit," ibid., vol. 7, p. 316 (emphasis added).

112. Cf. *WN* IV.i.4, 20–30. In the course of this discussion, Smith did note that sophisticated manufactures may be useful for raising funds during a war because of their high value and small bulk.

113. "Second Report on Public Credit," *Papers*, vol. 7, p. 316. Hamilton, Madi-

son, and Jay, *The Federalist,* no. 12, pp. 91–92 (emphasis added). Cf. Hume "Of Money," p. 37: "in every kingdom, into which money begins to flow in greater abundance than formerly, everything takes a new face: labour and industry gain life; the merchant becomes more enterprising, the manufacturer more diligent and skillful, and even the farmer follows his plough with greater alacrity and attention."

114. "Second Report on Public Credit," *Papers,* vol. 7, p. 318.

115. Hamilton regarded the rate of interest as simply reflecting the abundance or scarcity of money. This was another case in which he did not enter into an analysis of the "real" forces that might determine interest rates. See "First Report on Public Credit," ibid., vol. 6, p. 71; and "Second Report on Public Credit," ibid., vol. 7, p. 318.

116. "Second Report on Public Credit," *Papers,* vol. 7, p. 321. Johnson, *Foundations,* pp. 123–26, suggests that Hamilton's understanding of the balance-of-payments problem facing the United States was the organizing principle of his whole program.

117. "Second Report on Public Credit," *Papers,* vol. 7, p. 325.

118. *Hamilton,* p. 227. See also McDonald, *Novus Ordo Seclorum,* p. 140.

119. H to unknown addressee, December 1779, *Papers,* vol. 2, pp. 244, n. 6, 245.

120. "Second Report on Public Credit," ibid., vol. 7, p. 331.

121. "Report on Manufactures," ibid., vol. 10, pp. 282, 296. Again the language is very similar to Hume ("Of Refinement in the Arts," in *Essays,* p. 271). See also McDonald, *Novus Ordo Seclorum,* pp. 140–41.

122. Nelson, *Liberty and Property,* pp. 37–51.

123. "Report on Manufactures," *Papers,* vol. 10, p. 313.

124. Ibid., pp. 231–32.

125. Ibid., p. 235.

126. The first American edition of the *Wealth of Nations* was published in 1789. The book was, however, well known among educated Americans before this (Teichgraeber, "Less Abused," p. 344.) Henry Cabot Lodge claims that Hamilton wrote a now lost commentary on the *Wealth of Nations* around 1782 (Alexander Hamilton, *The Works of Alexander Hamilton,* ed. Henry Cabot Lodge [New York: G. P. Putnam's Sons, 1904], vol. 3, p. 417, n. 1. There is no evidence for Lodge's contention, although it is clear that Hamilton was quite familiar with Smith by the time of his great reports.

127. Hamilton described Jefferson as "a disciple of Turgot" and a "pupil of Condorcet" ("The Examination, No. III," January 18, 1802, *Papers,* vol. 25, p. 501). Turgot was something of a bridge between Smith and the Physiocrats, although Smith was hardly generous in acknowledging his influence. Condorcet, one of the most enthusiastic of believers in human perfectibility, embraced Smithian political economy wholesale, publishing a 220-page summary of the *Wealth of Nations* in 1791 as part of the *Bibliothèque de l'homme public: ou analyse raisonée des principaux ouvrages françois et étrangers* (ed. M. de Cordorcet, M. de Paysonel, M. Le Chapelier). See Rothschild, *Adam Smith and Conservative Economics,* p. 75. Smith and the Physiocrats were frequently, if selectively, referred to approvingly by many Republicans. See Johnson, *Foundations,* pp. 72–100, 152–92; and Caton, *Politics of Progress,* p. 506, n. 65.

128. "Report on Manufactures," *Papers,* vol. 10, pp. 240–42.

129. Ibid., pp. 243–45.

130. Ibid. pp. 246, 249.

131. Caton, *Politics of Progress,* p. 473. In "Preindustrial Economics of Adam Smith," Caton comments on the difficulty that mainstream economics has had dealing with the uncertainty inherent in technological change.

132. "Report on Manufactures," *Papers,* vol. 10, p. 255. Owens interprets this as

an expression of Hamilton's concern with the perfection of human nature ("Surest Guardian," pp. 159–66).

133. "Report on Manufactures," *Papers,* vol. 10, p. 256.

134. Ibid., vol. 2, p. 635.

135. H to Laurens, September 11, 1779, ibid., p. 167.

136. Hamilton, Madison, and Jay, *The Federalist,* no. 11, p. 88.

137. Washington to H, August 10, 1796, Washington to H, November 2, 1796, *Papers,* vol. 20, pp. 362–66. See also Washington to Arthur Young, December 5, 1791, in George Washington, *George Washington: A Collection,* ed. W. B. Allen (Indianapolis, Ind.: Liberty Classics, 1988), pp. 558–61.

138. Thomas Jefferson, "Notes on the State of Virginia," Query XIX, *Life and Selected Writings,* p. 280.

139. "Report on Manufactures," *Papers,* vol. 10, pp. 241–42, 257.

140. Ibid., pp. 257–58, 260–61, 265, 293–96.

141. Jefferson and many Republicans shared these views. Along with the Anti-Federalists, they saw high finance and manufacturing as productive of dissipation and idleness. In *Capitalism,* pp. 90–91, however, Appleby contends that the work ethic was less a part of the republican vision than the "hope of widespread 'comfort'" (as distinct from luxury). See also Owens, "Surest Guardian," p. 144.

142. The discussion is very reminiscent of Necker, *Treatise,* vol. 2, chap. 4, pp. 199–200.

143. "Report on Manufactures," *Papers,* vol. 10, p. 262.

144. McCoy, *Elusive Republic,* pp. 209–35.

145. In "The Continentalist, No. III" (*Papers,* vol. 2, p. 663), he noted that it was common for Americans to misjudge the strength of Great Britain. Hamilton himself was at one time guilty of this error. See "The Farmer Refuted," *Papers,* vol. 1, pp. 155–60.

146. H to Washington, April 14, 1794, ibid., vol. 16, pp. 266–79.

147. Madison's desire to impose tariff duties that penalized certain nations was more in the interest of changing the "channels" of American trade than in stimulating manufacturing. In his speeches of April and May 1789 he emphasized again and again the unnatural or artificial relationship between the United States and Great Britain. See James Madison, *Papers of James Madison,* ed. William T. Hutchison (Chicago: University of Chicago Press, 1962–), vol. 12, pp. 71, 73, 98, 100, 110, 112, 127–30. Fisher Ames commented on Madison's heavy reliance on Smith (Letter to George Minot, May 29, 1789, in *Works of Fisher Ames,* ed. William B. Allen [Indianapolis, Ind.: Liberty Classics, 1983], p. 638).

148. "Report on Manufactures," *Papers,* vol. 10, p. 266–68.

149. Ibid., pp. 266–67, 340.

150. Ibid., p. 301. Necker dismissed complaints about the injustice of trade regulations, arguing that they were really complaints about "imaginary misfortune" (*De l'administration des finances de la France,* vol. 2, chap. iv, p. 198).

151. "Report on Manufactures," *Papers,* vol. 10, p. 286.

152. Hamilton, Madison, and Jay, *The Federalist,* no. 11, p. 90. Steuart offered an elaborate account of the various phases of growth that created different interests among nations, but Hamilton did not explicitly draw on it (Steuart, *Inquiry,* pp. 228, 260–65, 394).

153. Forsythe, *Taxation,* p. 61.

154. He recommended that certain materials of manufacture be exempted from duties and that there be drawbacks—that is, refunds—of duties on materials used in

manufacturing ("Report on Manufactures," *Papers,* vol. 10, pp. 305–6).

155. In *Liberty and Property,* pp. 80–89, 150, 156–57, Nelson argues that a capital shortage was the chief problem for manufacturers and notes a proposal of Gallatin's for direct loans to manufacturers as evidence that Hamilton did not really want to encourage manufactures. Hamilton's failure to propose such a measure hardly warrants the conclusion that he "was not an advocate of American manufacturing." He probably thought direct loans were simply a bad idea. They would be as unpopular as bounties—if not more so—and very risky. Furthermore, Hamilton's entire financial scheme was designed to increase the supply of capital in the nation. Nelson also notes that Hamilton did not give manufacturers what they really wanted; namely, very high levels of protection. But, as I note below, Hamilton did not think this was good economic policy, whatever the politics of the issue. Hamilton eventually realized that the Federalists had lost control of the cities. This was part of a general realization that more "popular" measures were necessary. See H to Bayard, April 16–21, 1802, *Papers,* vol. 25, pp. 605–10.

156. "Report on Manufactures," ibid., vol. 10, p. 297.

157. Ibid., p. 299. Bounties were subsidies given for the production of specific commodities. Smith was severely critical of the practice. See, for example, *WN* IV.v.a.24, 37; *WN* IV.viii.15,53–54; *WN* V.ii.k.38.

158. "Report on Manufactures," *Papers,* vol. 10, pp. 299, 301–2.

159. Ibid., pp. 303, 310.

160. Ibid., pp. 304, 309.

161. Ibid., p. 291.

162. An active commerce is one that is carried out in the nation's own ships.

163. Caton, *Politics of Progress,* p. 475. As we have seen, however, Hamilton was not simply a mercantilist.

164. "Second Draft of the Report on the Subject of Manufactures," *Papers,* vol. 10, p. 52.

165. Hamilton, Madison, and Jay, *The Federalist,* no. 71, p. 432.

166. See, especially, Flaumenhaft, *Effective Republic,* pp. 69–132.

167. Jefferson, *Life and Selected Writings,* pp. 121–24.

168. McCoy, *Elusive Republic,* pp. 236–59. In *Capitalism,* pp. 104–5, Appleby rejects McCoy's linking of the Republicans with the classical republican tradition and argues that they embraced a progressive commercial vision of the future. But her reconsideration of Jeffersonian political economy also ends on a pessimistic note. Contemporary capitalism is no longer a force for producing equality. A consideration of Hamilton's more optimistic outlook would seem to be warranted.

169. David Hume, "Of the Rise and Progress of the Arts and Sciences," in *Essays,* p. 130.

170. David Hume, "Of the Populousness of Ancient Nations," in ibid., p. 420. See also Hume's "Of Commerce," in ibid., pp. 260–64; "Of Taxes," in ibid., pp. 344–45; and "Of Interest," in ibid., pp. 299–301.

171. Steuart, *Inquiry,* pp. 265–69.

172. "Report on a Plan for the Further Support of Public Credit," January 16, 1795, *Papers,* vol. 18, p. 109.

173. "Defense of the Funding System," July 1795, ibid., vol. 19, p. 59.

174. Ibid., p. 52. Cf. Hamilton's favorite poet, Alexander Pope, "An Essay on Man," in *Poetry and Prose of Alexander Pope,* ed. Aubrey Williams (Boston: Houghton Mifflin, 1969), p. 155: "Virtue alone is happiness below."

175. "Defense of the Funding System," *Papers,* vol. 19, pp. 60–61.

176. For example, "Second Report on Public Credit," ibid., vol. 7, pp. 314–15; and "Report on Manufactures," ibid., vol. 10, p. 282.

177. See Owens, "Surest Guardian," pp. 69–77, 152–58, 290–94.

178. Ralph Lerner, "Commerce and Character: The Anglo-American as New-Model Man," *William and Mary Quarterly* 36, no. 1 (1979):13.

179. Hume, "Of Commerce," p. 261.

180. "Draft of Washington's Eighth Annual Message to Congress," November 10, 1796, *Papers,* vol. 10, p. 385. See also H to Jonathan Dayton, October-November 1799, *Papers,* vol. 23, p. 603.

181. "Draft of Washington's Farewell Address," July 30, 1796, ibid., vol. 20, pp. 265, 280.

182. See his *The Effective Republic.*

183. Caton, *Politics of Progress,* p. 477. Cf. Hamilton, Madison, and Jay, *The Federalist,* no. 35, pp. 214–17. Caton notes Hamilton's anticipation of de Tocqueville regarding the place of lawyers in American political culture. At the Constitutional Convention, Gouverneur Morris remarked that "the Busy haunts of men not the remote wilderness was the proper school of political talents" (James Madison, *Notes of Debates in the Federal Convention of 1787 Reported by James Madison* [New York: W. W. Norton, 1969], p. 271).

CONCLUSION

1. Consider the remarkable and generally unacknowledged dependence on Hamilton's thinking that is evident in Henry Clay's "Speech on Tariff" of March 30–31, 1824, in *The Papers of Henry Clay,* ed. James F. Hopkins (Lexington: University of Kentucky Press, 1963), vol. 3, pp. 683–730. Note, in particular, Clay's contention (p. 718) that without a balanced economy America risked "demoralization" (that is, a loss of morality) and his praise (p. 720) of Napoleon's criticism of "modern systematizers." It must be added that Hamilton did not advocate a protective tariff. He thought there were more effective and less divisive ways to encourage manufactures.

2. For a recent and thorough account of current practice as well as theory on economic development, especially in the newly industrializing countries, see Stephen Haggard, *Pathways from the Periphery: The Politics of Growth in the Newly Industrializing Countries* (Ithaca, N.Y.: Cornell University Press, 1990). Haggard points to the significant role that government has played in the economic development of these countries, especially in the early stages of industrialization.

3. Alexander Rosenberg, *Economics: Mathematical Economics or Science of Diminishing Returns* (Chicago: University of Chicago Press, 1992), p. 230. In addition, see his critique of Milton Friedman's notion that economists can neglect reflecting on the realism of their assumptions because the scientific status of economics rests not upon this but upon its capacity to make predictions. Rosenberg points to the inability of economists to make anything more than generic predictions and to their failure to improve the accuracy of their predictions, something that would be an essential criterion for success in any other natural or social science (chap. 3). Rosenberg, however, understates the usefulness of mainstream economics, first as a practical rule of thumb and second as a political corollary to the classical liberalism out of which it originated.

4. Milton Friedman described as "mischievous" Smith's suggestion that the state has a broad duty to erect and maintain certain public works and institutions. "Adam Smith's Relevance for 1976," in *Adam Smith and the Wealth of Nations: Bicentennial Es-*

says, 1776–1976, ed. Fred F. Glahe (Boulder, Colo.: Colorado Associated University Press, 1978), p. 13. Some free-market advocates have criticized Smith for more fundamental reasons. The Austrian School objects to Smith for many of the same reasons I have advanced here. See Rothbard, *Economic Thought,* pp. 433–74. Yet they seem to want to have their cake and eat it too, in that they continue to share Smith's faith that economics is a science.

5. Caton includes Hamilton's views among the "industrial critiques" of Smith's political economy in "Preindustrial Economics of Adam Smith," pp. 846–49.

6. This was grasped clearly by Carl Menger when he wrote disapprovingly of Smith's "one-sided rationalistic liberalism" and his "not infrequently impetuous effort to do away with what exists." *Investigations into the Method of the Social Sciences,* trans. Francis J. Nock (New York: New York University Press, 1985), p. 177.

7. I do not mean to minimize the differences between Aristotle and Machiavelli on the issue of statesmanship, merely to point to the common ground they make against Smith (cf. Strauss, *Natural Right and History,* p. 178). Consider, in this regard, Smith's remarkable plan for an imperial union that would diffuse the "colonial disturbances," in part, by distracting the leading men of North America from their desire to be statesmen and legislators by showing to them the "dazzling" prizes to be gained in British politics (*WN* IV.vii.c.74–76).

8. See Kurt Riezler, "The Philosopher of History and the Modern Statesman," *Social Research* 13, no. 3 (1946):368–80, esp. 372–73.

9. There is a certain enthusiasm for Hamilton today among liberal planners. See, for example, Michael Lind, *The Next American Nation: The New Nationalism and the Fourth American Revolution* (New York: Free Press, 1995), pp. 371–76, 384.

10. Hamilton advocated what today would probably be described as a policy of economic nationalism. But it is important to stress that Hamilton did not see the nation as an organic whole, as, say, List did. Hamilton's commercial republicanism regarded the United States an independent nation dedicated to universal principles of justice. Much could be said about the relevance of Hamilton's example to the "substance" of the development policies of recent decades, but it is perhaps more appropriate for me to address myself in my closing remarks to the "style" of those policies. Since World War II the theory of economic development has been dominated by two schools of thought: structuralism and dependency theory. (For discussions of these theories see Arndt, *Economic Development,* pp. 119–26; and Gilpin, *Political Economy of International Relations,* pp. 273–88.) These theories have had their greatest practical influence in Latin America. Although structuralism is similar in many respects to Hamilton's advocacy of policies for national development, it shares with dependency theory a tendency to blame or indict the structure of the international trading system for impeding growth in the developing world. The reader will recall Hamilton's comment that such observations should not be made in "a spirit of complaint." Hamilton sought to make clear that development was a national responsibility as well as a national concern.

11. Hamilton, Madison, and Jay, *The Federalist,* no.17, p. 118.

12. "Report on Manufactures," *Papers,* vol. 10, p. 154.

13. Letter to Benjamin Austin, January 9, 1816, in Thomas Jefferson, *The Portable Thomas Jefferson,* ed. Merril D. Peterson (New York: Viking Press, 1975), p. 548–49.

14. Franklin D. Roosevelt, "Commonwealth Club Address, September 23, 1932, reprinted in *New Deal Thought,* ed. Howard Zinn (Indianapolis, Ind.: Bobbs-Merrill, 1966), p. 50.

D'Alembert, Jean. *Preliminary Discourse to the Encyclopedia of Diderot.* Translated by Richard N. Schwab. Indianapolis, Ind.: Bobbs-Merrill, 1963.

Ames, Fisher. *Works of Fisher Ames.* Edited by William B. Allen. Indianapolis, Ind.: Liberty Classics, 1983.

Appleby, Joyce. *Capitalism and a New Social Order: The Republican Version of the 1790s.* New York: New York University Press, 1984.

Aristotle. *Nicomachean Ethics.* Translated by Martin Ostwald. Indianapolis, Ind.: Bobbs-Merrill, 1962.

———. *The Politics.* Translated by Carnes Lord. Chicago: University of Chicago Press, 1984.

Arndt, H. W. *Economic Development: The History of an Idea.* Chicago: University of Chicago Press, 1987.

———. *The Rise and Fall of Economic Growth.* Chicago: University of Chicago Press, 1984.

Bacon, Sir Francis. *A Selection of His Works.* Edited by Sidney Warhaft. Indianapolis, Ind.: Odyssey Press, 1981.

Bagehot, Walter. "Adam Smith and Our Modern Economy." In *Economic Studies,* edited by Richard Holt Hutton. Stanford, Calif.: Academic Reprints, 1953.

———. "Adam Smith as a Person." In *Bagehot's Historical Essays.* Garden City, N.Y.: Anchor Books, 1965.

———. "The American Constitution at the Present Crisis." In *Bagehot's Historical Essays.* Garden City, N.Y.: Anchor, 1965.

———. *The English Constitution.* Ithaca, N.Y.: Cornell University Press, 1963.

Banning, Lance. *The Jeffersonian Persuasion: Evolution of a Party Ideology.* Ithaca, N.Y.: Cornell University Press, 1979.

Beard, Charles. *An Economic Interpretation of the Constitution.* New York: Free Press, 1913.

Bladen, Vincent. *From Adam Smith to Maynard Keynes.* Toronto: University of Toronto Press, 1973.

Blainey, Geoffrey. *The Causes of War.* New York: Free Press, 1973.

Blaug, Mark. *Economic Theory in Retrospect.* Homewood, Ill.: Richard D. Irwin, 1968.

Brown, Vivienne. *Adam Smith's Discourse: Canonicity, Commerce, and Conscience.* New York: Routledge, 1994.

Bryce, James. *The American Commonwealth.* 2 vols. London: Macmillan, 1933.

Buchanan, James, and Gordon Tullock. *The Calculus of Consent.* Ann Arbor: University of Michigan Press, 1962.

Burke, Edmund. *Reflections on the Revolution in France.* New York: Library of Liberal Arts, 1955.

Caton, Hiram. *The Politics of Progress: Origins and Development of the Commercial Republic, 1600–1835.* Gainesville: University of Florida Press, 1988.

———. "The Preindustrial Economics of Adam Smith." *Journal of Economic History* 45, no. 4 (1985):833–53.

Ceaser, James. *Liberal Democracy and Political Science.* Baltimore, Md.: Johns Hopkins University Press, 1990.

Chamley, P. E. "The Conflict between Montesquieu and Hume: A Study in the Origins of Adam Smith's Universalism." In *Essays on Adam Smith,* edited by Andrew S. Skinner and Thomas Wilson. Oxford: Clarendon Press, 1975.

Charnwood, Lord. *Abraham Lincoln.* New York: Henry Holt, 1917.

Clay, Henry. *The Papers of Henry Clay.* 10 vols. Edited by James F. Hopkins. Lexington: University of Kentucky Press, 1959–.

Cohen, Edward S. "Justice and Political Economy in Commercial Society: Adam Smith's Science of a Legislator." *Journal of Politics* 51, no. 1 (1989):50–72.

Condercet, M., M. de Peysonel, and M. Le Chapelier, eds. *Bibliotèque de l'homme public: ou analyse raisonée des principaux ouvrages françois et étrangers.* Paris, 1790.

Connant, Michael. *The Constitution and the Economy.* Norman: University of Oklahoma Press, 1991.

Cooke, Jacob. *Alexander Hamilton.* New York: Charles Scribner's Sons, 1982.

Cropsey, Joseph. *Political Philosophy and the Issues of Politics.* Chicago: University of Chicago Press, 1977.

———. *Polity and Economy: An Interpretation of the Principles of Adam Smith.* The Hague: Martinus Nijhoff, 1957.

Danford, John. "Adam Smith, Equality, and the Wealth of Sympathy." *Journal of Political Science* 24, no. 4 (1980):674–95.

Elkins, Stanley, and Eric McKitrick. *The Age of Federalism: The Early American Republic, 1788–1800.* New York: Oxford University Press, 1993.

Fallows, James. *Looking at the Sun: The Rise of a New East Asian Political System.* New York: Pantheon, 1994.

Fitzgibbons, Athol. *Keynes's Vision: A New Political Economy.* New York: Oxford University Press, 1988.

Flaumenhaft, Harvey. *The Effective Republic: Administration and Constitution in the Thought of Alexander Hamilton.* Durham, N.C.: Duke University Press, 1992.

Forbes, Duncan. "Sceptical Whiggism, Commerce and Liberty." In *Essays on Adam Smith,* edited by Andrew S. Skinner and Thomas Wilson. Oxford: Clarendon Press, 1975.

———. "Scientific Whiggism: Adam Smith and John Millar." *Cambridge Journal* no. 7 (August 1954):643–70.

Forsythe, Dall W. *Taxation and Political Change in the Young Nation.* New York: Columbia University Press, 1977.

Friedman, Milton. "Adam Smith's Relevance for 1976." In *Adam Smith and the Wealth of Nations: Bicentennial Essays, 1776–1976,* edited by Fred F. Glahe. Boulder: Colorado Associated University Press, 1978.

Frisch, Morton. *Alexander Hamilton and the Political Order.* Lanham, Md.: University Press of America, 1991.

Galbraith, John K. *Economics and the Public Purpose.* Boston: Houghton Mifflin, 1973.

Gilpin, Robert. *The Political Economy of International Relations.* Princeton, N.J.: Princeton University Press, 1987.

Grampp, W. D. "Adam Smith and the American Revolutionists." *History of Political*

Economy 11 (Summer 1979):179–91.

Green, Donald P., and Ian Shapiro. *Pathologies of Rational Choice Theory.* New Haven, Conn.: Yale University Press, 1994.

Haakonssen, Knud. *The Science of a Legislator: The Natural Jurisprudence of David Hume and Adam Smith.* Cambridge, England: Cambridge University Press, 1981.

Hacker, Louis M. *Alexander Hamilton in the American Tradition.* New York: McGraw-Hill, 1957.

Haggard, Stephen. *Pathways from the Periphery: The Politics of Growth in the Newly Industrializing Countries.* Ithaca, N.Y.: Cornell University Press, 1990.

Hamilton, Alexander. *The Law Practice of Alexander Hamilton.* 5 vols. Edited by Julius Goelbels and Joseph Smith. New York: Columbia University Press, 1964–1981.

———. *The Papers of Alexander Hamilton.* Edited by Harold C. Syrett. 27 vols. New York: Columbia University Press, 1961–1987.

———. *The Works of Alexander Hamilton.* 12 vols. Edited by Henry Cabot Lodge. New York: G. P. Putnam's Sons, 1904.

Hamilton, Alexander, James Madison, and John Jay. *The Federalist.* New York: Mentor, 1961.

Hamilton, Allan McLaine. *The Intimate Life of Alexander Hamilton.* New York: Charles Scribner's Sons, 1911.

Hammond, Bray. *Banks and Politics in America.* Princeton, N.J.: Princeton University Press, 1957.

Hamowy, Ronald. *The Scottish Enlightenment and the Theory of Spontaneous Order.* Carbondale: University of Southern Illinois Press, 1987.

Harpham, Edward. "Liberalism, Civic Humanism, and the Case of Adam Smith." *American Political Science Review* 78 (September 1984):772–73.

Hirschman, Albert O., *The Passions and the Interests: Political Arguments for Capitalism before Its Triumph.* Princeton, N.J.: Princeton University Press, 1977.

Hobbes, Thomas. *Leviathan.* Harmondsworth, England: Penguin Books, 1968.

Hollander, Samuel. *The Economics of Adam Smith.* Toronto: University of Toronto Press, 1973.

———. *The Economics of David Ricardo.* Toronto: University of Toronto Press, 1979.

Hont, Istvan, and Michael Ignatieff. "Justice and Needs in the *Wealth of Nations.*" In *Wealth and Virtue: The Shaping of Political Economy in the Scottish Enlightenment,* edited by Istvan Hont and Michael Ignatieff. Cambridge, England: Cambridge University Press, 1983.

Hume, David. *Essays: Moral, Political and Literary.* Edited by Eugene Miller. Indianapolis, Ind.: Liberty Classics, 1985.

Jefferson, Thomas. *The Life and Selected Writings of Thomas Jefferson.* Edited by Adrienne Koch and William Peden. New York: Modern Library, 1944.

———. *The Portable Thomas Jefferson.* Edited by Merril D. Peterson. New York: Viking Press, 1975.

Johnson, E. A. J. *The Foundations of American Economic Freedom: Government and Enterprise in the Age of Washington.* Minneapolis: University of Minnesota Press, 1973.

Kennedy, Paul. *The Rise and Fall of the Great Powers: Economic Change and Military Conflict from 1500 to 2000.* London: Fontana Press, 1989.

Keynes, John Maynard. *The General Theory of Employment, Interest and Money.* London: Macmillan, 1973.

Kukathas, Chandran. *Hayek and Modern Liberalism.* Oxford: Clarendon Press, 1989.

Kuttner, Robert. *The End of Laissez-Faire: National Purpose and the Global Economy after the Cold War.* New York: Alfred A. Knopf, 1994.

Lerner, Ralph. "Commerce and Character: The Anglo-American as New-Model Man." *William and Mary Quarterly* 36, no. 1 (1979):3–26.

Letwin, William. "The Economic Policy of the Constitution." In *Liberty, Property and the Foundations of the American Constitution,* edited by Ellen Frankel Paul and Howard Dickman. Albany: State University of New York Press, 1989.

Lind, Michael. *The Next American Nation: The New Nationalism and the Fourth American Revolution.* New York: Free Press, 1995.

List, Friedrich. *The National System of Political Economy.* Translated by Sampson S. Lloyd. New York: Longmans, Green, 1904.

Locke, John. "Some Considerations of the Consequences of the Lowering of Interest, and Raising the Value of Money." In *Locke on Money.* Oxford: Clarendon Press, 1991.

———. *Two Treatises of Government.* Edited by Peter Laslett. New York: New American Library, 1963.

Machiavelli, Niccolò. *The Prince.* Translated by Harvey C. Mansfield Jr. Chicago: Chicago University Press, 1985.

Madison, James. *Notes of Debates in the Federal Convention of 1787 Reported by James Madison.* New York: W. W. Norton, 1969.

———. *Papers of James Madison.* Edited by William T. Hutchison. Chicago: University of Chicago Press, 1962–.

Malthus, Thomas Robert. *Principles of Political Economy.* New York: Augustus M. Kelley, 1986.

Manent, Pierre. *La Cité de l'homme.* Paris: Fayard, 1994.

Mansfield, Harvey C., Jr. "Social Science and the Constitution." In *Confronting the Constitution,* edited by Allan Bloom. Washington D.C.: AEI Press, 1990.

Marshall, Alfred. *Principles of Economics.* London: Macmillan, 1920. Reprint London: Macmillan, 1974.

Marshall, John. *John Marshall: Major Opinions and Writings.* Edited by John Roche. New York: Bobbs-Merrill, 1967.

———. *Life of George Washington.* 5 vols. New York: Wm. H. Wise, 1925.

Marx, Karl. *The Marx-Engels Reader.* Edited by Robert C. Tucker. New York: W. W. Norton, 1978.

McCloskey, Donald. *The Rhetoric of Economics.* Madison: University of Wisconsin Press, 1985.

McCoy, Drew R. *The Elusive Republic: Political Economy in Jeffersonian America.* Chapel Hill: University of North Carolina Press, 1980.

McDonald, Forrest. *Alexander Hamilton: A Biography.* New York: W. W. Norton, 1979.

———. "The Constitution and Hamiltonian Capitalism." In *How Capitalist Is the Constitution?* edited by Robert A. Goldwin and William S. Schambra. Washington, D.C.: American Enterprise Institute, 1982.

———. *Novus Ordo Seclorum.* Lawrence: University Press of Kansas, 1985.

McNally, David. *Political Economy and the Rise of Capitalism.* Berkeley: University of California Press, 1988.

Meek, Ronald. *Social Science and the Ignoble Savage.* Cambridge, England: Cambridge University Press, 1975.

Melon, Jean. "Essai politique sur le commerce." In *Économistes-financiers du XVIII siècle,* edited by Eugène Daire. Paris: Guillamin, 1843.

Menger, Carl. *Investigations into the Method of the Social Sciences.* Translated by Francis J. Nock. New York: New York University Press, 1985.

Minowitz, Peter. *Profits, Priests, and Princes: Adam Smith's Emancipation of Economics from Politics and Religion.* Stanford, Calif.: Stanford University Press, 1993.

Mitchell, William C., and Randy T. Simmons. *Beyond Politics: Markets, Welfare, and the Failure of Bureaucracy.* Boulder, Colo.: Westview Press, 1994.

Montesquieu, Baron de. *The Spirit of the Laws.* Translated by Anne M. Cohler, Basia Carolyn Miller, and Harold Samuel Stone. New York: Cambridge University Press, 1989.

Mueller, Dennis. *Public Choice II.* Cambridge, England: Cambridge University Press, 1989.

Muller, Jerry Z. *Adam Smith in His Time and Ours: Designing the Decent Society.* New York: Free Press, 1993.

Mun, Thomas. *England's Treasure by Foreign Trade.* London, 1664. In *Masterworks of Economics,* edited by Leonard D. Talbott. 3 vols. New York: McGraw Hill, 1973.

Necker, Jacques. *De l'administration des finances de la France.* Paris, 1784.

Nelson, John R., Jr. *Liberty and Property: Political Economy and Policy Making in the New nation, 1789–1812.* Baltimore, Md.: Johns Hopkins University Press, 1987.

Owens, Mackubin Thomas. "The Surest Guardian of Liberty: Hamiltonian Statesmanship and the Creation of the American Union." Ph.D. diss., University of Dallas, 1982.

Palgrave's Dictionary of Political Economy. 3 vols. London: MacMillan, 1899. S.v. "Political Economy," by Henry Sedgwick.

Pangle, Thomas L. *Montesquieu's Philosophy of Liberalism: A Commentary on The Spirit of the Laws.* Chicago: University of Chicago Press, 1973.

Plato. *Republic.* Translated by Allan Bloom. New York: Basic Books, 1968.

Quesnai, François. *China: A Model for Europe.* Translated by Lewis A. Maverick. San Antonio, Tex.: Paul Anderson, 1946.

Rae, John. *Life of Adam Smith.* New York: Augustus M. Kelley, 1964.

Rahe, Paul A. *Republics: Ancient and Modern: Classical Republicanism and the American Revolution.* Chapel Hill: University of North Carolina Press, 1992.

Rashid, Salim. "Adam Smith's Interpretation of the History of Economics and Its Influence in the 18th and 19th Centuries." *Quarterly Review of Economics and Business* 27, no. 3 (1987):56–69.

———. "Adam Smith's Rise to Fame: A Reexamination of the Evidence." *The Eighteenth Century* 23, no. 1 (1992):64–85.

Redman, Deborah. "Adam Smith and Isaac Newton." *Scottish Journal of Political Economy* 40, no. 2 (1993):210–30.

Reich, Robert. *The Work of Nations: Preparing Ourselves for 21st Century Capitalism.* New York: Alfred A. Knopf, 1991.

Ricardo, David. *The Principles of Political Economy and Taxation.* London: Everyman's Library, 1984.

Riezler, Kurt. "The Philosopher of History and the Modern Statesman." *Social Research* 13, no. 3 (1946):368–80.

Roosevelt, Franklin D. "Commonwealth Club Address." September 23, 1932. Reprinted in *New Deal Thought,* edited by Howard Zinn. Indianapolis, Ind.: Bobbs-Merrill, 1966.

Rosenberg, Alexander. *Economics: Mathematical Economics or Science of Diminishing Returns.* Chicago: University of Chicago Press, 1992.

Rosenberg, Nathan. "Adam Smith on the Division of Labor: Two Views or One?" *Economica* 32 (May 1965):127–39.

————. "Another Advantage of the Division of Labor." *Journal of Political Economy* 84, no. 6, pt. 1 (1976):861–68.

Rothbard, Murray. *Economic Thought before Adam Smith: An Austrian Perspective on the History of Economic Thought.* Hants, England: Edward Elgar, 1995.

Rothschild, Emma. "Adam Smith and Conservative Economics." *Economic History Review* 45, no. 1 (1992):74–96.

Rotwein, Eugene. *David Hume: Writings on Economics.* Madison: University of Wisconsin Press, 1970.

Rousseau, Jean-Jacques. *The First and Second Discoures.* Edited by Roger D. Masters. Translated by Judith R. Masters. New York: St. Martin's Press, 1978.

Say, Jean Baptiste. *Treatise on Political Economy.* New York: Augustus M. Kelley, 1964.

Schumpeter, Joseph. *History of Economic Analysis.* New York: Oxford University Press, 1954.

Skidelsky, Robert. *The Road from Serfdom.* New York: Penguin, 1995.

Skinner, Andrew S. "Adam Smith: An Economic Interpretation of History." In *Essays on Adam Smith,* edited by Andrew S. Skinner and Thomas Wilson. Oxford: Clarendon Press, 1975.

————. "Adam Smith: Philosophy and Science." *Scottish Journal of Political Economy* 19 (November 1972):307–19.

Smith, Adam. *Correspondence of Adam Smith.* Edited by E. C. Mossner and T. S. Ross. Glasgow ed. Oxford: Oxford University Press, 1977; Indianapolis, Ind.: Liberty Classics, 1987.

————. *Essays on Philosophical Subjects.* Edited by W. L. D. Wightman and J. C. Bryce. Glasgow ed. Oxford: Oxford University Press, 1980; Indianapolis, Ind.: Liberty Classics, 1982.

————. *An Inquiry into the Nature and Causes of the Wealth of Nations.* Edited by R. H. Campbell and A. S. Skinner. 2 vols. Glasgow ed. Oxford: Oxford University Press, 1976; Indianapolis, Ind.: Liberty Classics, 1981.

————. *Lectures on Jurisprudence.* Edited by R. L. Meek, D. D. Raphael, and L. G. Stein. Glasgow ed. Oxford: Oxford University Press, 1978; Indianapolis, Ind.: Liberty Classics, 1982.

————. *Lectures on Rhetoric and Belles Lettres.* Edited by J. C. Bryce. Glasgow ed. Oxford: Oxford University Press, 1983; Indianapolis, Ind.: Liberty Classics, 1985.

————. *The Theory of Moral Sentiments.* Edited by David D. Raphael and Alec Macfie. Glasgow ed. Oxford: Oxford University Press, 1976; Indianapolis, Ind.: Liberty Classics, 1982.

Sowell, Thomas. *Classical Economics Reconsidered.* Princeton, N.J.: Princeton University Press, 1974.

Steuart, James. *An Inquiry into the Principles of Political Economy.* Edited by Andrew Skinner. Chicago: University of Chicago Press, 1966.

Stevens, David. "Adam Smith and the Colonial Disturbances." In *Essays on Adam Smith,* edited by Andrew S. Skinner and Thomas Wilson. Oxford: Clarendon Press, 1975.

Stewart, Dugald. "Account of the Life and Writings of Adam Smith." In *Essays on Philosophical Subjects.* Glasgow ed. Oxford: Oxford University Press, 1980. Indianapolis, Ind.: Liberty Classics, 1982.

Stigler, George. "Smith's Travels on the Ship of State." In *Essays on Adam Smith,* edited by Andrew S. Skinner and Thomas Wilson. Oxford: Clarendon Press, 1975.

Stimson, Shannon C. "Reflections on the Economic Interpretation of the Constitution."

In *Writing a National Identity: Political, Economic, and Cultural Perspectives on the Written Constitution,* edited by Vivian Hart and Shannon C. Stimson. Manchester, England: Manchester University Press, 1993.

———. "Republicanism and the Recovery of the Political in Adam Smith." In *Critical Issues in Social Thought,* edited by Murray Milgate and Cheryl B. Welch. New York: Academic Press, 1989.

Stourzh, Gerald. *Alexander Hamilton and the Idea of Republican Government.* Stanford, Calif.: Stanford University Press, 1970.

Strauss, Leo. "An Epilogue." In *Essays in the Scientific Study of Politics,* edited by Herbert J. Storing. New York: Holt, Rinehart, and Winston, 1962.

———. *Natural Right and History.* Chicago: University of Chicago Press, 1953.

Teichgraeber, Richard. *Free Trade and Moral Philosophy: Rethinking the Sources of the Wealth of Nations.* Durham, N.C.: Duke University Press, 1986.

———. "Less Abused Than I Had Reason to Expect: The Reception of the *Wealth of Nations* in Great Britain." *The Historical Journal* 30, no. 2 (1987):337–66.

Viner, Jacob. *The Long View and the Short: Studies in Economic Theory and Policy.* Glencoe, Ill.: Free Press, 1958.

———. *Studies in the Theory of International Trade.* Clifton, N.J.: Augustus M. Kelley, 1965.

Washington, George. *George Washington: A Collection.* Edited by W. B. Allen. Indianapolis, Ind.: Liberty Classics, 1988.

Weber, Max. *The Protestant Ethic and the Spirit of Capitalism.* New York: Charles Scribner's Sons, 1958.

Webster, Pelatiah. *Political Essays.* New York: B. Franklin, 1969.

White, Leonard. *The Federalists: A Study in Administrative History.* New York: Macmillan, 1948.

Wilson, Woodrow. *The New Freedom.* Englewood Cliffs, N.J.: Prentice Hall, 1961.

Winch, Donald. *Adam Smith's Politics: An Essay in Historiographic Revision.* Cambridge, England: Cambridge University Press, 1978.

———. "Science and the Legislator: Adam Smith and After." *Economic Journal* 93 (September 1983):501–20.

Wright, Colin. "Competing Conceptions of Political Economy." In *From Political Economy to Economic—and Back?* Edited by James Nicholls and Colin Wright. San Francisco: ICS Press, 1990.